Reforms and Economic Transformation in India

STUDIES IN INDIAN ECONOMIC POLICIES

India's Reforms: How they Produced Inclusive Growth

Reforms and Economic Transformation in India

Reforms and Economic Transformation in India

Edited by

Jagdish Bhagwati

Arvind Panagariya

OXFORD
UNIVERSITY PRESS

OXFORD
UNIVERSITY PRESS

Oxford University Press is a department of the University of Oxford.
It furthers the University's objective of excellence in research, scholarship,
and education by publishing worldwide.

Oxford   New York
Auckland   Cape Town   Dar es Salaam   Hong Kong   Karachi
Kuala Lumpur   Madrid   Melbourne   Mexico City   Nairobi
New Delhi   Shanghai   Taipei   Toronto

With offices in
Argentina   Austria   Brazil   Chile   Czech Republic   France   Greece
Guatemala   Hungary   Italy   Japan   Poland   Portugal   Singapore
South Korea   Switzerland   Thailand   Turkey   Ukraine   Vietnam

Oxford is a registered trademark of Oxford University Press
in the UK and certain other countries.

Published in the United States of America by
Oxford University Press
198 Madison Avenue, New York, NY 10016

Library of Congress Cataloging-in-Publication Data
Reforms and economic transformation in India / edited by Jagdish Bhagwati,
Arvind Panagariya.
p. cm.—(Studies in Indian economic policies)
Includes bibliographical references and index.
ISBN 978-0-19-991520-0 (cloth : alk. paper)   1. India—Economic policy—1991–
2. Industrial policy—India—History—21st century.   3. Commercial policy—
India—History—21st century.   4. India—Economic conditions—1991–   I. Bhagwati,
Jagdish N., 1934–   II. Panagariya, Arvind.
HC435.3.R44 2013
338.954—dc23
2012010951

ISBN: 978-0-19-991520-0

1 3 5 7 9 8 6 4 2
Printed in the United States of America
on acid-free paper

In Memory of
Abid Hussain
a pioneer among early reformers in India

CONTENTS

SERIES EDITORS' NOTE

Reforms and Economic Transformation in India is the second volume in the series *Studies in Indian Economic Policies*. The series bring out scholarly studies of past and future economic policies and their impact on India. It is our intention to include volumes authored by single or paired authors as well as collections of essays by different authors devoted to closely related themes in the series. The series is not wedded to any specific method of analysis or viewpoint but does seek a policy focus and high standards of economic and political analysis.

The origins of the series lie in the Columbia Program on Indian Economic Policies, generously funded by the John Templeton Foundation. Formally launched on October 1, 2009, the program has undertaken a series of research projects with the participation of leading economists interested in the study of India. The fruits of these projects are the bases of the first two volumes in the series.

We expect to bring out several additional volumes based on the research undertaken by the program and to also include other studies relevant to assessing Indian economic policies. We thank the John Templeton Foundation for supporting the Columbia Program, and Oxford University Press, especially Terry Vaughn and Catherine Rae, for making this series possible.

Jagdish Bhagwati and Arvind Panagariya
Columbia University
July 2012

PREFACE

This volume, the second in the series produced by the Columbia Program on Indian Economic Policies, turns to the analysis of the reforms from a different viewpoint than the first. It takes as its starting point the fact that while the reforms have undoubtedly delivered in terms of poverty reduction and associated social objectives, the impact has not been as substantial as it has been in other reform-oriented economies such as South Korea and Taiwan in the 1960s and 1970s and in China more recently. This is a puzzle whose explanation lies, we believe, in the fact that India's reforms have had a significantly smaller impact on transforming the Indian economy. In a nutshell, the reforms have missed key ingredients and have thus had limited impact on the transformation of the Indian economy in its sectoral output and employment composition among agriculture, industry, and services, and within and across enterprises within sectors.

The empirical analysis in the present volume therefore points systematically to the lacuna in Indian reforms and the direction in which future reforms could go. It also complements the first volume in the series by marshaling further new evidence that the transformation of the economy also has an upside. The papers at the end of this volume give new evidence that reinforces the findings of the first volume. Not only has poverty declined among all social groups, including the historically disadvantaged ones, but the wage and education gap between the disadvantaged and the upper-caste groups has declined. Moreover, the socially disadvantaged have also shared in the increased prosperity as entrepreneurs. These findings indicate that the social transformation has been a beneficial aspect of the reforms.

Like the research papers in the first volume, those in the present one have profited from presentations at two major conferences that the Columbia Program organized. The first of these was held at Columbia University in New York on November 4–6, 2010, and the second one under the joint auspices of Columbia University and the National Council on Applied Economic Research (NCAER) in New Delhi on March 31–April 1, 2011. Dr. Rajesh Chadha, Senior Fellow, NCAER, collaborated with us for the second conference and oversaw its superb execution, while Dr. Shashanka Bhide, NCAER's acting director general at that time, provided overall leadership for it. We are indebted to both of them.

We had the good fortune to get the participation of leading scholars, policymakers, and journalists in India between the two conferences. Thus, with gratitude, we acknowledge the contributions of Shankar Acharya, former chief economic advisor, Government of India; Jay Panda, member of the Lok Sabha; and Y. V. Reddy, former governor of the Reserve Bank of India; who were all generous enough to undertake the long journey from New Delhi to New York and offer their thoughtful commentaries at the first conference.

At the Delhi conference, we benefited from the participation of Sunil Jain, opinion editor, *Financial Express*; Bimal Jalan, former governor of the Reserve Bank of India and member of the Rajaya Sabha; Vijay Kelkar, chairman of the Thirteenth Finance Commission; Pradeep Mehta, secretary general of CUTS; Rakesh Mohan, professor at Yale University; Nandan Nilekani, chairman of the Unique Identification Authority of India; T. N. Ninan, chairman of the Business Standard Ltd.; Jay Panda, member of the Lok Sabha; Sharad Raghavan, reporter, *Financial Express*; Govinda Rao, director of the National Institute of Public Finance and Policy; and N. K. Singh, member of the Rajya Sabha.

The volume has greatly benefited from the formal comments by the discussants of the papers at the two conferences. Accordingly, we express our gratitude to Barry Bosworth, Brookings Institution; Rupa Chanda, Indian Institute of Management at Bangalore; Pravin Krishna, Johns Hopkins University; Thomas Reardon, Michigan State University; Michael Smitka, Washington and Lee University; and Jan Svejnar, University of Michigan.

It is also our pleasure to thank Rana Hasan of the Asian Development Bank and Karl Jandoc of the University of Hawaii, Manoa, the authors of Chapter 2 of the volume. They had prepared an earlier version of their essay independently of the Columbia Program, and it came to our notice just as we were beginning to prepare the manuscript of the present volume. We were very pleased that they not only offered the paper for inclusion in the volume but also agreed to do extensive revisions to it. They have filled what would otherwise have been a major gap in the volume.

Our final thanks go to the OUP team, especially Terry Vaughn and Catherine Rae, who have assisted us at various points during the preparation of the volume, and to Ananth Panagariya who has helped with the cover design.

CONTRIBUTORS

Reshad N. Ahsan, Lecturer, Department of Economics, University of Melbourne, Melbourne, Australia.

Laura Alfaro, Professor of Business Administration, Harvard Business School, Harvard University, Cambridge, MA.

Jagdish Bhagwati, University Professor of Economics and Law, Columbia University, New York, NY.

Anusha Chari, Associate Professor of Economics, University of North Carolina at Chapel Hill, Chapel Hill, NC.

Rajeev Dehejia, Professor, Robert F. Wagner Graduate School of Public Service, New York University, NY.

Pinelopi Goldberg, William K. Lanman, Jr., Professor of Economics, Yale University, New Haven, CT.

Nandini Gupta, Associate Professor of Finance, Kelley School of Business, Indiana University, Bloomington, IN.

Viktoria Hnatkovska, Assistant Professor of Economics, University of British Columbia, Vancouver, Canada.

Rana Hasan, Principal Economist, India Resident Mission, Asian Development Bank, New Delhi, India.

Karl Robert L. Jandoc, Graduate Student, University of Hawaii, Manoa.

Amit Khandelwal, Associate Professor, Finance and Economics, Columbia Business School, Columbia University, New York, NY.

Rajeev Kohli, Ira Leon Rennert Professor of Business, Columbia Business School, New York, NY.

Amartya Lahiri, Professor of Economics, University of British Columbia, Vancouver, Canada.

Devashish Mitra, Professor of Economics and Gerald B. and Daphna Cramer, Professors of Global Affairs, Syracuse University, Syracuse, NY.

Arvind Panagariya, Professor of Economics and Jagdish Bhagwati, Professor of Indian Political Economy, Columbia University, New York, NY.

Nina Pavcnik, Professor of Economics, Dartmouth College, Hanover, NH.

Asha Sundaram, Senior Lecturer, Faculty of Commerce, University of Cape Town, Cape Town, South Africa.

Reforms and Economic
Transformation in India

CHAPTER 1

Introduction

JAGDISH BHAGWATI AND ARVIND PANAGARIYA

There is now compelling evidence—systematically gathered in the first volume of the present series, *India's Reforms: How They Produced Inclusive Growth*—that the post-1991 reforms not only helped accelerate and sustain growth but also led to reduced poverty among all social groups.

Moreover, citizens now overwhelmingly acknowledge the benefits that accelerated growth has brought them and express greater optimism regarding the future. And, as voters, they reward the governments that deliver superior economic outcomes and punish those that fail to do so. Thus, for example, performing governments in Orissa, Bihar, and Gujarat have been returned to power, while the nonperforming one in West Bengal has been ousted.

THE REFORMS-LED REDUCTION IN POVERTY HAS BEEN LESS DRAMATIC IN INDIA

These favorable outcomes are tempered by the important qualification that the reduction in poverty for each percentage-point growth in gross domestic product (GDP) has been smaller in India than in the fast-growing economies of South Korea and Taiwan in the 1960s and 1970s, and China more recently. Whereas two decades of sustained rapid growth in these cases proved sufficient to virtually eliminate poverty, approximately one-fifth to one-fourth of Indians remain in poverty, even by the standards of a modest poverty line.

THE KEY ROLE OF TRANSFORMATION

We believe that at the heart of this slow pace of poverty alleviation in India has been the slow transformation of the primarily agrarian economy into a modern, industrial one. Whereas manufacturing grew rapidly in South Korea,

Taiwan, and China, it has grown at only moderate rates in India during the rapid-growth phase. Manufacturing's share of GDP rapidly rose in the afore-mentioned countries but has remained stagnant in India.

More important, rapid growth in labor-intensive manufacturing—consisting of apparel, footwear, toys, and light consumer goods—was at the heart of the transformation in South Korea, Taiwan, and China. In contrast, capital and skilled labor intensive sectors such as engineering goods, petroleum refining, auto parts and automobiles, telecommunications, software, and pharmaceuticals have propelled India's growth.

As a result, while rapid movement of workers out of agriculture into industry and services accompanied growth in South Korea, Taiwan, and China, such movement has been modest at best in India. Thus, for example, even though agriculture's share of GDP in India declined from 30 percent in the early 1990s to below 15 percent in 2010–11, the shift in employment has been so slow that the absolute number of workers in agriculture has yet to show a perceptible decline.[1] The small proportionate shift in the workforce from agriculture to industry and services has been offset by a rising number of total workers.

THREE BROAD THEMES

Against this background, the present volume pursues three broad themes related to the ongoing economic transformation in India.

The chapters in Part One ask why the transformation in India in terms of the movement of workers out of agriculture into industry and services has been slower than in other similarly fast-growing economies. These chapters also address what India needs to do to speed up this transformation.

In Part Two, the authors analyze the transformation that reforms have brought about within and across enterprises. For instance, they investigate the impact of privatization on enterprise profitability and that of the end to the licensing regime on the nature of competition among enterprises.

Finally, Part Three focuses on the manner in which the reforms have helped promote social transformation. In this section, the authors analyze the impact the reforms have had on the fortunes of the socially disadvantaged groups.

CONTENTS OF VOLUME: AN ANALYTICAL SYNOPSIS

The volume contains nine original essays. Of these, the first four study transformation at the level of broad sectors, the next three within and across enterprises, and the remaining two across social groups.

Part One: Reforms and the Transformation within Manufacturing and Services

In Chapter 2, Hasan and Jandoc subject the firm-level data in India's manufacturing sector to a systematic analysis with a view to understanding the reasons behind its very different size distribution compared to other countries, notably China. Pooling the data on the firms in the organized as well as unorganized manufacturing sectors, the authors first show that, in 2005, an astonishing 84 percent of workers in manufacturing in India were employed in firms with forty-nine or fewer workers.[2] Large firms, defined as those employing two hundred or more workers, accounted for only 10.5 percent of the manufacturing workforce, with the remaining 5.5 percent of manufacturing workers employed in medium-size firms. In contrast, medium- and large-scale firms employed 23.3 and 51.8 percent of the workers, respectively, in China the same year.

Upon disaggregation by sectors, Hasan and Jandoc find that the firm size distribution varies dramatically across sectors, even within India. Thus, workers in the highly labor-intensive apparel sector are concentrated almost entirely in the small firms; medium- and large-scale firms are nearly absent. And even within small firms, most firms employ fewer than ten workers. Firms with four or fewer workers employed 79.2 percent of the apparel workers, and those with five to ten workers employed an additional 8.2 percent of the apparel workforce in 2005. The remaining 12.6 percent of the workers were spread across firms with eleven or more workers with only 5.3 percent in large firms of two hundred or more workers.

This distribution contrasts sharply with that in China, where medium- and large-scale firms accounted for a gigantic 87.7 percent of the apparel employment in 2005. The distribution also contrasts sharply with the more capital-intensive auto and auto parts sector within India, in which large-scale firms employed 50.3 percent of all workers in 2005.

Hasan and Jandoc focus on state-level data to search for the causes of the near absence of large-scale firms in the labor-intensive sectors. When they compare the firm size distributions of all manufacturing activity between states with flexible labor regulations and those with inflexible ones, they find little difference. However, when the sample is restricted to labor-intensive industries only, large-scale firms exhibit significantly larger shares of employees in states with flexible labor regulations. Given the fact that labor laws remain highly restrictive even in the states classified as relatively more flexible and thus hinder the emergence of medium- and large-scale firms in greater proportions, the existence of these state-level differences is particularly notable.

To be sure that other factors are not behind the state-level differences, Hasan and Jandoc also do a comparison between states with and without good infrastructure. But this comparison yields no real differences in the employment shares of large firms.

In Chapter 3, Sundaram, Ahsan, and Mitra study the impact of the reforms on the organized versus unorganized sectors. They begin by noting that insofar as economic reforms principally apply to organized manufacturing, it is likely that they would stimulate the latter at the expense of unorganized manufacturing. But it is also possible that accelerated growth in organized manufacturing would lead to the expansion of unorganized manufacturing through both demand and supply externalities. On the demand side, accelerated growth in large firms may pave the way for the growth of smaller firms that supply critical inputs to them. On the supply side, innovations and skill creation in the organized sector may help bring down costs in the unorganized sector. Thus, in principle, the two sectors may exhibit either substitutability or complementarity in growth. The question is ultimately an empirical one.

The authors note that, at the aggregate level, output has been rising in both organized and unorganized sectors at an approximately equal pace, indicating complementarity between the two sectors. Using more detailed firm-level data for the years 1989–90, 1994–95, and 2000–01 for the fifteen largest states, they further find that states and sectors in which organized industry exhibited faster growth also saw faster growth in unorganized industry. Thus, the evidence points to strong complementarity in the growth of output in the organized and unorganized sectors.

The authors also study the link between economic policy and the degree of complementarity between the organized and unorganized sectors. They find that trade liberalization on average boosts employment, output, and value added in unorganized manufacturing. In states with rigid labor laws, this positive effect of trade liberalization is stronger in enterprises with more than five workers. In view of the existing findings in the literature that trade liberalization generates weaker output effects in organized manufacturing in states with inflexible labor laws, this finding suggests that when labor laws are stringent trade liberalization leads to movement further away from the organized sector. The finding thus strengthens the view that labor laws remain a key barrier to India's transformation to a modern economy.

In contrast to Chapters 2 and 3, which focus on manufacturing, Chapter 4 examines the transformation within the service sector. Authors Dehejia and Panagariya show that the preponderance of employment in small enterprises with low average labor productivity, which Hasan and Jandoc observe in manufacturing, also characterizes services in India. Exploiting the extensive firm-level service sector data collected by the National Sample Survey Organization (NSSO) for 2001–02 and 2006–07 (excluding data for retail trade and financial services), they show that in the latter year, 73 percent of service sector workers were employed in firms with four or fewer workers, which accounted for only 35 percent of the output.[3] Thus, the bulk of the employment in services is also in small firms with low per-worker output. The authors conclude, "The transformation to a modern economy would require not just the movement of workers from agriculture to industry... but also a movement of workers from the smaller to larger services enterprises."

Dehejia and Panagariya further find that a very large increase in services productivity has characterized the post-reform growth in services. Their calculations yield annual compound productivity growth rates of 3 percent or more in a number of states, with Maharashtra, Gujarat, Kerala, and Andhra Pradesh exhibiting rates in excess of 4.5 percent. Interestingly, with the possible exception of Kerala, these states are often identified as those with more flexible labor markets. The authors hypothesize that this productivity growth has resulted at least in part from more effective use of previously underutilized labor.

An important observation that critics sometimes raise is that the service sector has dominated growth in India, though reforms had focused principally on manufacturing. This criticism can be challenged at least partially on factual grounds.

The massive growth in telecommunications and outsourcing services has been the direct result of economic reforms. But there is also a grain of truth to the question of why the services that were not directly subject to reforms have also grown more rapidly in the post-reform era. In their ongoing research, Dehejia and Panagariya address this issue.

They hypothesize that liberalization has helped services growth in two other ways. First, improved access to high-quality tools and equipment due to liberalization has helped many of the service activities that are themselves non-traded in character. Second, the demand for many services depends on the size of the rest of the economy. Therefore, growth in manufacturing can stimulate service growth. The authors' preliminary investigation finds encouraging evidence in support of these hypotheses.

An important aspect of economic transformation in the service sector is also the modernization of retail trade. Just as the labor market in India has been dominated by employment in the unorganized sector, retail trade has been populated by millions of tiny unorganized sector shops. Strict labor market regulations have discouraged the entry of large firms in labor-intensive manufacturing; in the same vein, outright prohibition of supermarkets and hypermarkets has until recently resulted in retail trade becoming the exclusive preserve of small establishments. While this prohibition on domestic investors ended in the early 2000s, with supermarket chains such as Reliance and Bharti emerging in the major cities, India has continued to exclude foreign multibrand retail companies such as Walmart and Tesco from entry on the ground that this would decimate small retail shops.

In Chapter 5, Kohli and Bhagwati address this issue. They begin by noting that the share of organized retail in total retails sales grew from 3.3 percent in

2005 to 4.8 percent in 2009. If this growth is sustained, the share of organized retail would grow to 9.1 percent by 2016.

They argue that the fears that this growth would crush millions of small "mom-and-pop" retailers are unfounded. This is a common fear when restrictions on the expansion of the larger retailers, even those of entirely domestic origin, are proposed. When the Japanese restrictions on such expansion were repealed under US pressure, there was a similar fear. But little of what had been feared actually transpired. The experience in other countries such as China and Thailand has been similar.

Kohli and Bhagwati argue that small retailers have several advantages over the big retailers. For instance, since Indian customers lack refrigerators and cars, most of them do their shopping daily and from local stores "down the road" or "around the corner." Large retail stores are simply not accessible to them. Likewise, they often seek personal rapport with their shopkeeper: this is not possible with a Walmart employee. Local shopkeepers are also able to use space far more efficiently than their large counterparts; indeed, these shopkeepers use much of the store space to stock supplies.

Kohli and Bhagwati additionally point to some direct benefits from the entry of multinational retailers. The latter not only will bring cheaper imports to Indian customers but will also buy products of Indian manufacturers for sales abroad. Thus, they will help build the critical market links between Indian consumers and foreign suppliers as well as between Indian suppliers and foreign customers. The authors point out that the evidence is extremely strong that the productivity in agriculture, and attendant prosperity in the countryside, follows the entry of multinational retailers, since they catalyze the spread of refrigeration, storage, and other productivity-enhancing changes.

Part Two: Reforms and the Transformation within and across Enterprises

While Part One focuses more broadly on the transformation of manufacturing and services from their current predominantly unorganized form to the organized one, Part Two focuses on policy-led transformation at the level of the enterprise.

In Chapter 6, Gupta studies the important but neglected issue of privatization. Despite considerable liberalization and expansion of the private sector, the public sector remains dominant in India. Firms owned by the central government alone contributed more than 11 percent of GDP in 2005 and just forty-seven listed government-owned firms accounted for 22 percent of the total market capitalization of the Bombay Stock Exchange as of February 28, 2011. But as Gupta points out, "government-owned firms are highly inefficient due to surplus employment, rent-seeking activities by politicians, protection from competitive forces, and the absence of market-based incentives for workers." According to her, though 158 central-government-owned firms posted positive profits in 2009, 59 firms reported cumulative losses summing to 158 billion rupees.

The developments in telecommunications and airlines in the post-1991 reform era illustrate the power of the private sector. In 1990, more than one hundred years after phones were introduced in India, there were still only five million telephones in the country. But the entry of private providers in the early 1990s, followed by the implementation of the New Telecom Policy of 1999, transformed the telecommunications landscape in India. By the end of September 2010, India had a staggering 723 million telephone subscribers with private sector companies accounting for nearly 90 percent of the subscribers. Air travel within India has been similarly transformed. The private sector accounted for 82 percent of the market in 2010 compared to total absence in the early 1990s.

These examples suggest that, in the long run, the role of public sector units (PSUs) can be diluted through the expansion of the private sector, a process under way in almost all sectors. But a very large number of PSUs run in loss and keeping them afloat through subsidy has high social costs.[4] Gupta's comprehensive analysis of privatization episodes in India offers compelling evidence in support of this hypothesis.

Gupta studies various partial and full privatizations by the Indian government and finds that the favorable impact is many times larger when privatization involves the transfer of management into private hands, rather than just the sale of minority equity. Between 1991 and 2010, the central government raised approximately 960 billion rupees through minority equity sales and outright privatization. Of 247 central PSUs, 46 were subjected to minority equity sales without transfer of management. In addition, the National Democratic Alliance, which ruled from 1998 to 2004, undertook strategic sales involving transfer of management into private hands for fourteen enterprises.

Gupta finds that the enterprises subject to the minority equity sales experienced a significant increase in average sales, gross fixed assets, profits, net worth, and cash profits in the post-sale phase. She shows that, compared with enterprises that have been selected for privatization but have not yet sold any equity, a ten percentage point increase in private equity leads to an increase in annual sales of 3.3 percent, returns to sales of 3.8 percent, and net worth of 17 percent, on average. Disinvested enterprises also experience a significant increase in access to loans and show no decline in employment or wage compensation.

These gains magnify when privatization includes the transfer of management. Gupta shows that the sales and returns to sales increase on average by 23 percent and 21 percent, respectively, following such privatizations. These improvements in performance are not accompanied by layoffs or falling worker compensation. One reason for larger gains when privatization involves the transfer of ownership is that it ends political interference in PSUs and allows them to operate entirely on the basis of commercial considerations.

The analysis by Gupta makes a powerful case for the privatization of PSUs as another weapon in the government's reform arsenal that can speed up the modernization of the Indian economy. Needless to say, privatization of some of the largest PSUs—which are in sectors such as electricity, mining, and minerals—is not at issue at present. For example, privatization of the National Thermal Power Corporation, the Oil and Natural Gas Corporation Ltd., or GAIL (India) Ltd. is far off.

But it would make sense to gradually begin privatizing many manufacturing and services enterprises. For instance, keeping firms such as Air India, HMT Watches Ltd., Indian Drugs and Pharmaceuticals Ltd., Hindustan Cables Ltd., and National Jute Manufacturers Corporation Ltd. in the public sector makes little sense.

Among the reforms India undertook early on was the liberalization of imports of intermediate inputs. In Chapter 7, Goldberg, Khandelwal, and Pavcnik report on their research on this liberalization's impact on a specific aspect of firm activity: product innovation and its contribution to manufacturing growth. The authors argue that the post-1991 reforms led to a large expansion of the volume and variety of imported inputs. This improved access to inputs led to the birth of new product varieties. The authors estimate that the new products accounted for 25 percent of the manufacturing output growth with the share being as high as 50 percent in chemicals and fabricated metals.

In Chapter 8, the final essay in Part Two, Alfaro and Chari report on their research on how the end of licensing requirements for investments and imports has impacted the nature of competition among firms. These authors track the registered firms in India from 1989 to 2005 using the data collected by the Center for Monitoring the Indian Economy (CMIE). For each registered firm, CMIE records the birth year and evolution along with such characteristics as product, revenues, and profits.

Alfaro and Chari find that a massive entry of new firms, including foreign firms, has taken place since the reforms. A measure of this entry is that the average market share of incumbent firms in total sales declined from 99 to 79 percent between 1989 and 2005. Correspondingly, the average market share of new entrants incorporated after 1991 increased from 1 to 24 percent over the same period. Similar patterns emerge in terms of firm shares in assets. Alfaro and Chari find that all indicators point to increased competition: the average firm size has declined, the dispersion in firm size distribution has risen, and the concentration ratio—however measured—has gone down.

An interesting finding of Alfaro and Chari, which resonates with several of the essays in Part Two, is that the entry of firms takes place from the left tail of the firm size distribution, meaning that new firms are invariably small. By itself this is not surprising; new firms in most countries are small, but the more dynamic and successful among them quickly grow large. What seems to be different in India is that even after twenty years of concerted reforms, the largest firms remain the large incumbent firms. While Alfaro and Chari do not draw this inference, our own suspicion is that labor market rigidities discourage even otherwise dynamic new entrants from growing large in India.

Part Three: Reforms and Social Transformation

India has had a long history of discrimination against certain castes and tribes, widely known as the Scheduled Castes and Scheduled Tribes. These castes and tribes, so called because of their being formally listed in specific schedules of the constitution, lag behind average Indians in various spheres of life such as education, wages, and consumption expenditures. A key objective of development policy in India has been to uplift these castes and tribes. Therefore, any discussion of India's economic transformation would be incomplete without some assessment of how the reforms and accompanying growth have been reshaping their fortunes. This is the task undertaken in Part Three of the book.

In Chapter 9, Hnatkovskay and Lahiri begin by reviewing their earlier work (with S. Paul), which compellingly demonstrated that the gaps between Scheduled Castes and Tribes on the one hand, and non-scheduled caste groups on the other, have seen a decline between 1983 and 2004–05 in terms of wages and education. The gaps have declined when measured against mean and median wages and education levels as well as intergenerational mobility rates. Regarding the latter, Scheduled Caste and Scheduled Tribe children changed their status relative to their parents in terms of wages and education faster than the children of non-scheduled castes did with respect to their parents between 1983 and 2004–05.

The authors go on to examine the variation across states, seeking an explanation of these trends. They find growth to be the key explanatory variable: higher growth has almost always been associated with faster convergence of education attainment rates and wages. Initial per-capita income also matters: the higher it is, the slower the convergence. An examination of the relationship between quota-based job reservations for the Scheduled Castes and Tribes and convergence reveals that their initial level rather than future expansions have mattered more. Convergence has been faster in the states that had more generous quotas initially, with future expansions playing no role.

The inescapable conclusion flowing from the analysis by Hnatkovskay and Lahiri is that, by catalyzing and sustaining growth, reforms have significantly contributed to the convergence in education and wages across castes. But this is not all: liberalizing reforms have also been an important key to stimulating entrepreneurship among the Scheduled Castes and Scheduled Tribes.

In the final chapter of the book, Chapter 10, Dehejia and Panagariya offer the first systematic analysis of entrepreneurship according to social groups, consisting of the Scheduled Castes, Scheduled Tribes, Other Backward Castes, and forward castes.

The authors begin by drawing attention to a nascent group of thirty Dalit (formerly untouchable) entrepreneurs who have acquired the status of "crore-pati" or millionaire within a short period in the post-reform era. There is no known history of Dalit entrepreneurs succeeding under the license raj. But liberalization opened the doors of corporate India to all, and successful Dalit entrepreneurs have begun to emerge. While no Dalit entrepreneurs have yet joined the ranks of dollar billionaires, a handful of rupee billionaires have emerged. According to Dehejia and Panagariya, Milind Kamble, who owns a construction business and founded the Dalit Indian Chamber of Commerce and Industry in April 2005, puts the matter thus, "Including mine, most of the big Dalit-owned businesses are fifteen years old. With the emergence of globalization and the disappearance of the License-Permit Raj, many opportunities appeared and many of us jumped on them. Multinationals started rushing in, and business expanded in a big way." Kamble also tells the story of a visit by thirty Dalit crorepatis to the Planning Commission.

Going beyond anecdotal accounts, Dehejia and Panagariya provide more systematic data on entrepreneurship by social groups in the service sector. The service sector surveys conducted by the NSSO in 2001–02 and 2006–07 ask the owners of proprietor and partnership (though not corporate and cooperative) enterprises to identify their social group from among the Scheduled Castes, Scheduled Tribes, Other Backward Castes, or other (i.e., forward castes). This allows the authors to identify the value added, workers employed, and number of enterprises by social groups within proprietor and partnership enterprises.

Dehejia and Panagariya find that the picture which emerges from entrepreneurship data is consistent with that emerging from data on poverty, wages, and per-capita consumption: while the Scheduled Castes and Scheduled Tribes remain well behind the non-scheduled castes, they have handsomely shared in the growth the reforms have generated. To quote the authors,

> We find that the SC and ST groups do lag behind other social groups in terms of their shares in GVA [gross value added], workers employed and number of enterprises owned in a large number of services sectors covered by our data. But the presence of these groups in entrepreneurial activity is far from negligible. More importantly, there is no truth whatsoever to the assertions by many left-of-center observers that growth is leaving these groups behind. The ST entrepreneurs, who have been at the greatest disadvantage, have also made the largest

gains between 2001–02 and 2006–07. Overall, in terms of workers employed and enterprises owned, the SC entrepreneurs have a presence in services sectors that is not far out of line with the SC share in the population, but they are in enterprises with below-average productivity. As a result, their share in the GVA is well below their population share. But they, too, have grown alongside other entrepreneurs. (see Chapter 10)

An interesting point that Dehejia and Panagariya make is that, at least between 2001–02 and 2006–07, the forward castes seem to be in somewhat of a retreat in terms of both output share and workers employed. The major gainers have been other backward castes. It turns out that the most serious competition to the Scheduled Caste and Scheduled Tribe entrepreneurs has come from these Other Backward Castes rather than the forward castes.

CONCLUDING OBSERVATIONS

To conclude, the systematic reforms since 1991 have helped the Indian economy grow much faster than in the past and made significant differences in the lives of people from virtually all backgrounds. But the progress has been slower than what could have been achieved. Part One demonstrates that the process of drawing the workforce out of agriculture into industry and services could have been much faster than has been the case to date. In addition, even within industry and services, employment remains predominantly in the unorganized sector of the economy. This analysis points to stringent labor laws as the key impediment to workers moving from agricultural to non-agricultural employment, or from informal manufacturing and services employment to the formal sector.

The empirical analysis in Part Two of the deleterious effects of the slowdown in privatization, the lack of enthusiasm for liberalizing trade, and the continuing barriers to the growth of new large-scale firms also testifies to the fact that these shortfalls in reforms have prevented India from benefiting more fully from the reforms begun in earnest in 1991.

NOTES

1. Data from India usually relate to its fiscal year, which begins on April 1 and ends on March 31. Thus, year 2010–11 covers the period from April 1, 2010 to March 31, 2011.
2. In India, the organized manufacturing sector consists of firms registered under the Factories Act of 1948. All with ten workers using power and twenty workers even if not using power and engaged in manufacturing activity are required to register under this Act. All other firms are included in unorganized sector. The

Annual Survey of Industries (ASI) surveys the firms in the organized sector every year while the National Sample Survey Organization (NSSO) surveys the firms in the unorganized sector at irregular intervals.

3. Specifically, these services include hotels and restaurants; transport, storage and communications; real estate, ownership of dwellings, and business services; and education, health, and other community services.

4. Air India alone received more than US$10 billion in subsidies during fiscal year 2010–11.

PART ONE

Reforms and the Transformation within Manufacturing and Services

CHAPTER 2

Labor Regulations and Firm Size Distribution in Indian Manufacturing

RANA HASAN AND KARL ROBERT L. JANDOC

INTRODUCTION

There exists a large and growing literature that seeks to understand the policy determinants of industrial performance. In this chapter, we use data from establishment-level surveys of India's manufacturing sector to contribute to this literature. The specific issue we examine is how the size of Indian manufacturing establishments in terms of employment is distributed. We also provide evidence on how one element of policy—labor regulations—may be contributing to this size distribution.

Our interest in the size distribution is driven by the close link between establishment size and various dimensions of industrial performance, including average wages and labor productivity found internationally.[1] Indeed, at least since Moore's (1911) study of daily wages of Italian working women in textile mills, the finding that wages are higher in larger enterprises has been confirmed repeatedly in different contexts. As noted by Oi and Idson in their review of the relationship between firm size and wages in mostly industrialized countries, the facts Moore uncovered had not changed nearly a century later:

A worker who holds a job in a large firm is paid a higher wage, receives more generous fringe benefits, gets more training, is provided with a cleaner, safer, and generally more pleasant work environment. She has access to newer technologies and superior equipment. She is, however, obliged to produce standardized as opposed to customized goods and services, and for the most part to perform the work in tandem with other members of a larger team. The cost of finding a job with a small firm is lower. The personal relation between employee and employer may be closer, but layoff and firm failure rates are higher, resulting in less job security. (1999, p. 2207)

To the extent that an important part of this correlation is a causal relationship between a firm's size and its productivity and wages, any factor that constrains firm size will have adverse implications for the growth of productivity and wages. Therefore, an understanding of the size distribution of enterprises in India and the factors that explain it can be key to an analysis of the potential constraints to enterprise growth and, ultimately, economic growth more broadly.

We begin by examining how employment is distributed across manufacturing enterprises of different sizes in India. As noted by the pioneering work of Dipak Mazumdar (see, for example, the works cited in Mazumdar 2003), the size distribution of Indian manufacturing enterprises is characterized by a "missing middle" whereby employment tends to be concentrated in small and large enterprises. After confirming that this pattern continues to hold even as recent as 2005, we turn our attention to whether India's industrial labor regulations may be one of the drivers of the missing middle phenomena. In particular, we examine whether states coded by recent literature as having relatively flexible or inflexible labor regulations differ in the distribution of enterprises across different size groups. Our findings suggest that labor regulations do have an impact.

The remainder of this chapter is organized as follows. In the next section, we describe our data on Indian manufacturing establishments. In the third section, we use these data to document the distribution of employment by enterprise size groups in Indian manufacturing. Similar information from other countries in the region complements the data and highlights some policy issues. The main finding is that in India, as elsewhere, large firms on average are more productive and pay better than smaller firms; however, a unique feature of the Indian firm size distribution is the overwhelming importance of smaller enterprises in accounting for total manufacturing employment—an important phenomenon described in greater detail in the fourth section. The implication is that a very large proportion of Indian workers are employed in low-productivity and low-wage enterprises. The fifth section indicates some reasons why the Indian size distribution looks the way it does. One of these reasons has to do with labor regulations, which the sixth section discusses in greater detail before turning to an empirical investigation of the links between labor regulations and the size distribution of Indian enterprises. The final section concludes.

DATA

The main sources of data used in this study are nationally representative surveys of formal and informal manufacturing firms in India. The Annual Survey of Industries (ASI) gathers information on "registered" or formal sector firms that are covered by Sections 2m(i) and 2m(ii) of the 1948 Factories Act and by the 1966 Bidi and Cigar Workers Act—particularly those firms that use electricity and hire more than ten workers, and those that do not use electricity but nevertheless employ twenty or more workers. The ASI also covers certain utility industries such as power and water supply. Units with one hundred or more workers are categorized under the *census* sector and are completely enumerated,[2] while the rest are categorized under the *sample* sector and are surveyed based on a predetermined sampling design.

The "unregistered" or informal sector firms are covered by the National Sample Survey Organization (NSSO) Survey of Unorganized Manufacturing Enterprises. The surveys are follow-ups to the different economic censuses conducted by the NSSO. Informal firms engaged in manufacturing are classified as: (a) *own-account manufacturing enterprises* (OAMEs) if they operate without any hired worker employed on a fairly regular basis, (b) *non-directory manufacturing establishments* (NDMEs) if they employ fewer than six workers (household and hired workers taken together), or (c) *directory manufacturing establishments* (DMEs) if they employ a total of six or more household members and hired workers.

For this study, we combine ASI and NSSO data from three years: 1994–95, 2000–01, and 2004–05 for the ASI, and 1994–95, 2000–01, and 2005–06 for the NSSO. The first two years match up very well across the two data sources. This is less so for the last year of data, but it is unavoidable given data availability. For expositional convenience we refer to the years covered by the data as 1994, 2000, and 2005.

From this combined dataset we mainly use four variables: employment, output, capital, and value added. Employment includes all workers in the firm, including production workers, employees holding supervisory or managerial positions, and working proprietors.[3] Output is the sum total of the value of manufactured products and by-products, the value of other services rendered, and the value of other incidental receipts of the firm. Capital is defined as the value of total assets minus the value of land and buildings. We use the net value (net of depreciation) for ASI but the gross market value for NSSO. Although our measure of capital is imperfect, we use it minimally and only for the purpose of determining labor intensive industries.[4] Value added is computed by deducting total output from total inputs (fuels, raw materials, etc.) of the firm. We deflate the current rupee values using wholesale price indices of manufacturing industries used by Gupta, Hasan, and Kumar (2009).

We have employed some measures to filter and clean the data that are used in this study. First, there are a substantial number of firms that failed to report output (or reported zero output), especially in the 2000 and 2005 rounds of the ASI. Second, some variables have outliers and implausible values (e.g., one firm reports employing four million workers). We conduct our analysis by excluding nonmanufacturing firms involved in industries such as recycling and agriculture, including firms in the ASI which are reported to be "open" during the survey period,[5] and dropping firms with very high values for employment (i.e., firms reporting employment greater than 50,000).

We also restrict our attention to fifteen major Indian states (using pre-2000 boundaries of three large states). The states are: Andhra Pradesh, Assam, Bihar (including what is now Jharkhand), Gujarat, Haryana, Karnataka, Kerala, Madhya Pradesh (including what is now Chhattisgarh), Maharashtra, Orissa, Punjab, Rajasthan, Tamil Nadu, Uttar Pradesh (including what is now Uttarakhand) and West Bengal. This not only makes it easier to compare data across years, but also allows us to use available information on state-level labor regulations in our analysis of the links between labor regulations and firm size distribution.

For some of our analysis, we need information on the manufacturing industries firms operate in. Since the 1994 data use India's NIC-1987 industrial classification, the 2000 data use the NIC-1998 classification, and the 2005 data use the NIC-2004 classification, we employ a concordance that maps three-digit NIC-1998 and NIC-2004 codes into unique two-digit NIC-1987 codes. This gives us a total of sixteen aggregated industries.

Table 2.1 reports the number of firms surveyed and their implied population statistics. There are 26,000–47,000 firms surveyed across the different ASI rounds, while there are 72,000–196,000 enterprises surveyed across the NSSO rounds. Based on the population weights provided in the various datasets, the sample firms represent eleven to sixteen million Indian firms per year.

Table 2.2 provides some summary statistics for the main variables we use in this study. In addition to the mean, we provide the median, the tenth percentile, and the ninetieth percentile values of the variables to give us a sense of their distribution. As expected, firms in the formal sector have higher value added, output, employment, and capital per worker. What is surprising, however, is

Table 2.1 NUMBER OF FIRMS IN ASI AND NSSO DATASETS: 1994, 2000, AND 2005

Dataset	1994		2000		2005	
	Sample	Population	Sample	Population	Sample	Population
ASI	47,121	97,846	26,611	106,205	33,838	110,873
NSSO	142,780	11,575,745	196,385	16,306,696	72,109	16,496,285
of which:						
OAME	110,899	9,908,945	129,921	14,163,075	48,049	14,182,576
NDME	19,010	1,112,885	42,384	1,556,979	15,311	1,669,454
DME	12,871	553,915	24,080	586,642	8,749	644,255

Note: ASI = Annual Survey of Industries; NSSO = National Sample Survey Organisation (Survey of Unorganised Manufacturing Enterprises); OAME = own-account manufacturing enterprises; NDME = non-directory manufacturing enterprises; DME = directory of manufacturing enterprises.
Source: Authors' computations based on ASI and NSSO datasets.

Table 2.2 SUMMARY STATISTICS ON VALUE ADDED, OUTPUT, EMPLOYMENT, AND CAPITAL PER WORKER

1994	Value Added (Thousands of 1993 Rupees)				Output (Thousands of 1993 Rupees)				Number of Workers				Capital per Worker (Thousands of 1993 Rupees)			
	Mean	p10	Median	p90	Mean	p10	Median	p90	Mean	p10	Median	p90	Mean	p10	Median	p90
ASI	8,168.07	39.22	565.16	7,189.04	38,409.49	321.11	3,671.39	50,088.76	77	7	21	125	62.40	0.66	13.28	119.18
OAME	9.66	1.13	6.08	20.73	19.42	1.64	8.93	38.63	2	1	2	3	1.59	0.01	0.21	3.84
NDME	44.26	7.90	28.91	85.68	112.86	13.73	53.07	244.72	3	2	3	5	7.99	0.24	3.00	20.91
DME	143.17	10.42	77.80	291.67	496.34	25.28	136.60	1,022.40	9	1	7	14	9.92	0.14	2.60	25.23
2000	Mean	p10	Median	p90	Mean	p10	Median	p90	Mean	p10	Median	p90	Mean	p10	Median	p90
ASI	7,917.53	(2,325.51)	450.79	8,547.78	49,746.25	-	3,295.66	63,525.63	69	6	18	118	102.28	1.35	26.42	205.11
OAME	11.30	1.70	7.39	24.74	22.72	2.17	10.61	47.17	2	1	2	3	1.86	0.02	0.45	4.46
NDME	58.57	13.51	42.75	115.77	153.23	22.01	70.25	303.56	3	2	3	5	7.34	0.39	2.97	17.00
DME	209.59	30.16	138.22	410.74	1,095.84	54.70	273.33	1,697.95	10	6	8	16	12.15	0.36	3.73	27.12
2005	Mean	p10	Median	p90	Mean	p10	Median	p90	Mean	p10	Median	p90	Mean	p10	Median	p90
ASI	11,516.14	(2,523.05)	532.17	10,662.03	73,166.21	-	4,171.86	83,088.75	70	7	19	126	111.86	1.31	28.71	223.02
OAME	11.25	1.59	6.49	25.24	21.48	1.84	8.48	45.19	2	1	1	3	1.85	0.01	0.33	4.34
NDME	72.19	16.17	50.55	129.82	216.83	24.93	84.76	369.25	3	2	3	5	8.12	0.43	3.21	19.02
DME	307.18	44.39	179.24	533.10	1,271.42	73.94	386.96	2,284.86	10	6	8	16	13.52	0.36	4.21	31.88

Notes: p10 and p90 denote 10th and 90th percentile values, respectively. Monetary values are adjusted to 1993 prices using wholesale price indices for different industries. See Gupta, Hasan, and Kumar (2009) for details.
Source: Authors' computations based on ASI and NSSO datasets.

Table 2.3 TOTAL VALUE ADDED, OUTPUT, AND EMPLOYMENT BY YEAR AND DATASET

Dataset	1994			2000			2005		
	Value Added	Output	Employment	Value Added	Output	Employment	Value Added	Output	Employment
	(Billions of 1993 Rupees)		(Millions)	(Billions of 1993 Rupees)		(Millions)	(Billions of 1993 Rupees)		(Millions)
ASI	798.76	4,233.99	7.52	840.56	7,935.00	7.30	1,276.50	14,493.53	7.70
NSSO	224.24	675.06	28.24	374.18	1,709.70	35.18	474.98	2,504.75	35.02
of which:									
OAME	95.73	221.68	20.04	160.05	486.47	24.21	157.21	526.60	23.04
NDME	49.21	142.33	3.46	91.19	344.38	5.03	120.05	603.29	5.41
DME	79.30	311.04	4.73	122.95	878.86	5.94	197.72	1,374.87	6.58

Note: Monetary values are adjusted to 1993 prices using wholesale price indices for different industries.
Source: Authors' computations based on ASI and NSSO datasets.

that a large number of these formal-sector firms have fewer than ten workers, as can be seen by the low tenth percentile value for number of workers.

While formal firms tend to have a higher number of workers per firm, the vast majority of workers are employed in informal firms. Table 2.3 shows that around 80 percent of workers are employed in the informal sector; of these informal sector workers, around 70 percent belong to OAMEs, working on their own account. Although employing fewer workers overall, the formal sector produces disproportionately more value added and output than the informal sector.

INDIAN MANUFACTURING AND THE
"GOOD JOBS" PROBLEM

As figure 2.1 clearly indicates, a very large share of workers in India's manufacturing sector—almost 85 percent in 2005—are employed in enterprises with fewer than fifty workers.[6] This share is considerably higher than that in many comparator countries in the Asia-Pacific region.

This employment distribution pattern has important welfare implications. First, large enterprises on average are more productive (figure 2.2) and—not unrelated—pay higher wages (figure 2.3). Accordingly, the preponderance of Indian manufacturing employment in small-sized firms means low wages for a large fraction of workers. It also means high levels of wage inequality: the distributions implicit in the figures shown here yield Gini coefficients of 0.35 in India versus 0.16 in Korea and 0.13 in Taipei, China.

A more disaggregated look at the distribution of Indian manufacturing employment by firm size helps frame policy issues more sharply. Figure 2.4, which considers the distribution of workers by finer size groups than those considered so far, indicates that much employment is accounted for by firms with fewer than five workers. Moreover, as the figure also shows, the overwhelming majority of these microenterprises are OAMEs.

Figure 2.5 presents the distribution of workers once again, but this time omitting the OAMEs. While the figure continues to show how important small enterprises are to manufacturing employment in India, it highlights a second feature of the distribution of employment by firm size in India—the relatively low share of manufacturing employment in firms with 51–200 workers.

As can be seen from the two figures, both features of the employment distribution are present in each of the three years of our data. In the absence of panel data—which would enable us to examine how given enterprises evolved in size—these features of the size distribution suggest some combination of the following: the transition from microenterprise to small enterprise seems difficult, and the transition from small to medium enterprise also seems difficult.

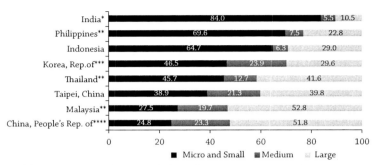

*India's manufacturing employment includes workers in own-account manufacturing enterprises.
**Includes imputation for the self-employed based on differentials between labor force survey and enterprise survey/census data.
***Data on Korean microenterprises are not available.
****Adds 5.9 million self-employed (see ADB 2009 for more details).
Note: Micro and small: 1–49 workers in all economies except Thailand (1–50 workers); medium: 50–199 in all economies except Thailand (51–200 workers); large: 200 or more workers in all economies except Thailand (more than 200 workers).

Figure 2.1
Share of Manufacturing Employment by Enterprise Size Groups (percent)
Source: ADB (2009).

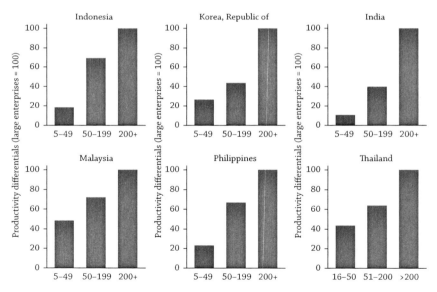

Figure 2.2
Productivity (Value Added per Worker) Differentials by Enterprise Size Groups (large enterprises = 100)
Source: ADB (2009).

Given the size–productivity–wage relationship discussed earlier, the patterns above strongly suggest that understanding what prevents Indian enterprises of different size groups from expanding is critical insofar as the goal of generating better paying jobs is concerned. Given that microenterprises—especially

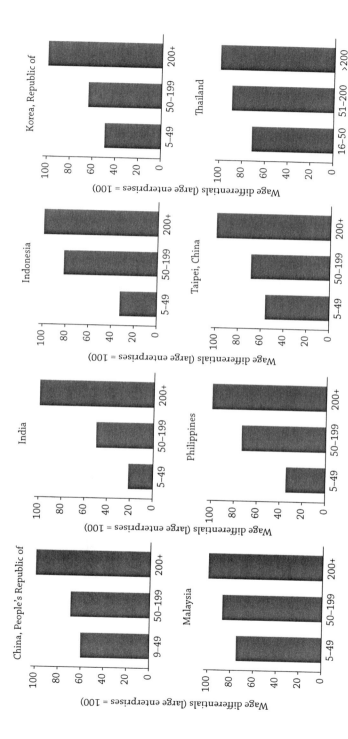

Figure 2.3
Wage Differentials by Enterprise Size Groups (large enterprises = 100)
Source: ADB (2009).

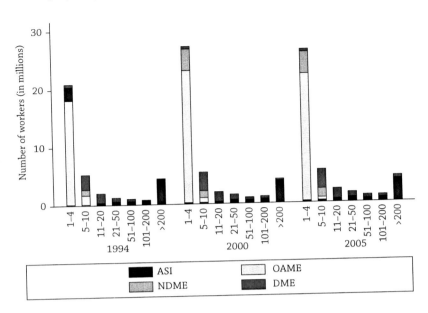

Figure 2.4
Number of Workers by Firm Size and Type (millions)
Source: Authors' computations based on ASI and NSSO datasets.

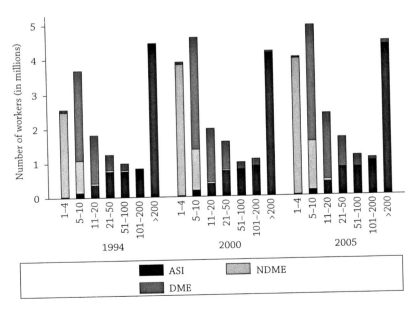

Figure 2.5
Number of Workers by Size and Firm Type, Without OAME Workers (millions)
Source: Authors' computations based on ASI and NSSO datasets.

the OAMEs—are likely to have very different characteristics and face different constraints in their operations and growth than small- and medium-sized enterprises, we separate OAMEs from the larger firms as we discuss their prospects for growth.

THE OWN-ACCOUNT MANUFACTURING ENTERPRISES

As noted earlier, the OAMEs comprise very small enterprises that do not hire even one worker from outside the family on a regular basis. Tables 2.4 and 2.5 show us which industries the OAMEs operate in and where they are located. OAMEs are mostly based in rural areas. Moreover, they are mostly confined to a few industries, namely wood/wood products, food products, beverages, and textiles and textile products.

Why are there so many OAMEs? Do they possess the potential to grow and expand? Will they eventually become significant employers? It is beyond the scope of this paper to shed detailed light on these issues. However, it is useful to consider the results of some recent research on this issue from another South Asian country, Sri Lanka, and examine what implications there may be for the case of India.

As de Mel, McKenzie, and Woodruff (2008) argue, understanding the OAMEs is very crucial for guiding policies on industrial development and

Table 2.4 OAME WORKERS BY INDUSTRY AFFILIATION (PERCENT)

Industry	1994	2000	2005
Food products	20	18	15
Beverages, tobacco	12	14	20
Textiles	11	9	7
Textile products	10	19	24
Wood/wood products	22	20	17
Paper/paper products	1	1	1
Leather/leather products	1	1	1
Basic chemicals	1	1	2
Rubber/plastic/petroleum/coal	0	0	0
Non-metallic	9	7	5
Metals and alloys	0	0	0
Metal products	3	3	3
Machinery	0	1	1
Electrical machinery	0	0	0
Transport	0	0	0
Other manufacturing	10	6	4
Total	100	100	100

Source: Authors' computations based on NSSO datasets.

Table 2.5 OAME WORKERS BY URBANITY AND INDUSTRY AFFILIATION
(PERCENT)

Industry	1994		2000		2005	
	Rural	Urban	Rural	Urban	Rural	Urban
Food products	74	26	83	17	83	17
Beverages, pobacco	76	24	80	20	83	17
Textiles	66	34	73	27	59	41
Textile products	69	31	69	31	69	31
Wood/wood products	84	16	90	10	90	10
Paper/paper products	39	61	34	66	52	48
Leather/leather products	58	42	54	46	27	73
Basic chemicals	48	52	46	54	72	28
Rubber/plastic/petroleum/coal	44	56	47	53	53	47
Non-metallic	80	20	87	13	87	13
Metals and alloys	19	81	53	47	43	57
Metal products	69	31	70	30	76	24
Machinery	70	30	74	26	62	38
Electrical machinery	27	73	52	48	51	49
Transport	46	54	43	57	47	53
Other manufacturing	66	34	48	52	40	60
Total	73	27	77	23	76	24

Source: Authors' computations based on NSSO datasets.

employment generation. In particular, it can help determine whether the focus of policy should be on helping microenterprises grow or on the constraints to growth facing those employers operating relatively larger enterprises. The issue is still unsettled in the literature. In a useful summary of the debate in this area, de Mel, McKenzie, and Woodruff note that while scholars such as Peruvian economist Hernando de Soto[7] tend to consider microenterprise owners as capitalists-in-waiting held back by credit constraints, weak property rights, and burdensome regulation, a very different view comes from other scholars such as Viktor Tokman. Tokman (2007), along with the International Labour Organisation (ILO), believes that these workers are the product of the "failure of the economic system to create enough productive employment" and that, given the opportunity for regular salaried work, they may be more than willing to make the change and abandon their businesses.

Recent evidence suggests that the Tokman and ILO view has the upper hand. In a systematic comparison of wage workers, own-account workers, and employers in Sri Lanka, de Mel, McKenzie, and Woodruff (2008) find that in a wide range of ability measures and cognitive tests, own-account workers and wage workers perform very similarly and their scores are below those of entrepreneurs who operate larger enterprises. Moreover, they also find that parents of entrepreneurs are more educated than parents of wage workers, who in turn cannot be distinguished from parents of own-account workers in terms of educational achievement. Employers are also more motivated (important for running a business) and more tenacious (important for making the business grow) than own-account workers, according to industrial psychology tests. Taken together, the findings of this study cast doubt on the idea that owners of microenterprises are capable of growing their businesses.

There is some suggestive evidence to support these findings in the Indian context as well. Figure 2.6 describes the distribution of education for different categories of nonagricultural workers using data from the 2004–05 NSS Employment-Unemployment Survey. The self-employed are divided into employers and own-account workers, while wage earners are divided into regular and casual workers. The figure shows that the own-account workers look a lot like casual wage laborers, while employers and regular wage workers are fairly similar. Among both the own-account and casual wage workers, a large share of workers has less than primary education, and very few have tertiary education.

Interestingly, as figure 2.7 reveals, similarities also exist between per-capita expenditures across Indian households relying on own-account income and casual wage employment, and across households relying on regular wage employment and income from being a self-employed employer. Both these patterns suggest important differences between microenterprise owners and entrepreneurs of larger enterprises. Indeed, it is quite plausible that the vast majority of microenterprises are unlikely to expand and become employers.

To the extent that this is correct, the policy imperative of generating good jobs has to focus on understanding the barriers to growth for larger enterprises. Accordingly, we omit the OAMEs in the rest of our analysis and focus on understanding the distribution of employment by size groups for all other enterprises.

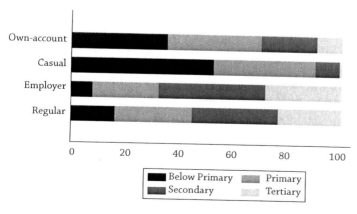

Figure 2.6
Distribution of Education by Type of Employment in India (percent)

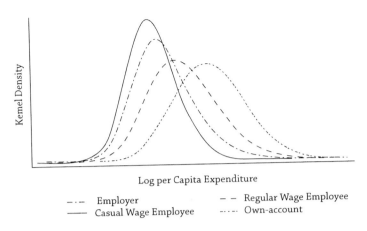

Figure 2.7
Household Per Capita Expenditure by Type of Employment in India (Rupees)
Source: Authors' computations based on the 2004–2005 NSS Employment-Unemployment Survey.

UNDERSTANDING THE SIZE DISTRIBUTION
OF EMPLOYMENT IN NON-OAMES

What is causing the appearance of the missing middle? A host of factors affect the pattern of size distribution. To a certain extent, the pattern will reflect industrial composition. If technology in a given industry is characterized by economies of scale, we can expect larger plant size. In general, the more capital (machines) required in a production process, the greater the scope for reaping economies of scale and thus the larger the optimum size of enterprises. For example, automobile production requires far more capital per unit of labor than apparel production, and economies of scale are very important to the production process. As a result, the typical automobile plant will be much larger than an apparel plant.

This can be seen quite clearly in figure 2.8, which contrasts the distribution of non-OAME employment across size groups in apparel and motor vehicles and parts in India. While there is a mass of employment in very small apparel enterprises, the situation is very different in motor vehicles. Since total employment generated by non-OAMEs in apparel is about four times that of motor vehicles and parts (2.6 million workers versus around 671,000 workers in 2005) in the fifteen major states, this will certainly exert a large influence on the distribution of employment across size groups in manufacturing as a whole.[8] Including the OAMEs reinforces this message even more strongly. For example, in India's apparel sector, close to 80 percent of employment is accounted for by enterprises with fewer than five workers. This may be compared to a figure of around 37 percent of employment when the OAMEs are excluded (as in figure 2.8)! Appendix figure 2.A1 presents the analog to figure 2.8 when the OAMEs are included.

In this way, the size distribution of enterprises in an economy will depend to some extent on the industrial composition of the economy. Since lower

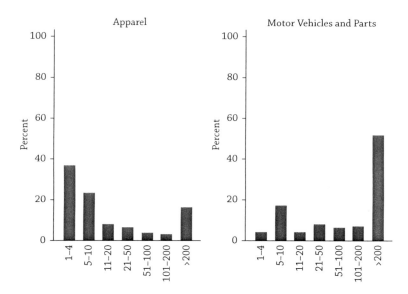

Figure 2.8
Employment Share by Firm Size: Apparel vs. Motor Vehicles and Parts, 2005
Source: Authors' computations based on ASI and NSSO datasets.

income countries will tend to have a composition dominated by simpler-to-pro-duce products like apparel and footwear, metal products, and furniture—low incomes on average will mean greater demand for these types of products—we can expect a concentration of small enterprises in these countries.

But as noted by Mazumdar (2009), the effects of broad industrial composition should not be exaggerated. This is because the size distribution within the same industry can show significant variations across countries. Thus, while apparel can be manufactured in small establishments where one or a few tailors work on basic sewing machines, production can also occur in large establishments using sophisticated machines (for example, machines for spreading and cutting cloth). Figure 2.9 compares the distribution of employment across size groups in China and India for apparel products (excluding OAMEs from the Indian distribution). Appendix figure 2.A2 presents the analog to figure 2.9 when the OAMEs are included for the Indian distribution.[9] Large enterprises account for much more of total employment in apparel in China than in India.[10] The very different distri-butions between these two countries strongly suggest very different production technologies for a broadly similar set of products and very different implications for firm size distribution. Indeed, these two distributions are entirely consist-ent with the qualitative description provided by the McKinsey Global Institute (2001) of the structure and production technologies of Indian apparel producers compared to their Chinese and Sri Lankan counterparts.

As Mazumdar (2009) argues, a number of factors can explain the coex-istence of firms of different sizes within a given product line, including the

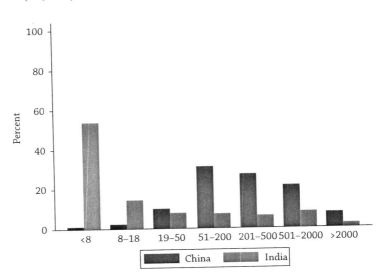

Figure 2.9
Employment Share by Firm Size in China and India: Apparel, 2005
Source: Authors' computations based on ASI and NSSO datasets for India and ADB (2009) for China.

transition of production technologies from "crafts" traditions to modern methods (especially important in textiles and apparel); product market differentiation whereby low income consumers demand low-quality, low-priced products (especially important in countries with large rural populations such as India); differential access to finance (especially problematic for smaller firms); transaction costs; and wide range of government policies encompassing industrial regulations, trade policy, and even labor market regulations.

Understanding which factors are key is important from a policy point of view. In this context, analysis of detailed microlevel survey data can be helpful. In what follows, we illustrate how the survey data we have access to can be used to examine how one element of regulation, namely labor regulations, may be affecting the firm size distribution. (For an analysis of how recent changes in trade policy have affected the firm size distribution, see Nataraj 2011.)

LABOR MARKET REGULATIONS AND FIRM SIZE DISTRIBUTION

Labor Regulations in India

Why should labor regulations affect the firm size distribution? It is useful to first consider the different channels through which labor regulations can affect firms and then consider what the implications of these channels are for the firm size distribution. First, labor regulations can increase directly the cost of hiring workers, for example, through minimum wage stipulations and provisions for mandated benefits (such as health care and pensions). Second, labor regulations can affect the speed and cost of *adjusting* employment levels via regulations governing hiring and layoffs and changes to conditions of service for incumbent workers. Third, labor regulations can influence the relative bargaining power of workers and firms by regulating the conditions under which industrial disputes arise and are settled.

If labor regulations apply uniformly to all firms, then the size *distribution* of firms is unlikely to be affected. However, if labor regulations apply only to a subset of firms—for example, firms above a certain size—then the size distribution of firms may be affected. In the context of Indian manufacturing, various aspects of labor regulation kick in depending on whether a firm has seven, fifty, or one hundred workers or more (see below), while other regulations apply at thresholds of ten and twenty workers.[11] To the extent that these regulations impose significant costs on employers, we can expect firms to be incentivized to stay below the relevant thresholds, all else being equal. In other words, one would expect to see a bunching up of firms operating just under the various thresholds.

It needs to be recognized, however, that in a developing country context, the *strength* of enforcement of a given labor regulation is unlikely to be equal across firms that come under the regulation's ambit. To the extent that larger firms are easier to monitor, stricter enforcement of labor regulations and firm size are likely to go hand in hand. Thus, the "bite" of labor regulations will probably not be felt exactly at the various legal thresholds associated with the regulations but somewhere in their neighborhood. For example, a regulation that kicks in at seven workers may well be enforced effectively among firms with a much larger number of workers.

In addition, the effect of labor regulations on the size distribution of firms may be more pronounced in certain industries. By definition, labor-intensive industries are those in which labor makes up a relatively high share of total production costs. They are also often the industries in which rapid adjustments in employment levels are needed—as in the case of apparel producers facing frequent changes in consumer preferences regarding clothing styles. Thus, if labor regulations apply with greater force to larger firms (whether by design or on account of stricter enforcement), the effects on size distribution are more likely to be picked up in labor-intensive industries.[12]

Which specific labor regulations may be affecting the size distribution of Indian manufacturing firms? Perhaps the single most important piece of labor legislation affecting Indian manufacturing firms is the Industrial Disputes Act (IDA). In addition to laying down procedures for the investigation and settlement of industrial disputes, the IDA also governs the conditions under which layoff, retrenchment, and closure of firms can take place, and the appropriate level of compensation in each case (dealt with in Chapters V and VB of the IDA).

Until 1976, the provisions of the IDA on retrenchments or layoffs were fairly uncontroversial. The IDA allowed firms to lay off or retrench workers according to economic circumstances as long as certain requirements—such as the provision of sufficient notice, severance payments, and the order of retrenchment among workers (last in, first out)—were met. An amendment in 1976 (the introduction of Chapter VB), however, made it compulsory for employers with more than three hundred workers to seek the prior approval of the appropriate government before workers could be dismissed. A further amendment in 1982 widened the scope of this regulation by making it applicable to employers with one hundred or more workers. In some states, such as West Bengal, the threshold of one hundred was reduced to fifty workers or more.

Since government approval for retrenchments or layoffs is difficult to obtain, Chapter VB of the IDA is believed to have incentivized formal sector manufacturing firms in India to conserve on hiring labor—India's most abundant factor of production—and gravitate toward capital-intensive production processes and sectors (see Panagariya 2008 for a detailed discussion).[13]

However, the Chapter VB provisions of the IDA are not the only ones that may have created such incentives. The IDA also prescribes the terms under which employers may change "conditions of service" (dealt with in Sections 9A and 9B of Chapter IIA). Section 9A of the act requires that employees be given at least twenty-one days' notice before employers modify wages and other allowances, hours of work, rest intervals, and leave. According to some observers, including the Government of India's Task Force on Employment Opportunities, the "requirement of a 21 day notice can present problems when units have to redeploy labor quickly to meet the requirement, for example, for time bound export orders" (Planning Commission 2001, p. 156).

But the problem may be more serious than just delays caused by a twenty-one-day notice period. Along with the Industrial Employment (Standing Orders) Act, which requires all employers with one hundred or more workers (fifty in certain states) to inform workers of the specific terms of their employment, the provisions on service conditions seek to make labor contracts complete, fair, and legally binding. While these are laudable objectives, the problem, according to some analysts, is that the workings of India's Trade Union Act make it difficult to obtain the worker consent needed to execute changes in service conditions (including modifying job descriptions, moving workers from one plant to another, etc.). The Trade Union Act allows any seven workers in the enterprise to form and register a trade union, but has no provisions for union recognition (for example, by a secret ballot).[14] The result has been multiple unions within the same establishment, with rivalries between unions so common that a requirement of workers' consent for enacting changes "can become one of consensus amongst all unions and groups, a virtual impossibility" (Anant 2000, p. 251).

In summary, certain elements of India's labor regulations have the potential to create strong incentives for firms to conserve on hiring workers. Since these incentives can be expected to arise as firms approach the thresholds of seven, fifty, and one hundred workers due to the regulations discussed above (and ten and twenty workers owing to other regulations which also impinge on labor issues), India's labor regulations may well have affected the size distribution of manufacturing firms. In particular, based on the assumption that very large sized firms—with, say, two hundred or more workers (i.e., double the one-hundred-worker threshold employed by Chapter VB of the IDA)—are better placed to comply with these regulations and still be profitable, small- and medium-sized firms can be expected to be the most affected by labor regulations and thus less prevalent in the Indian manufacturing landscape.

It is important to note that not all analysts agree that India's labor laws have made for a rigid labor market. In particular, a counterargument to the views above is that the rigidity inducing regulations have been either ignored (see Nagaraj 2002) or circumvented through the increased usage of temporary (casual) or contract workers (Ramaswamy 2003).[15] Since many provisions of Indian labor regulations, including those of the IDA, cover only "regular" workers, firms have an incentive to hire temporary and contract workers instead. While the Contract Labour (Regulation and Prohibition) Act, which regulates the employment of contract labor, provides for the abolition of contract labor in work that is of a perennial nature and is carried out by regular workers in the same or similar establishments (under Section 10 of the act), the share of contract labor in Indian manufacturing has increased considerably over time and may have served to reduce the bite of labor regulations (Ahsan and Pages 2007).[16,17]

At the same time, it needs to be recognized that some major industrial disputes have arisen over contract labor (regarding "regularization" and union recognition, for example), and some amount of uncertainty will always accompany the use of contract labor for getting around other labor regulations. Ultimately, whether or not India's labor laws have created significant rigidities in labor markets is an empirical issue.

Evidence on Labor Regulations and Firm Size Distribution

How can we test whether India's labor regulations have affected the firm size distribution? We follow Besley and Burgess (2004), who examine variation in labor regulations across India's states to develop a measure of the stance of labor regulations at the state level. As per the Indian constitution, states are given control over various aspects of regulation (and enforcement). Labor market regulation is one such area, and various studies—starting with Besley and Burgess—have attempted to codify state-level differences in labor regulation. If labor regulations do generate incentives to remain small, then states deemed to have "inflexible" ("flexible") labor regulations should have a firm size distribution that is characterized by greater prevalence of smaller (larger) firms.

Unfortunately, quantifying differences in labor market regulations across states—a critical step in evaluating whether labor regulations have affected different dimensions of industrial performance—has proved to be contentious. For example, Besley and Burgess evaluate state-level amendments to the IDA—arguably the most important set of labor regulations governing Indian industry—and code legislative changes across major states as pro-worker, neutral, or pro-employer. Bhattacharjea (2006), however, has argued that deciding objectively whether an individual amendment to the IDA is pro-employer or pro-worker is difficult. Even if individual amendments can be so coded, the actual workings of the regulations can hinge on judicial interpretations of the amendments. Moreover, if noncompliance with the regulations is widespread, then even an accurate coding of amendments loses its meaning.

A recent study that considers these complexities is that by Gupta, Hasan, and Kumar (2009, henceforth GHK). GHK's starting point is the state-level indexes/assessments of labor regulations developed by Besley and Burgess (2004), Bhattacharjea (2009), and OECD (2007). While the Besley and Burgess measure relies on amendments to the IDA as a whole, the Bhattacharjea assessment focuses exclusively on Chapter VB of the IDA—the section that deals with the requirement for firms to seek government permission for layoffs, retrenchments, and closures. Moreover, Bhattacharjea considers not only the content of legislative amendments but also judicial interpretations to Chapter VB. Finally, Bhattacharjea carries out his own assessment of legislative amendments rather than relying on that of Besley and Burgess.

The OECD study, on the other hand, is based on a survey of experts and codes progress in recent years in introducing changes not only to regulations dealing with labor issues but also to the relevant administrative processes and enforcement machinery. The regulations covered by the survey go well beyond the IDA and include the Factories Act, the Trade Union Act, and Contract Labour Act, among others. Within each major regulatory area, a number of issues is considered. Scores are assigned on the basis of whether or not a given state has introduced changes. A higher score is given for changes that are deemed to be pro-employer. The responses on each individual item across the various regulatory and administrative areas are aggregated into an index that reflects the extent to which procedural changes have reduced transaction costs vis-à-vis labor issues.

GHK compare the stance of state-level labor regulations proposed by each of the three studies and find similarities across them.[18] In particular, they note that diametrically opposite classifications of labor regulations for a given state—such as a state classified as having flexible (inflexible) regulations by one measure and inflexible (flexible) by another—are unusual. They thus assign scores of 1, 0, and -1 (denoting flexible, neutral, and inflexible regulations, respectively) to each state based on information from the three studies and then adopt a simple majority rule to come up with a composite index of labor regulations. The advantage of this approach is that if a particular methodology or data source used by one of the underlying studies is subject to measurement error, it will be ignored due to the majority rule.

In what follows, we use the GHK composite index to categorize states in terms of whether their labor regulations are flexible or inflexible.[19] Five states are deemed to have flexible labor regulations: Andhra Pradesh, Karnataka, Rajasthan, Tamil Nadu, and Uttar Pradesh. The remaining ten states are deemed to have inflexible labor regulations: Assam, Bihar, Gujarat, Haryana, Kerala, Madhya Pradesh, Maharashtra, Orissa, Punjab, and West Bengal.

Figure 2.10 shows the 2005 distribution of employment in formal (i.e., ASI firms) and informal (i.e., NSSO firms, but excluding the OAMEs) manufacturing firms across two types of states (those with inflexible and flexible labor regulations as per the GHK measure) and five size groups (1–9 employees, 10–49 employees, 50–99 employees, 100–199 employees, and 200 or more

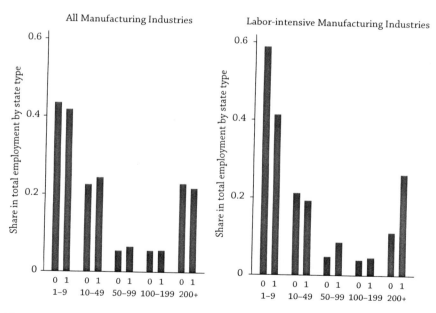

Figure 2.10
Employment Share by Firm Size and Labor Regulation, 2005
Notes: States are distinguished in terms of whether they have inflexible (0) or flexible (1) labor regulations. Firms are distinguished by size groups defined in terms of number of employees.
Source: Authors' computations based on ASI and NSSO datasets.

employees).[20] The definition of the size groups are influenced by the key employment thresholds at which various regulations impinging on labor issues take effect—around ten for the Factories Act and Trade Union Act, fifty for certain provisions of the IDA and the Industrial Employment (Standing Orders) Act, and one hundred for Chapter VB of the IDA.

The distributions shown in the first panel are constructed using all sixteen manufacturing industries. As is quite clear, they are quite similar across inflexible and flexible labor regulation states. More than 40 percent of manufacturing employment in both types of states is accounted for by firms with fewer than ten employees; firms with either ten to forty-nine employees or two hundred or more employees account for between 20 and 25 percent of manufacturing employment each; and medium-sized firms with 50–99 employees and 100–199 employees account for around 5 percent of total manufacturing employment each.[21] Differences in the share of total manufacturing employment accounted for by firms in a given size group are never larger than two percentage points across the two types of states.

To some extent, the distribution of employment for *both* types of states is consistent with their being affected by labor regulations. First, the largest share of employment is accounted for by the smallest firm size group, a category that is least subject to labor regulations. Second, employment shares are the lowest for medium-sized firms, the category in which the main potentially rigidity-inducing regulations kick in (i.e., in the neighborhoods of fifty and one hundred workers, if not at precisely those thresholds once imperfections in monitoring and labor regulation enforcement are allowed for). Finally, larger shares of employment are accounted for by firms with two hundred or more workers. While these large firms would certainly face the full weight of labor regulations, their large size should also put them in a better position to profitably comply with the costs of regulations compared to medium-sized firms.

On the face of it, however, not finding significant differences in the distribution of firm size across flexible and inflexible labor regulation states suggests that other, non-labor-related factors may well explain the observed firm size distributions.[22] But, it is possible that the bite of labor regulations is felt more in labor-intensive industries. If so, differences between the distribution of firm size across state type should be more apparent if we restrict attention to labor-intensive industries. The second panel of figure 2.10 (right side panel) allows a comparison of the firm size distribution across state type for labor-intensive industries.[23] The picture changes quite dramatically. The flexible labor regulation states have a significantly smaller share of manufacturing employment in 1–9 employee firms (seventeen percentage points smaller, to be precise); they also have a considerably higher share of employment in firms with two hundred or more employees (15 percentage points higher). The patterns are similar, though not as dramatic, if we use data from 1994 and if states are partitioned on the basis of GHK's Besley-Burgess measure.

Since labor-intensive industries are the ones in which the costs of labor are a significant share of total production costs, the findings that states categorized as having inflexible labor regulations have a much higher share of manufacturing employment in very small sized firms (i.e., firms which are hardly subject to any labor regulation), and that states with flexible labor regulations have a much larger share of manufacturing employment in large firms (i.e., firms which would be subject to the full force of India's labor regulations and likely to find their profitability significantly affected by the costs of labor regulation relative to their counterparts in more capital-intensive industries) are suggestive of a causal link between labor regulations and firm size distribution.

The case for a causal link would be strengthened if we could be more certain that our partition of states is more influenced by labor regulations than by anything else—for example, some aspect of the business environment unrelated to labor regulations. We thus consider how the distribution of firm size varies across states partitioned on the basis of another characteristic, one likely to have significant bearing on the prospects of manufacturing firms in general and not specifically those operating in labor-intensive industries. In particular, we use the work of Kumar (2002) and partition states into ones with relatively better or worse physical infrastructure. We then examine how the size distribution of firms varies across these two types of states. As before, we carry out this exercise for the entire sample of enterprises as well as those belonging to labor-intensive industries only.

Figure 2.11 shows the resulting distributions of employment. Interestingly, when all manufacturing industries are considered (left-hand side panel), states with better infrastructure have a smaller share of total manufacturing employment in the smallest firms (fewer than ten employees). For all other size groups, states with better infrastructure have higher shares of manufacturing employment. The differences are rarely large, however. More important, restricting attention to labor-intensive industries does not yield dramatically different distributions of employment across state type when states are distinguished in terms of infrastructure quality. This is unlike the case of figure 2.10 where labor-intensive industries are characterized by large differences in employment shares across state type when states are distinguished on the basis of labor market regulations.

We now turn to an analysis of the size distribution of employment and related issues using data for formal manufacturing firms alone. As noted in the second section, ASI data allow us to distinguish between production workers and other employees, and also allow the former to be subdivided into two categories that can be treated as regular workers and contract workers

All Manufacturing Industries   Labor-intensive Manufacturing Industries

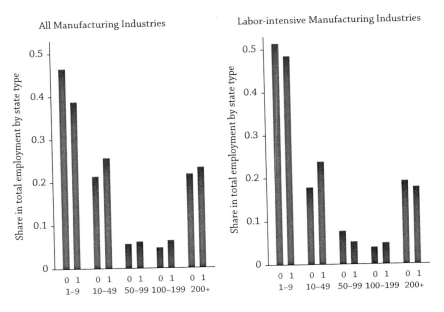

Figure 2.11
Employment Share by Firm Size and Infrastructure, 2005
Notes: States are distinguished in terms of whether they have weak (0) or strong (1) infrastructure. Firms are distinguished by size groups defined in terms of number of employees.
Source: Authors' computations based on ASI and NSSO datasets.

("workers employed directly" and "workers employed through contractors" being the exact terms used in the ASI surveys). The data also allow analysis by age of enterprise (or, as described in the ASI survey questionnaire, "year of initial production").

In what follows, we work with four size groups instead of the previous five. This is because we exclude formal enterprises with fewer than ten regular workers, since the Factories Act—which encompasses the universe of formal manufacturing firms—applies to firms with ten or more regular workers.[24] The four size groups, based on the number of regular workers, are: 10–49 workers, 50–99 workers, 100–199 workers, and 200 or more workers. Insofar as the employment shares are concerned, we also construct these using data on regular workers. Figure 2.12 is the ASI data analog to figure 2.10 and shows a very similar pattern: states with flexible labor regulations have smaller (larger) employment shares in smaller (larger) sized firms when attention is restricted to labor-intensive industries.

What is interesting in the case of ASI data is that this pattern is further reinforced when the ASI firms are restricted to those that started production after 1982.[25] As may be recalled, 1982 was the year that Chapter VB of the IDA was amended to lower the threshold above which employers would have to seek formal permission from the government to lay off or retrench workers

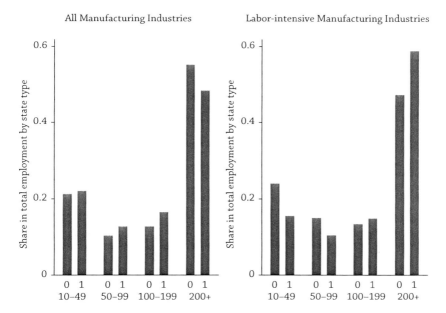

Figure 2.12
Employment Share by Firm Size and Labor Regulation in the Formal Sector, 2005
Notes: States are distinguished in terms of whether they have inflexible (0) or flexible (1) labor regulations.
Firms are distinguished by size groups defined in terms of number of regular production workers.
Source: Authors' computations based on ASI data.

(i.e., from three hundred workers to one hundred workers). Thus, as may be seen by comparing the first and second panels of figure 2.13, the differentials in employment shares across flexible and inflexible labor regulation states are accentuated when firms are restricted to those that started production after 1982.[26]

Interestingly, and consistent with figure 2.13, table 2.6 reveals that of the firms operating in 2005, a greater number had been established (commenced production, strictly speaking) in states with flexible labor regulations after 1982 (first two column of the upper and lower panels).[27] This is true in the aggregate as well as for every size group. However, this was not always the case. Prior to 1976, when Chapter VB of the IDA was first introduced, a greater number of firms operated in inflexible labor regulation states (last two columns of the upper and lower panels). Again, this is true both in the aggregate as well as for every size group. This pattern is particularly stark when we restrict attention to large firms in labor-intensive industries (lower panel of table 2.6). Thus, more than three times as many of the enterprises established after 1982 with two hundred or more workers are in states with flexible labor regulations. In contrast, focusing on firms established prior to 1976, the number of such enter-

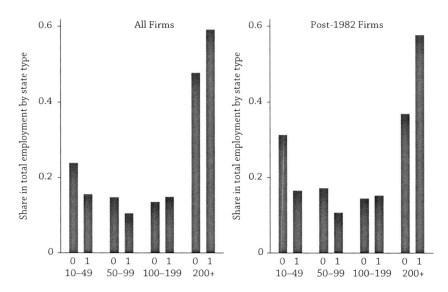

Figure 2.13
Employment Share by Firm Size and Labor Regulation in the Labor-Intensive Formal Sector,
2005
Notes: States are distinguished in terms of whether they have inflexible (0) or flexible (1) labor regulations.
Firms are distinguished by size groups defined in terms of number of regular production workers.
Source: Authors' computations based on ASI data.

Table 2.6 NUMBER OF FIRMS IN 2005 BY YEAR OF INITIAL PRODUCTION,
STATE LABOR REGULATION, AND INDUSTRY TYPE

Size Groups (regular workers)	Post-1982		1976–1982		Pre-1976	
	Inflexible LR	Flexible LR	Inflexible LR	Flexible LR	Inflexible LR	Flexible LR
All industries						
10–49	16,889	16,984	2,652	1,686	3,532	2,075
50–99	2,304	2,869	336	339	706	401
100–199	1,219	1,704	166	240	674	405
200+	877	1,154	214	236	758	471
Labor-intensive industries						
10–49	3,512	4,144	420	272	567	376
50–99	550	813	78	56	164	107
100–199	234	578	35	30	99	84
200+	151	559	51	61	98	69

Notes: States are distinguished in terms of whether they have inflexible or flexible labor regulations (LR).
Firms are distinguished by size group defined in terms of number of regular production workers.
Source: Authors' computations based on ASI data for 2005.

Table 2.7 THE USE OF CONTRACT WORKERS

Size Groups (workers)	Firms with Contract Workers (%)			Average Share of Contract Workers (%)		
	1994	2000	2005	1994	2000	2005
All industries						
10–49	18	21	25	11	14	17
50–99	30	38	46	19	24	31
100–199	30	38	46	16	21	29
200+	32	43	50	13	19	27
Labor-intensive industries						
10–49	17	22	26	13	17	20
50–99	26	39	46	18	30	37
100–199	27	37	43	16	22	30
200+	35	39	42	16	21	26

Note: Firms are distinguished by size group defined in terms of number of production workers (i.e., on regular plus contract basis).
Source: Authors' computations based on ASI data.

prises in flexible labor regulation states was lower than that in inflexible labor regulation states.

No analysis of the effects of labor regulation on employment patterns would be complete without a look at the issue of contract labor. Table 2.7 depicts the propensity of firms to hire contract workers, as well as the share of contract workers among all production workers across different firm size groups. The size groups used here are defined on the basis of all production workers (both regular and contract workers) rather than only regular workers as above.

An examination of the first three columns of table 2.7 reveals that the propensity of firms to hire contract workers has increased over time and for each of the four size groups. Interestingly, within any given year a large increase in the propensity to hire contract workers takes place as we go from firms with 10–49 production workers to firms with 50 or more workers. Whereas around a quarter of firms with 10–49 workers used contract workers in 2005, almost half of firms with 50–99 workers did so (regardless of whether we consider all industries together or restrict attention to labor-intensive industries only). The propensity increases over the subsequent two size groups when all industries are considered, but not as dramatically. Interestingly, among only labor-intensive industries in 2005, firms with 50–99 workers are most likely to use contract workers.

A similar pattern emerges when we examine, across firms, the average share of contract workers employed (i.e., the ratio of contract workers to all production workers). According to 2005 data (last column of table 2.7), the share of contract workers almost doubles from an average of 17 percent for firms with 10–49 workers to 31 percent for firms with 50–99 workers and tends to stabilize beyond this size group. The corresponding increase for labor-intensive industries is from 20 percent to 37 percent. Interestingly, the average share of contract workers peaks for the group of firms with 50–99 workers. In fact, the share of contract workers peaks in firms with 50–99 workers across all industries, not only labor-intensive ones.

It needs to be noted that while the use of contract workers should afford firms some "flexibility" regarding labor regulations, it is not a very desirable solution to the potential rigidities labor regulations cause. From the perspective of workers, the higher wages and income stability that come with longer, more stable tenure will always be preferable to contract work. From the perspective of employers, Section 10 of the Contract Labour (Regulation and Prohibition) Act creates uncertainties about the legitimate employment of contract work in firms' production processes. Indeed, the year 2011 has witnessed a series of strikes across the country, especially in the motor vehicles and parts industry (Varma 2011); the hiring of contract workers has been an underlying issue in many cases, suggesting that flexibility earned through contract workers may be a short-term solution for firms.

CONCLUSION

In this chapter, we have used establishment-level data from the Indian manufacturing industry to examine the distribution of firms across employment size groups. Like Mazumdar (2003) and Mazumdar and Sarkar (2008), we find the Indian size distribution to be characterized by a preponderance of very small enterprises and a "missing middle," even in data from as recent as 2005. We have also discussed why such a pattern—especially small firms accounting for a large share of employment—can represent welfare losses. Like the extensive international literature on the issue, we find both average wages and labor productivity to be much lower in small firms than in large firms.

We have also examined the possible effects of labor regulations on firm size and its distribution. Using available measures of labor regulations across Indian states, we find that as far as labor-intensive industries are concerned, states with more flexible (inflexible) labor regulations tend to have a greater share of employment in larger (smaller) firms. Moreover, this is more evident among firms established after 1982, when an amendment to the IDA—perhaps the single most important piece of legislation affecting labor-related issues for

Indian manufacturing—required firms with one hundred or more workers to seek permission from the government to lay off or retrench employees. Taken together, the results are suggestive of a link between labor regulations and firm size distribution.

ACKNOWLEDGMENT

This chapter is an extensively revised version of our earlier work, "The Distribution of Firm Size in India: What Can Survey Data Tell Us?" (Asian Development Bank Economics Working Paper Series, no 213). We are indebted to Arvind Panagariya for detailed discussions on the possible effects of India's labor regulations, which motivated the extensions to our original analysis that appear here. We would also like to thank Pranab Bardhan, Dipak Mazumdar, and K. V. Ramaswamy for useful comments and suggestions. Of course, any errors are our responsibility. The views presented here are those of the authors and not necessarily those of the Asian Development Bank, its executive directors, or the countries that they represent.

APPENDIX

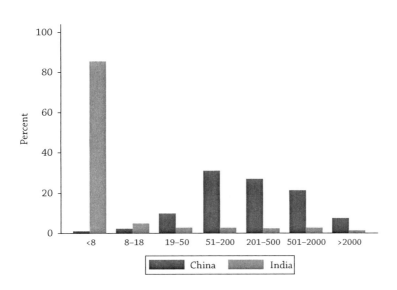

Figure 2.A2
Employment Share by Firm Size in China and India Including OAMEs: Apparel, 2005
Source: Authors' computations based on ASI and NSSO datasets for India and ADB (2009) for China.

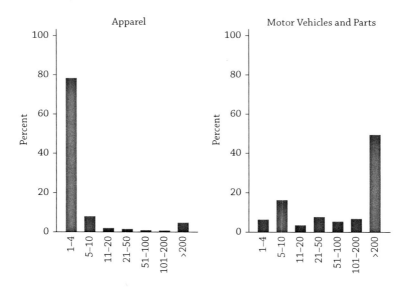

Figure 2.A1
Employment Share by Firm Size Including OAMEs: Apparel vs. Motor Vehicles and Parts, 2005
Source: Authors' computations based on ASI and NSSO datasets.

NOTES

1. The terms *enterprise* (or firms) and *establishment* are often used interchangeably in this chapter. These are distinct concepts. An establishment is a single physical location at which business is conducted or where services or industrial operations are performed. An enterprise or firm is a business organization consisting of one or more domestic establishments under common ownership or control. For companies with only one establishment, the enterprise and the establishment are the same.
2. From 1997–1998 to 2003–2004, only units having 200 or more workers were covered in the census sector. See India's Ministry of Statistics and Program Implementation website, http://mospi.nic.in/stat_act_t3.htm, for more details.
3. ASI microdata allow production workers to be further subdivided into two categories: those hired "directly" and "workers employed through contractors." Directly hired workers include all "regular" or permanent workers. Others, including casual labor hired on daily wages, are classified under the second category. Regular workers receive a number of benefits and protections not available to other workers.
4. The capital-intensity ranking of industries hardly changes when we use the market value of plant and machinery instead of our preferred measure. The capital-intensive industries are: machinery, electrical machinery, transport, metals and alloys, rubber/plastic/petroleum/coal and paper/paper products. The labor-intensive industries are: beverages and tobacco, textile products, wood/wood products, leather/leather products, and non-metallic products. The remaining

industries are not as clearly distinguishable and include: food products, textiles, basic chemicals, metal products, and other manufacturing.

5. Firms in the ASI are also classified based on their status, i.e., whether they are "open" or "closed" for the reference year and "non-operative" for at least three years prior to the reference year.

6. See box 3.1 of ADB (2009, page 23) for details on data sources and methodology pertaining to figure 2.1.

7. For instance, de Soto 1989.

8. Of course, the relationship between production technology and the optimum size of enterprises can be quite complex and one that has changed over time. Moreover, other factors matter for firm size, such as the nature and evolution of transaction costs. See Section 4 of ADB (2009) for more details.

9. Including OAMEs in the Indian distribution reveals that more than 80 percent of employment in Indian apparel is accounted for by enterprises with fewer than 8 employees (as opposed to around 53 percent depicted in figure 2.9).

10. A question that arises is why firms of different sizes seem to coexist in the same broad product line. One reason is to be found in the diversity in quality of the product. While there are certainly exceptions, it is generally the case that higher-quality products require greater mechanization and more tasks. Accordingly, the optimal size of the enterprise increases.

11. As discussed in the second section of this paper, the Factories Act governs manufacturing firms with ten workers (twenty if the firm's production process doesn't use power). The act requires firms to comply with a variety of regulations related to both labor and non-labor issues. Manufacturing firms with ten or more workers also come under the purview of the Employees State Insurance Act which mandates a variety of health- and social security-related benefits for workers.

12. There are two caveats to this observation, however. First, larger firms may well have greater wherewithal to absorb the higher costs associated with labor regulations. Second, certain regulations may affect capital-intensive industries to a greater extent. For example, regulations that raise the cost of settling industrial disputes can exacerbate the "holdup problem" for owners of capital. It is not much of a stretch to imagine that such holdup problems would be a greater concern for firms operating in capital-intensive industries. Ahsan and Pagés (2007) find evidence consistent with this view.

13. Consistent with the idea that India's labor regulations have encouraged capital-intensive production processes and sectors, Hasan, Mitra, and Sundaram (2010) find that capital–labor ratios are higher in India than other countries with similar levels of development and factor endowments for a majority of manufacturing industries.

14. An amendment to the Trade Union Act in 2001 raised the minimum number of workers that can form a trade union in the case of enterprises with one hundred or more workers. In such enterprises, the minimum has been set at 10 percent of the total number of workers up to a maximum of one hundred workers. Additionally, one-third or five officers of the trade union, whichever is less, are permitted to be outsiders in the case of organized sector enterprises as per the 2001 amendment.

15. For a detailed review of Indian labor regulations and the debate surrounding the issue of rigidity, see Anant et al (2006).

16. The act applies to all establishments employing at least twenty workers as contract labor on any day in the preceding twelve months, and to every contractor

employing twenty or more contract workers in the same period. The act provides for the registration of establishments of the principal employer employing contract labor and the licensing of contractors. The principal employer must provide facilities such as rest room, canteens, first aid, etc., if the contractor fails to do so. The principal employer must also ensure that the contractor pays the wages due to the laborers.

17. The share of contract labor in manufacturing has increased from around 12 percent in 1985 to 23 percent in 2002 (Ahsan and Pagés 2007). Certain states have seen a particularly sharp rise in the use of contract labor. Andhra Pradesh, which has seen the largest increase, passed a law in 2003 permitting contract labor employment in so-called core activities of firms and widening the scope of non-core activities (Anant et al. 2006).

18. For the purpose of their study, GHK consider time-invariant measures of state-level labor regulations. They also make two important changes to the original coding of Besley and Burgess. First, based on the arguments of Bhattacharjea (2006), they treat labor regulations in Gujarat as neutral rather than pro-worker. Second, they deem Madhya Pradesh's labor regulations to be neutral rather than mildly pro-employer.

19. We checked our results using GHK's time-invariant measure of state-level labor regulations based on only the Besley and Burgess coding of amendments to the IDA. Results were quite similar, something which is not surprising given that the two state-level measures only differ for two states. Kerala is considered a flexible labor regulation state, while Uttar Pradesh considered an inflexible labor regulation state in GHK's time-invariant version of Besley and Burgess.

20. Employee data is used here since it is difficult to distinguish between different types of workers in the NSSO data.

21. Employment shares are specific to the type of state. More specifically, the employment share for any particular size group and state type is calculated by dividing the employment generated by manufacturing firms belonging to that particular size group in states with a common stance on labor regulations (i.e., inflexible or flexible) by the total manufacturing employment in those states.

22. Of course, this is conditional on our partition of states representing accurately their stance on labor regulations.

23. Recall that labor-intensive industries are: beverages and tobacco, textile products, wood/wood Products, leather/leather products, and non-metallic products. The capital intensive industries are: machinery, electrical machinery, transport, metals and alloys, rubber/plastic/petroleum/coal, and paper/paper products. The remaining industries, which are difficult to unambiguously classify, are: food products, textiles, basic chemicals, metal products, and other manufacturing.

24. We also apply some filters such as dropping firms which report having more total employees than production workers (i.e., regular workers plus contract workers). Fortunately, there are not too many such observations.

25. Firms failing to report the year in which they commenced production, or reporting it as earlier than 1800 or later than 2005, are dropped from this analysis.

26. The first panel of figure 2.13 is virtually identical to the second panel of figure 2.12; the only difference stems from the omission of firms with missing or implausible information on year of establishment.

27. As with all other data analysis in this chapter, the numbers reported in table 2.6 are generated using survey weights provided in the firm-level data.

REFERENCES

Ahsan, Ahmad, and Carmen Pagés. 2007. "Are All Labor Regulations Equal? Assessing The Effects Of Job Security, Labor Dispute and Contract Labor Laws in India." *World Bank Policy Research Working Paper* 4259, June.

Anant, T. C. A. 2000. "Reforming the Labour Market." In S. Gangopadhyay and W. Wadhwa, eds., *Economic Reforms for the Poor*. New Delhi: Konark.

Anant, T. C. A., R. Hasan, P. Mohapatra, R. Nagraj, and S. K. Sasikumar. 2006. "Labor Markets in India: Issues and Perspectives." In J. Felipe and R. Hasan, eds., *Labor Markets in Asia: Issues and Perspectives*. London: Palgrave Macmillan for the Asian Development Bank.

Asian Development Bank. 2009. *Key Indicators 2009: Enterprises in Asia: Fostering Dynamism in SMEs*. Manila, Philippines: Asian Development Bank.

Besley, Timothy, and Robin Burgess. 2004. "Can Regulation Hinder Economic Performance? Evidence from India." *The Quarterly Journal of Economics* 119(1):91–134.

Bhattacharjea, Aditya. 2006. "Labour Market Regulation and Industrial Performance in India: A Critical Review of the Empirical Evidence." *The Indian Journal of Labour Economics* 49(2):211–232.

Bhattacharjea, Aditya. 2009. "The Effects of Employment Protection Legislation on Indian Manufacturing." *Center on Democracy, Development and the Rule of Law Working Paper*, Number 96. Stanford University.

de Mel, S., D. McKenzie, and C. Woodruff. 2008. "Who Are the Microenterprise Owners? Evidence from Sri Lanka on Tokman v. de Soto." Policy Research Working Paper No. 4635. Washington, DC: World Bank.

de Soto, Hernando. 1989. *The Other Path: The Invisible Revolution in the Third World*. New York: Harper and Row.

Gupta, Poonam, Rana Hasan, and Utsav Kumar. 2009. "Big Reforms but Small Payoffs: Explaining the Weak Record of Growth in Indian Manufacturing." *India Policy Forum* 5: 59–123.

Hasan, Rana, Devashish Mitra, and Asha Sundaram. 2010. "The Determinants of Capital Intensity in Manufacturing: The Role of Factor Endowments and Factor Market Imperfections." Mimeo, Syracuse University.

Kumar, T. Ravi. 2002. "The Impact of Regional Infrastructure Investment in India." *Regional Studies* 36(2):194–200.

Mazumdar, Dipak. 2003. "Small and Medium Enterprise Development in Equitable Growth and Poverty Alleviation." In Christopher M. Edmonds, ed., *Reducing Poverty in Asia: Emerging Issues in Growth, Targeting and Measurement*. Chaltenham, UK: Asian Development Bank, Edward Elgar.

Mazumdar, Dipak. 2009. "A Comparative Study of the Size Structure of Manufacturing in Asian Countries." Study prepared for the Asian Development Bank.

Mazumdar, Dipak, and Sandip Sarkar. 2008. *Globalization, Labor Markets and Inequality in India*. Routledge: London and New York.

McKinsey Global Institute. 2001. *India: The Growth Imperative*. McKinsey & Company India Office.

Moore, H. 1911. *Laws of Wages: An Essay in Statistical Economics*. New York: Augustus M. Kelley.

Nagaraj, Rayaprolu. 2002. "Trade and Labor Market Linkages in India: Evidence and Issues." Economic Series Working Paper no. 50. East West Center, Hawaii.

Nataraj, Shanthi. 2011. "The Impact of Trade Liberalization on Productivity and Firm Size: Evidence from India's Formal and Informal Manufacturing Sectors." *Journal of International Economics* 85(2):292–301.

Oi, W., and T. L. Idson. 1999. "Firm Size and Wages." In Orley C. Ashenfelter and David Card, eds. *Handbook of Labor Economics Volume 3B*. Amsterdam: Elsevier B. V.

Panagariya, Arvind. 2008. *India: The Emerging Giant*. New York: Oxford University Press.

Planning Commission. 2001. *Report of Task Force on Employment Opportunities*. Report by the Government of India. New Delhi. Available at http://planningcommission. nic.in/aboutus/taskforce/tk_empopp.pdf.

Ramaswamy, K. V. 2003. "Liberalization, Outsourcing and Industrial Labor Markets in India: Some Preliminary Results." In S. Uchikawa, ed., *Labour Market and Institution in India, 1990s and Beyond*. New Delhi: Manohar.

Tokman, V. E. 2007. "Modernizing the Informal Sector." DESA Working Paper No 42. New York: United Nations.

Varma, Subodh. 2011. "Forces of Labour." *Times of India*. Special Report. November 6, page 18.

CHAPTER 3

Complementarity between Formal and Informal Manufacturing in India

The Role of Policies and Institutions

ASHA SUNDARAM, RESHAD N. AHSAN,
AND DEVASHISH MITRA

INTRODUCTION

Are formal and informal sector activities, within an industry, substitutes of each other or complements? In other words, if labor laws constrain formal sector activity (for which these restrictions are binding), is that at least partly made up for by informal sector activity (which is not under the purview of such laws) in that industry? Or do both formal and informal sector activities move in the same direction due to agglomeration effects such as labor-market pooling, location of input suppliers close to where most of an industry's activity is located, various kinds of linkage effects, as well as sometimes relationships based on outsourcing of economic activities from formal sector to informal sector firms? In such cases, it is quite possible that not only will there be a positive correlation between formal and informal sector activity but that this relationship will be even stronger in regions or states where the labor laws make for a less restrictive or a more flexible labor market. An alternative hypothesis could be that this correlation is stronger where labor laws are more restrictive and make for a more rigid labor market, as outsourcing from formal sector to informal sector firms might actually be aimed at getting around these restrictive laws.

The study of the informal manufacturing sector and its linkages with formal manufacturing is important from the public policy point of view for a number of reasons. Producers in the informal sector use outdated technologies and as a result have lower productivity, which in turn leads to lower wages. Around 80 percent of manufacturing employment is in the informal sector, even though its contribution to manufacturing value added is only about 20 percent (which by itself implies a much lower productivity in informal manufacturing compared to formal manufacturing). Thus, a study of the relationship between the formal and informal manufacturing sectors is important for sharpening our understanding of the factors that lead to poverty reduction. Agglomeration externalities arising in the process of manufacturing sector growth can benefit the informal sector through various kinds of spillovers. We study such issues in this chapter. In addition, we investigate whether informal sector activity is affected by trade liberalization and whether the link between formal and informal sector activity can be explained by the former outsourcing to the latter, possibly to get around labor laws that might be restrictive.

A casual look at the broad Indian sectoral data on formal and informal employment, output, and value added shows that within the manufacturing sector, the share of informal sector employment has been rising slowly over time—from about 75 percent in 1989 to roughly 81 percent in 2000—while its share in value added has been stable (with minor fluctuations) at around 20 percent. It is also true that value added has been rising over time in both the informal and formal manufacturing sectors. On the other hand, employment in the formal sector has remained static or has even been mildly declining, while in the informal sector it has been rising steadily. These observations imply that while in the case of value added we get a percent-to-percent match in the growth of formal and informal manufacturing (indicative of some degree of complementarity between the two sectors), the growth in population or the labor force has mainly been absorbed by the informal manufacturing sector.

Our cross-state, cross-industry analysis also shows strong positive correlation between formal and informal sector activities (employment, output, and value added). This correlation lends significant support to the complementarity hypothesis. Here, however, the elasticity of informal sector activity at the industry level with respect to the corresponding formal industry-level activity variable (employment, output, or value added) is less than unitary, which is indicative of a move toward formal production within an industry and shows that the opposite effect in aggregate data may be due to changes in the industrial composition of the economy. We also find some evidence that the positive impact of formal sector activity on informal manufacturing is bigger in states with more flexible labor markets. Labor-market pooling makes sense only if hiring and firing are not too restricted. High firing costs lead to both limited hiring and limited firing, since employers do not want to hire a worker and be stuck with that person even in bad times or if the worker turns out to be unproductive or incompetent. Thus, with less restrictive labor market policies, workers located in such regions will have greater probability of employment in formal sector firms. That alone will act as an incentive for potential employees to also seek jobs in the informal sector enterprises in such a region.

We explore the effect of labor-market restrictions on the complementarity or substitutability of formal and informal manufacturing activity, as well as how trade liberalization affects informal manufacturing activity, by categorizing Indian states as either pro-labor or pro-employer, which we will call "rigid" and "flexible," respectively. As explained in our data section, the classification is from Gupta, Hasan, and Kumar (2009).

Our results also seem to suggest that the positive relationship between formal and informal sector activity is stronger in industries that use more capital-intensive techniques in the formal sector. Since our measure of labor or capital intensity of an industry is the observed technique in use in the formal sector, our results may be interpreted as saying that the industries where formal sector firms are relatively more successful at outsourcing look more capital intensive, primarily because the production activities they outsource are relatively more labor intensive. Hence, these results suggest outsourcing between the formal and informal manufacturing sectors in India, leading to stronger complementarity between formal and informal sector activity.

In fact, we also find some direct evidence—albeit weak—that outsourcing by formal sector firms to informal sector firms leads to higher informal sector output in states with more flexible labor markets. Additionally, we find evidence that greater formal sector activity is associated with a greater proportion of informal enterprises selling their output (or contracting to sell their output) to another enterprise or a middleman/contractor.

Finally, trade liberalization seems to boost employment, output, and value added in informal manufacturing (with just a few exceptions). This positive effect of trade liberalization is stronger in enterprises with more than five workers in states with rigid labor laws. On the other hand, earlier work by Mitra and Ural (2007) shows that the positive impact of trade liberalization on formal sector employment, output, and value added is greater in states with more flexible labor markets. This leads to the following interpretation: rigid labor laws constrain the growth of formal manufacturing, with the remainder of the growth picked up by informal manufacturing. This might also mean that the trade liberalization induced structural change—in terms of the shares of the formal and informal sectors in output, value added, and employment is more desirable where labor markets are more flexible. In other words, the change in composition between formal and informal activities is not skewed toward the latter in the case of such states.

In the context of our analysis it is important to understand that rigid labor laws constrain the ability of formal sector firms to hire and fire workers in response to shocks to technology, relative prices of output and inputs, and the macroeconomic environment. Thus adjustment is restricted, which can have an adverse impact on the functioning of private firms and therefore efficiency at all levels. Additionally, the realization of the beneficial effects of trade reforms requires substantial labor reallocation—both intersectoral and intrasectoral. Rigid labor laws can constrain such reallocation. Panagariya (2001) has argued that rigid labor laws raise the costs for employers and also constrain the size of firms by discouraging them from employing more than a fairly small number of permanent workers. He also argues that the costs of such rigid labor laws go beyond those incurred by existing entrepreneurs, as these laws also discourage entry. It is important to note that labor laws are expected to impact mainly formal or organized manufacturing firms. However, due to agglomeration externalities, possible competition effects, and outsourcing possibilities, these labor laws may have spillover effects on informal sector firms as well.

INDIAN POLICY AND INSTITUTIONAL FRAMEWORK

The Trade Reforms in India

The general elections of 1991 brought to power a new government that inherited probably the world's most complex and restrictive trade regime and, at the same time, a very severe external payments problem. Upon request, the International Monetary Fund (IMF) granted loans to the government of India, albeit on the condition of major and deep economic reforms. The reforms were initiated instantly. Many members in the new cabinet had been cabinet members in past governments that had tried to avoid IMF loans precisely to avoid these conditions. These members were also strong believers in inward-looking trade policies and the use of tariffs as a primary source of revenues. Thus, the reforms came as a surprise.

The maximum tariff was reduced from 400 to 150 percent in July 1991, 110 percent in February 1992, 85 percent in February 1993, 64 per cent in February 1994, and roughly 45 percent by 1997–98. The mean tariff went from 128 percent before July 1991 to 94 percent in February 1992, 71 percent by February 1993, 55 percent in February 1994, and roughly 35 percent by 1997–98. The standard deviation of tariffs during this period went down from forty-one percentage points to roughly fifteen. While some of the non-tariff barriers were reduced, many others were completely eliminated. Other major trade reform objectives included the removal of most licensing and other non-tariff barriers on all imports of intermediate and capital goods, the broadening and simplification of export incentives, the removal of export restrictions, the elimination of the trade monopolies of the state trading agencies, the simplification of the trade regime, and so on.

Labor Markets: Regulations and Rigidity

We describe here some salient features of the labor market regulations in India. First, labor issues fall in the concurrent list of the constitution over which the central (federal) government and individual state governments have legislative authority. The state governments have the authority to amend central statutes, introduce subsidiary legislations, and enforce most labor regulations irrespective of who enacted them. Thus there may be considerable variation in labor markets across India's states.

Second, India's labor laws have significantly added to the implicit costs of hiring and firing workers. The Industrial Disputes Act (IDA) requires firms employing more than one hundred workers to obtain the permission of state governments in order to retrench or lay off workers, and states are often unwilling to grant such permission (see Datta-Chaudhuri 1996). There are additional provisions for job security in the Industrial Employment (Standing Orders) Act, applicable to all employers with one hundred or more workers (fifty in certain states), which require worker consent for modification of job descriptions or interplant transfers of workers in response to changing market conditions. This makes adjusting labor input in response to economic shocks very difficult. The problems are further accentuated by India's Trade Union Act (TUA) that allows any seven workers in an enterprise to form and register a trade union. This can lead to multiple unions within the same firm; consensus among them on issues related to wage setting, employment, retrenchment, hiring, and firing is required but becomes almost impossible to achieve (see Anant 2000).

Very minimal labor regulations apply to firms with fewer than ten workers if the firm uses power (or twenty workers if not using power). Such firms are not part of the organized sector and are not subject to the Factories Act of 1948. Once the firm crosses the threshold size (ten with power, twenty without), the firm has to register under the Factories Act, joining the organized or formal sector and becoming subject to numerous regulations relating to facilities, worker safety, overtime work, employment of women and children, and setting up of retirement funds. Reaching a threshold size of fifty employees requires the firm to provide health insurance and makes it subject to the worker–management dispute settlement process under the IDA. As mentioned earlier, the other restrictions on retrenching, firing, and reassigning workers under the IDA apply to firms with one hundred or more employees (see Panagariya 2008 for further details).

Thus, from a casual reading of such labor laws, one would infer that they are likely to encourage the growth of the informal or unorganized sector at the cost of the organized sector. These laws probably also prevent firms within the organized sector from growing.

DATA

The unorganized sector and formal sector data we use for this study come from three main sources. A detailed description of all variables along with data sources (and details on their construction and cleaning) is presented in Appendix A2. The unorganized sector data are the enterprise-level data from the national-level Survey of Unorganized Manufacturing and Repairing Enterprises by India's National Sample Survey Organization (NSSO). The data cover unorganized manufacturing and repairing enterprises, broadly defined as enterprises employing fewer than ten workers if using power or fewer than twenty workers if not using power. These enterprises are not required to register under the Factories Act of 1948 (see various reports by the NSSO on the unorganized manufacturing sector in India for a detailed definition of enterprises covered under the survey). We restrict our analysis to manufacturing and exclude repairing enterprises. The terms "unorganized manufacturing sector," "informal manufacturing sector," and "unregistered manufacturing sector" are often used interchangeably in India. We use three rounds of repeated cross-section data for the years 1989–90, 1994–95, and 2000–01. The data we use cover fifteen major Indian states. We collapse the enterprise-level data in different ways to obtain total output, value added, and employment for rural and urban sectors, for each state, for each of the three years, and for each three-digit industry under the Indian National Industrial Classification (NIC).

We also construct a variable that measures the proportion of informal enterprises that sell their output (or are on contract to sell) to another enterprise or a middleman/contractor for the year 2000. We argue that this can be used as a measure of outsourcing activity for informal enterprises. This is no doubt an imperfect measure of outsourcing since we are not able to observe if the informal enterprise sells to a large formal firm. However, we posit that subcontracting between large formal firms and microenterprises most likely occurs through middlemen and can be captured by this indicator variable for each firm.

Unorganized sector enterprises produce a large variety of products, including flour milling, slaughtering, sun-drying fish, wooden furniture and baskets, lace, embroidery, rope, medicated water and low-end medicines, tooth powder, agricultural metal tools, metal utensils, batteries, valves, cables, bulbs, and electric fans. Unorganized manufacturing enterprises in India are classified into household enterprises that do not hire workers (called own-account manufacturing enterprises or OAMEs), enterprises hiring fewer than six workers including household and hired workers (called non-directory manufacturing enterprises or NDMEs), and enterprises hiring six or more workers including household and hired workers (called directory manufacturing enterprises or DMEs). DMEs were not surveyed in the 1989–90 data round. We perform our analysis separately for each enterprise type.

Our formal sector data are from the Annual Survey of Industries (ASI), conducted by India's Central Statistical Organization. The ASI covers firms registered under the Central Factories Act of 1948. Hence, for our study and in the Indian context in general, the formal sector is associated with larger firm size and consists of firms that are registered under a central authority.

A lot fewer labor regulations apply to unorganized enterprises, and they are also relatively loosely enforced. We use formal sector output, value added, and employment for each of the fifteen states, for each year and three-digit industry. Since we do not have this information separately for rural and urban areas, we use total state-level figures.

We obtain corresponding information on the value of outsourcing in manufacturing by formal sector firms from the Prowess database collected by the Centre for Monitoring the Indian Economy (CMIE). This database has been used previously by Topalova and Khandelwal (2011). It consists of all firms traded on India's major stock exchanges as well as other public sector enterprises. Together these firms represent 70 percent of output in the organized industrial sector in India (Topalova and Khandelwal 2011). The firms in the sample were asked to report their annual expenditure on outsourcing manufacturing activities as well as professional services. Given our focus in this chapter on manufacturing outsourcing between formal and informal Indian firms, we construct our aggregate outsourcing measure using only the manufacturing outsourcing data. In particular, we aggregate the firm manufacturing outsourcing data to the industry-state level. Table 3.1B indicates that the there is Rs. 181.9 million worth of manufacturing outsourcing in the mean industry-state cell in the sample. This translates to approximately US$3.65 million. Interestingly, the amount of outsourcing in 1993 was only Rs. 17.7 million, which indicates that the vast majority of outsourcing has occurred since 1993. Unfortunately, we are unable to tell if outsourcing is to an unorganized manufacturing enterprise. Hence, our outsourcing measure is a proxy for the "outsourcing intensity" of an industry. All monetary values are converted to constant 1993 rupees using an industry-level wholesale price index.

We also use data on the labor intensity of each three-digit industry in the formal sector. Labor intensity is measured using the ASI data and is defined as the ratio of wage bill to value added in each industry. We use this data to look at the differential association between formal and unorganized sector activity across industries with varying labor intensities in their formal-sector production techniques. In addition, we rely on India's diverse institutional environment across states to examine the relationship between formal sector activity, outsourcing, and unorganized sector activity in states with differing labor policies and exposure to international markets.

We classify states into states with flexible labor laws and states with relatively more rigid labor laws on the basis of a labor regulation index from Gupta, Hasan, and Kumar (2009). This partition is based on combining information from Besley and Burgess 2004, Bhattacharjea 2008 (see also Bhattacharjea 2006), and OECD 2007. While Besley and Burgess create an index of the extent to which labor laws in each state are pro-employee or pro-employer based on the cumulative pro-employee or pro-employer amendments to the

IDA, Bhattacharjea characterizes state-level differences in labor market flexibility based on his own assessments of legislative amendments and judicial interpretations of Chapter VB of the IDA. The OECD study creates an index based on an aggregation of responses to a survey to identify the areas in which states have made specific changes to the implementation and administration of all labor laws, including the IDA. Gupta, Hasan, and Kumar take each of the three studies; partition states into those with flexible, neutral, or inflexible labor regulations; and then come up with a composite labor market regulation indicator variable using a simple majority rule across the different partitions: Andhra Pradesh, Karnataka, Rajasthan, Tamil Nadu, and Uttar Pradesh are classified as pro-employer or flexible labor market states; the remaining are pro-employee or relatively rigid labor market states (includes what was classified as neutral as well as inflexible in the prior stage).

Our state-level, employment-weighted protection measures are from Hasan, Mitra, and Ural (2007). These state-level measures of trade protection are at three levels of aggregation: the state as a whole, as well as urban and rural sectors within states. In particular, industry-level tariff rates and non-tariff barrier (NTB) coverage rates for agricultural, mining, and manufacturing industries are weighted by state and sector-specific employment shares (see Appendix A2 for details). Similar measures have also been created by Topalova (2010).

RESULTS

The Relationship between the Formal and Informal Manufacturing Sectors

Tables 3.1A and 3.1B show that while informal sector employment in manufacturing rose fairly rapidly between 1989–2000, formal sector employment had been mildly falling over time. Value added, on the other hand, had been growing more or less at the same pace in both informal and formal manufacturing. All this is seen in table 3.1C, which shows that the share of the informal sector in manufacturing value added has hovered around the 20 percent mark, while the employment share has grown from 75 percent in 1989 to 81 percent in 2000. Thus, while the value-added data is strongly indicative of complementarity between informal and formal manufacturing, no such inference can be drawn from the aggregate data on informal and formal manufacturing employment. We, therefore, next analyze more disaggregative data.

We start by looking at the relationship between formal and informal sector activity at the industry-state level over time. In other words, our unit of observation is an industry in a state in each of the years 1989, 1994, and 2000. In table 3.2A, we estimate a Tobit model with informal sector activity, measured by informal (or unorganized) sector employment, output, and value added,

Table 3.1A SUMMARY STATISTICS – INFORMAL SECTOR

	−1	−2	−3	−4	−5	−6
	By Survey Round			By Enterprise Type		
	1989	1994	2000	OAME	NDME	DME
All Regions						
Informal	35,942.80	40,780.10	47,823.80	31,661.90	6,155.30	6,817.60
Employment	[104,716]	[109,759]	[124,122]	[98,157]	[14,945]	[21,918]
Informal Output	542.6	829.9	1647.5	347.7	265.3	644.5
	[1,787.6]	[1,961.5]	[9,475.4]	[1,230]	[905.8]	[6,722.7]
Informal	236.4	337.9	494.9	173.7	100.2	140
Value Added	[653]	[813.7]	[995.2]	[462.9]	[300.9]	[409.5]
Rural						
Informal	27,519.70	28,728	31,551	25,300.50	2,554.80	2,895.70
Employment	[91,640]	[90,909]	[99,368]	[86,824.4]	[8,296]	[13,518]
Informal Output	273.8	324.5	510.8	233.3	65.2	121.3
	[1,047.3]	[1,168.6]	[1,589.8]	[1,091.2]	[185.6]	[431.1]
Informal Value	135.3 [427.9]	145.3	217.7	117.6	27.3	37.9
Added		[406.8]	[533.7]	[363.3]	[77.4]	[156.1]
Urban						
Informal	8,425.10	12,054.90	16,275.80	6,362.40	3,601.60	3,922.90
Employment	[22,045]	[33,511]	[38,172]	[18,915]	[9,065]	[12,804]
Informal Output	268.8	505.4	1136.7	114.4	200	523.2
	[1,303.5]	[1,321.3]	[9,250]	[310.5]	[848.8]	[6,695.1]
Informal	101.1	192.6	277.2	56.1	72.8	102.2
Value Added	[401.9]	[586.3]	[647.7]	[170.3]	[270.8]	[336.3]

Notes: 1) All monetary values are in millions of 1993 rupees. 2) The numbers in brackets are standard deviations. 3) OAME refers to own-account manufacturing firms that use only household workers. 4) NDMEs are non-directory manufacturing enterprises. These enterprises use outside workers with no more than five total workers. 5) DMEs are directory manufacturing enterprises and include enterprises with outside workers and more than five total workers.

regressed on corresponding formal sector activity variables. It is important to note here that no enterprises reported activity in some state-industry-sector-year cells. We exploit the information in these observations by coding them to zero, which necessitates the use of a Tobit analysis throughout this chapter.[1]

In all our pooled, multi-year regressions, we control for general unobservable time shocks as well as time-invariant, three-digit industry effects as well as state effects. A positive coefficient on formal sector activity would indicate that formal sector activity is associated with higher activity in the informal sector, consistent with outsourcing between the formal and informal manufacturing sectors. Columns 1, 2, and 3 of table 3.2A use employment, output, and value added to measure economic activity for OAMEs. Columns 4, 5, and 6 present corresponding results for NDMEs; columns 7, 8, and 9 do the same for DMEs.

Table 3.1B SUMMARY STATISTICS – FORMAL SECTOR

	–1	–2	–3	–4
	Overall	1989	1994	2000
Formal employment	11,757.80	12,134.90	11,655.60	11,488.50
	[34,436]	[45,625]	[27,187]	[27,443]
Formal output	6,681.60	4,404.50	6,135.80	9,468.80
	[17,136.4]	[9,484.9]	[13,462]	[24,376]
Formal value added	1,429.30	959.5	1,430.20	1,888.90
	[4,024.1]	[2,266.2]	[3,536.7]	[5504.3]
Tariff (all regions)	62.8 [30.7]	94.4 [15.7]	70.7 [4.93]	24.5 [2.97]
Tariff (urban)	86.9 [39.6]	131.7 [8.49]	93.8 [4.71]	36.8 [2.61]
Tariff (rural)	59.8 [29.7]	89.8 [16.7]	67.8 [4.74]	22.9 [2.89]
Outsourcing	181.9 [532.2]	14 [13.3]	17.7 [26.8]	502.1 [820.6]

Notes: 1) All monetary values are in millions of 1993 rupees. 2) The numbers in brackets are standard deviations.

Table 3.1C INFORMAL ACTIVITY SHARES
IN OVERALL MANUFACTURING

	1989	1994	2000
Employment	0.75	0.78	0.81
Output	0.11	0.12	0.15
Value added	0.2	0.19	0.21

Table 3.2A shows that formal sector employment, output, and value added are all positively related to informal sector employment, output, and value added. More important, coefficients are precisely estimated for all measures of economic activity across the three types of enterprises. Marginal effects are presented in table 3.2B. Again, effects are estimated precisely in most cases, except for DMEs in the rural sector. Results indicate that a 1 percent increase in formal sector employment is associated with a 0.2, 0.4, and 0.7 percent increase in informal sector employment in OAMEs, NDMEs, and DMEs, respectively. A 1 percent increase in formal sector output is associated with a 0.2, 0.7, and 1 percent increase in informal sector output for OAMEs, NDMEs, and DMEs, respectively. Value-added estimates are close to our output estimates. The results indicate that both formal and informal sector activities move in the same direction due to possible agglomeration effects such as labor-market pooling, location of input suppliers close to where most of an industry's activity is located, various kinds of linkage effects, and the possibility that formal sector firms outsource some of their production activities to informal sector firms. The less than unitary elasticity of informal sector employment, output, and value added in an industry with

Table 3.2A THE RELATIONSHIP BETWEEN THE FORMAL AND THE INFORMAL SECTOR

	(1)	(2)	(3)	(4)	(5)	(6)	(7)	(8)	(9)
	OAME = 1989, 1994, 2000			NDME = 1989, 1994, 2000			DME = 1994, 2000		
Dependent variable	Ln (Informal Empl.)	Ln (Informal Output)	Ln (Informal VA)	Ln (Informal Empl.)	Ln (Informal Output)	Ln (Informal VA)	Ln (Informal Empl.)	Ln (Informal Output)	Ln (Informal VA)
All regions (Tobit)									
Ln (corresponding formal sector variable)	0.275***	0.294**	0.277***	0.452***	0.711***	0.634***	0.692***	1.258***	1.051***
	(0.060)	(0.120)	(0.102)	(0.059)	(0.130)	(0.112)	(0.084)	(0.191)	(0.164)
Observations	1,951	1,951	1,923	1,951	1,951	1,921	1,307	1,307	1,286
Rural (Tobit)									
Ln (corresponding formal sector variable)	0.348***	0.520***	0.539***	0.547***	0.992***	0.869***	0.626***	1.507***	1.392***
	(0.083)	(0.171)	(0.145)	(0.085)	(0.198)	(0.171)	(0.132)	(0.320)	(0.280)
Observations	1,951	1,951	1,924	1,951	1,951	1,922	1,307	1,307	1,285
Urban (Tobit)									
Ln (corresponding formal sector variable)	0.272***	0.383***	0.316***	0.385***	0.684***	0.599***	0.680***	1.302***	0.929***
	(0.063)	(0.133)	(0.116)	(0.062)	(0.145)	(0.125)	(0.090)	(0.209)	(0.178)
Observations	1,951	1,951	1,922	1,951	1,951	1,920	1,307	1,307	1,287

Notes: 1) All regressions include 3-digit industry, state, and year effects. 2) Robust standard errors in parentheses. 3) *** p < 0.01, ** p < 0.05, * p < 0.1

Table 3.2B MARGINAL EFFECT OF FORMAL SECTOR ACTIVITY: THE RELATIONSHIP BETWEEN THE FORMAL AND THE INFORMAL SECTOR

	(1)	(2)	(3)	(4)	(5)	(6)	(7)	(8)	(9)
	OAME = 1989, 1994, 2000			NDME = 1989, 1994, 2000			DME = 1994, 2000		
Dependent Variable	Ln (Informal Empl.)	Ln (Informal Output)	Ln (Informal VA)	Ln (Informal Empl.)	Ln (Informal Output)	Ln (Informal VA)	Ln (Informal Empl.)	Ln (Informal Output)	Ln (Informal VA)
All Regions (Tobit)									
Ln (Corresponding Formal Sector Variable)	0.209***	0.223**	0.212**	0.442***	0.699***	0.625***	0.685***	1.236***	1.033***
	(0.058)	(0.101)	(0.087)	(0.569)	(0.127)	(0.110)	(0.083)	(0.188)	(0.161)
Rural (Tobit)									
Ln (Corresponding Formal Sector Variable)	0.334***	0.499***	0.517***	0.297***	0.554***	0.472***	0.042	0.199	0.175
	(0.079)	(0.163)	(0.139)	(0.093)	(0.185)	(0.159)	(0.041)	(0.174)	(0.156)
Urban (Tobit)									
Ln (Corresponding Formal Sector Variable)	0.261***	0.370***	0.308***	0.378***	0.673***	0.590***	0.644***	1.241***	0.889***
	(0.059)	(0.128)	(0.112)	(0.062)	(0.145)	(0.125)	(0.084)	(0.200)	(0.170)

Notes: 1) Marginal effects are for the year 1994 for the median industry and state by informal sector employment (see Appendix A1). 2) All continuous variables are set at their mean value for the relevant enterprise type. 3) Standard errors of the marginal effects are calculated using the delta method.

respect to the same variables in the same industry in the formal sector indicates that with positive growth, the structure of employment, output, and value added in the average manufacturing industry is moving toward formal production and away from informal production. The opposite structural change in the aggregate (that is shown in table 3.1C) might therefore be driven by compositional effects on the industrial structure of manufacturing.

We then examine the differential relationship between the formal and informal manufacturing sections across industries with varying labor intensities, by considering the interaction term between formal sector activity and observed formal sector labor intensity in an industry. Table 3.3A presents these results. Again, we arrange our columns as in table 3.2A, with results for regressions with employment, output, and value added for each of the three types of enterprises. Table 3.3B presents marginal effects for both the level term of formal sector activity and for the interaction between formal sector activity and labor intensity.

In table 3.3A, the coefficient of the interaction of formal sector activity with labor intensity is negative, indicating that the positive relationship between formal sector activity and informal sector activity is smaller in magnitude in industries that use more labor-intensive techniques in the formal sector. It also shows that at given levels of formal sector activity, informal sector activity is smaller in industries where formal sector production is observed to be more labor intensive. Coefficients are estimated precisely for NDMEs and DMEs for the rural, urban, and combined sectors in most cases, and for OAMEs in the rural sector. Overall, results seem to suggest that informal sector activity has greater magnitude in industries that use more capital-intensive techniques in the formal sector. Since our measure of the labor intensity of an industry is the observed technique in use in the formal sector, our results may not be inconsistent with our hypothesis that formal sector firms have an incentive to retain the more capital-intensive tasks in the production process and outsource more labor-intensive tasks to the informal sector, whose labor costs are lower. In other words, our results may be interpreted as saying that the industries in which formal sector firms are relatively more successful in outsourcing look more capital intensive, primarily because the production activities they outsource are relatively labor intensive. Hence, these results suggest outsourcing between the formal and informal manufacturing sectors in India, leading to stronger complementarity between formal and informal sector activity.

The Formal and Informal Sectors and the Institutional and Policy Environment

We next focus on the role of state-level policy and institutional environment in shaping the relationship between the formal and informal manufacturing sectors in India. First, we look at the role of labor market regulation, a pertinent

Table 3.3A LABOR INTENSITY AND THE RELATIONSHIP BETWEEN THE FORMAL AND THE INFORMAL SECTOR

Dependent Variable	(1)	(2)	(3)	(4)	(5)	(6)	(7)	(8)	(9)
	OAME = 1989, 1994, 2000			NDME = 1989, 1994, 2000			DME = 1994, 2000		
	Ln (Informal Empl.)	Ln (Informal Output)	Ln (Informal VA)	Ln (Informal Empl.)	Ln (Informal Output)	Ln (Informal VA)	Ln (Informal Empl.)	Ln (Informal Output)	Ln (Informal VA)
PANEL A: All regions (Tobit)									
Ln (corresponding formal sector variable)	0.095	−0.336	−0.242	−0.234	−1.485***	−0.960**	0.01	−1.746	−0.993
	(0.347)	(0.616)	(0.458)	(0.269)	(0.470)	(0.380)	(0.487)	(1.175)	(0.918)
Formal sector labor intensity X Ln (corresponding formal sector variable)	−0.092	−0.323	−0.264	−0.351***	−1.115***	−0.803***	−0.353	−1.543**	−1.039**
	(0.158)	(0.282)	(0.204)	(0.111)	(0.185)	(0.151)	(0.235)	(0.590)	(0.473)
Observations	1947	1947	1919	1947	1947	1917	1303	1303	1282
PANEL A: Rural (Tobit)									
Ln (corresponding formal sector variable)	−0.103	−0.936	−0.794	−0.346	−1.754**	−1.209*	−1.697**	−4.269**	−3.508**
	(0.449)	(0.800)	(0.570)	(0.349)	(0.786)	(0.733)	(0.832)	(2.114)	(1.785)
Formal sector labor intensity X Ln (corresponding formal sector variable)	−0.233	−0.751**	−0.681**	−0.458***	−1.406***	−1.051***	−1.205***	−2.999***	−2.514***
	(0.225)	(0.377)	(0.279)	(0.154)	(0.383)	(0.342)	(0.421)	(1.087)	(0.929)
Observations	1947	1947	1918	1947	1947	1920	1303	1303	1281
PANEL A: Urban (Tobit)									
Ln (corresponding formal sector variable)	0.173	−0.158	−0.091	−0.317	−1.531***	−1.054*	0.336	−1.138	−0.719
	(0.302)	(0.642)	(0.571)	(0.317)	(0.578)	(0.546)	(0.477)	(1.240)	(0.955)
Formal sector labor intensity X Ln (corresponding formal sector variable)	−0.051	−0.277	−0.208	−0.360***	−1.126***	−0.834***	−0.177	−1.252**	−0.838*
	(0.138)	(0.302)	(0.266)	(0.137)	(0.238)	(0.249)	(0.231)	(0.620)	(0.492)
Observations	1947	1947	1918	1947	1947	1916	1303	1303	1283

Notes:1) Labor intensity is defined for the formal sector at the 3-digit industry level as the ratio of wage bill to value added in each industry and is calculated using data from the ASI. 2) All

Table 3.3B MARGINAL EFFECT OF LEVELS AND THE INTERACTION

Labor Intensity and the Relationship between the Formal and the Informal Sector

Dependent Variable	(1)	(2)	(3)	(4)	(5)	(6)	(7)	(8)	(9)
	OAME = 1989, 1994, 2000			NDME = 1989, 1994, 2000			DME = 1994, 2000		
	Ln (Informal Empl.)	Ln (Informal Output)	Ln (Informal VA)	Ln (Informal Empl.)	Ln (Informal Output)	Ln (Informal VA)	Ln (Informal Empl.)	Ln (Informal Output)	Ln (Informal VA)
All regions (Tobit)									
Formal sector labor intensity XLn	−0.07	−0.242	−0.2	−0.345***	−1.107***	−0.797***	−0.351	−1.541***	−1.036**
(corresponding formal sector variable)	(0.12)	(0.211)	(0.155)	(0.11)	(0.184)	(0.15)	(0.234)	(0.59)	(0.472)
Ln (corresponding formal sector variable)	0.212***	0.231	0.217**	0.459***	0.736***	0.639***	0.711***	1.334***	1.079***
	(0.069)	(0.113)	(0.098)	(0.074)	(0.165)	(0.133)	(0.07)	(0.196)	(0.105)
Rural (Tobit)									
Formal sector labor intensity XLn	−0.218	−0.628**	−0.588**	0.3***	−1.236***	−0.847***	−0.665***	−2.985***	−2.458***
(corresponding formal sector variable)	(0.21)	(0.315)	(0.239)	(0.101)	(0.337)	(0.275)	(0.232)	(1.081)	(0.905)
Ln (corresponding formal sector variable)	0.339***	0.472***	0.489***	0.372***	0.926***	0.717***	0.391***	1.713***	1.48***
	(0.084)	(0.145)	(0.116)	(0.057)	(0.201)	(0.135)	(0.075)	(0.385)	(0.289)
Urban (Tobit)									
Formal sector labor intensity XLn	−0.049	−0.273	−0.204	−0.355***	−1.117***	−0.827***	−0.17	−1.237**	−0.823*
(corresponding formal sector variable)	(0.133)	(0.298)	(0.262)	(0.135)	(0.236)	(0.246)	(0.221)	(0.611)	(0.483)
Ln (corresponding formal sector variable)	0.264***	0.389***	0.319**	0.396***	0.712***	0.606***	0.661***	1.346***	0.939***
	(0.096)	(0.16)	(0.147)	(0.082)	(0.189)	(0.157)	(0.065)	(0.165)	(0.103)

Notes: 1) Marginal effects are for the year 1994 for the median industry and state by informal sector employment (see Appendix A1). 2) All continuous variables are set at their mean value for the relevant enterprise type. 3) Standard errors of the marginal effects are calculated using the delta method.

feature of the institutional environment for the relationship between the formal and informal sectors. We examine whether formal and informal sector activity are differentially related in states with varying regulatory environments in the labor market by adding an interaction term between formal sector activity and a dummy for the flexibility of state labor markets.

In a setting where the formal sector outsources to the informal sector to get around labor laws, one might expect the positive relationship between formal and informal sector activity to be stronger in states with less flexible labor markets. This would result in a negative coefficient on the interaction term between formal sector activity and the labor market flexibility dummy. However, it is possible that with some kind of positive spillovers through agglomeration externalities, complementarity between these two sectors would result in a positive relationship between formal and informal sector activity, especially in states with more flexible labor laws, where formal manufacturing might thrive (Besley and Burgess 2004). The possibility of labor-market pooling is enhanced only if hiring and firing are not too restricted. Employers do not want to hire a worker and be stuck with that person even in bad times or if the worker turns out to be unproductive or incompetent. Thus, with less restrictive labor market policies, workers located in such regions will have greater probability of gaining employment in formal sector firms. That by itself will act as incentive to also seek employment in the informal sector enterprises in such a region in the hopes of future formal sector employment. This in turn could enhance outsourcing possibilities by formal firms to informal firms. This would mean a positive sign on the coefficient of the interaction term.

From table 3.4A, we find evidence that formal sector activity is associated with greater informal sector activity in states with more flexible labor market regulation for DMEs and for NDMEs in the urban sector. For OAMEs, we find that the opposite is true. However, our coefficients are imprecisely estimated. Table 3.4B presents marginal effects, most of which are estimated precisely. Coefficients reported show the impact of formal sector activity on informal activity for a state and industry with median informal employment that has flexible labor laws (labor regulation dummy set to one) or rigid labor laws (labor regulation dummy set to zero).[2] For example, magnitudes indicate that, for NDMEs, a 1 percent increase in formal sector employment is associated with a 0.8 percent increase in informal employment in states with flexible labor laws, but only a 0.6 percent increase in informal employment in other states. Similarly, for DMEs, a 1 percent increase in formal employment is associated with a 0.9 percent increase in informal employment in states with flexible labor laws, and with a 0.7 percent increase in informal employment in other states. To summarize, these results tie in with our hypotheses of interdependence between the formal and informal manufacturing sectors and the role of labor regulation in determining this relationship. As mentioned earlier, labor-market pooling makes sense only if hiring and firing are not

LABOR MARKET REGULATIONS AND THE RELATIONSHIP BETWEEN THE FORMAL AND THE INFORMAL SECTOR

	(1)	(2)	(3)	(4)	(5)	(6)	(7)	(8)	(9)
	OAME = 1989, 1994, 2000			NDME = 1989, 1994, 2000			DME = 1994, 2000		
Dependent Variable	Ln (Informal Empl.)	Ln (Informal Output)	Ln (Informal VA)	Ln (Informal Empl.)	Ln (Informal Output)	Ln (Informal VA)	Ln (Informal Empl.)	Ln (Informal Output)	Ln (Informal VA)
PANEL A: All regions (Tobit)									
Ln (corresponding formal sector variable)	0.301***	0.350***	0.346***	0.408***	0.660***	0.592***	0.608***	1.143***	0.968***
	(0.081)	(0.131)	(0.099)	(0.089)	(0.212)	(0.169)	(0.092)	(0.218)	(0.135)
Labor market regulations X	-0.083	-0.189	-0.231	0.143	0.174	0.142	0.284*	0.423	0.293
Ln (corresponding formal sector variable)	(0.095)	(0.143)	(0.146)	(0.088)	(0.207)	(0.185)	(0.151)	(0.354)	(0.291)
Observations	1,951	1,951	1,923	1,951	1,951	1,921	1,307	1,307	1,286
PANEL A: Rural (Tobit)									
Ln (corresponding formal sector variable)	0.338***	0.550***	0.582***	0.497***	0.980***	0.878***	0.488***	1.288***	1.274***
	(0.102)	(0.190)	(0.141)	(0.104)	(0.241)	(0.197)	(0.157)	(0.397)	(0.362)
Labor market regulations X	0.034	-0.1	-0.149	0.163	0.039	-0.031	0.478**	0.834**	0.42
Ln (corresponding formal sector variable)	(0.082)	(0.138)	(0.142)	(0.113)	(0.251)	(0.205)	(0.189)	(0.413)	(0.375)
Observations	1,951	1,951	1,924	1,951	1,951	1,922	1,307	1,307	1,285
PANEL A: Urban (Tobit)									
Ln (corresponding formal sector variable)	0.284***	0.434***	0.390***	0.330***	0.601**	0.533***	0.610***	1.218***	0.858***
	(0.092)	(0.144)	(0.133)	(0.100)	(0.237)	(0.192)	(0.089)	(0.199)	(0.133)
Labor market regulations X	-0.037	-0.18	-0.254	0.178**	0.293	0.23	0.233*	0.3	0.244
Ln (corresponding formal sector variable)	(0.121)	(0.238)	(0.214)	(0.083)	(0.240)	(0.210)	(0.137)	(0.316)	(0.271)
Observations	1,951	1,951	1,922	1,951	1,951	1,920	1,307	1,307	1,287

Notes :1) "Labor market regulations" is a dummy variable that equals 1 if a state has relatively flexible labor laws (see Gupta, Hasan, and Kumar 2009). 2) All regressions include 3-digit industry, state, and year effects. 3) Robust standard errors in parentheses **clustered at the state level**. 4) *** $p < 0.01$, ** $p < 0.05$, * $p < 0.1$.

Table 3.4B MARGINAL EFFECT OF FORMAL SECTOR ACTIVITY

Labor Market Regulations and the Relationship between the Formal and the Informal Sector

Dependent Variable	(1)	(2)	(3)	(4)	(5)	(6)	(7)	(8)	(9)
	OAME = 1989, 1994, 2000			NDME = 1989, 1994, 2000			DME = 1994, 2000		
	Ln (Informal Empl.)	Ln (Informal Output)	Ln (Informal VA)	Ln (Informal Empl.)	Ln (Informal Output)	Ln (Informal VA)	Ln (Informal Empl.)	Ln (Informal Output)	Ln (Informal VA)
All regions (Tobit)									
Labor market regulation dummy = 1	0.145*	0.079	0.052	0.548***	0.832***	0.732***	0.891***	1.565***	1.259***
	(0.082)	(0.102)	(0.088)	(0.098)	(0.151)	(0.144)	(0.137)	(0.309)	(0.236)
Labor market regulation dummy = 0	0.23***	0.265***	0.266***	0.399***	0.65***	0.584***	0.601***	1.122***	0.951***
	(0.062)	(0.099)	(0.076)	(0.087)	(0.208)	(0.167)	(0.091)	(0.213)	(0.131)
Rural (Tobit)									
Labor market regulation dummy = 1	0.356***	0.431***	0.416***	0.472***	0.61***	0.433***	0.288***	1.468***	0.622***
	(0.085)	(0.16)	(0.143)	(0.081)	(0.158)	(0.091)	(0.055)	(0.277)	(0.117)
Labor market regulation dummy = 0	0.32***	0.538***	0.574***	0.28***	0.549***	0.475***	0.033***	0.17***	0.159***
	(0.096)	(0.185)	(0.138)	(0.058)	(0.134)	(0.106)	(0.011)	(0.058)	(0.049)
Urban (Tobit)									
Labor market regulation dummy = 1	0.233	0.225	0.116	0.507***	0.893***	0.761***	0.832***	1.508***	1.092***
	(0.142)	(0.241)	(0.203)	(0.098)	(0.184)	(0.176)	(0.12)	(0.275)	(0.211)
Labor market regulation dummy = 0	0.272***	0.42***	0.379***	0.324***	0.591**	0.525***	0.576***	1.159***	0.819***
	(0.088)	(0.139)	(0.129)	(0.098)	(0.233)	(0.189)	(0.083)	(0.19)	(0.127)

Notes: 1) Marginal effects are for the year 1994 for the median industry and state by informal sector employment (see Appendix A1). 2) All continuous variables are set at their mean value for the relevant enterprise type. 3) Standard errors of the marginal effects are calculated using the delta method.

too restricted. High firing costs lead to both limited hiring and limited firing, since employers do not want to be stuck with a new worker. With less restrictive labor market policies, workers located in such regions will have greater probability of employment in formal sector firms. That by itself will act as an incentive for them to also seek employment in informal sector enterprises in such a region.

We next study the effects of industry-level outsourcing by formal sector firms on informal sector output and how these effects vary by labor market flexibility. Table 3.1B clearly shows explosive growth in outsourcing by formal manufacturing firms. While we do not have a distinction between domestic and foreign outsourcing, it is not unreasonable to expect that a large number of informal sector enterprises would have benefited from this outsourcing. Table 3.5A clearly shows that the coefficient of the interaction between the labor market flexibility dummy and the natural logarithm of industry outsourcing is positive throughout and—in a number of cases, namely rural sector DMEs and urban sector OAMEs and NDMEs—significant as well. This shows evidence of complementarity between flexible labor laws and outsourcing in raising informal employment, output, and value added. This is supported by the positive marginal effects of formal sector industry-level outsourcing in relatively flexible labor market states across the board when we look at the combination of rual and urban sectors as well as separately for rural areas (see table 3.5B). In the case of OAMEs this is true only for urban areas (see table 3.5B). These marginal effects are precisely estimated for NDMEs in rural areas. Overall, we interpret this as indicating that formal sector outsourcing has a positive effect on informal sector activity in flexible labor market states. This is not difficult to explain. In states with relatively flexible labor laws, firms can respond more easily to shocks by changing their employment levels. As a result, there is greater need for and possibility of labor-market pooling. The probability of a person with the requisite skills or qualifications finding formal employment in such states should be higher. As a result, people are willing to accept informal employment in such regions as a stepping stone to formal employment. Such informal sector activity might be driven by formal sector firms outsourcing to informal sector firms. The informal sector employment can also provide some valuable experience in the interim.

Next we consider the impact on informal sector activity of greater exposure to international markets through trade and whether these trade liberalization effects interact with labor market institutions. We measure trade liberalization through a decrease in the state-level, employment-weighted tariff measure. Results are presented in table 3.6A in the usual format. These results indicate considerable heterogeneity by enterprise type. For OAMEs, greater trade exposure is associated with greater informal sector activity in the overall sector, and this result seems to be driven by the rural sector. Also, trade exposure effects do not seem to differ between states with flexible and those

Table 3.5A LABOR MARKET REGULATIONS AND THE RELATIONSHIP BETWEEN THE FORMAL SECTOR OUTSOURCING AND THE INFORMAL SECTOR

	(1)	(2)	(3)	(4)	(5)	(6)	(7)	(8)	(9)
	OAME = 1989, 1994, 2000			NDME = 1989, 1994, 2000			DME = 1994, 2000		
Dependent Variable	Ln (Informal Empl.)	Ln (Informal Output)	Ln (Informal VA)	Ln (Informal Empl.)	Ln (Informal Output)	Ln (Informal VA)	Ln (Informal Empl.)	Ln (Informal Output)	Ln (Informal VA)
PANEL A: All regions (Tobit)									
Ln (industry outsourcing)	-0.081	-0.167	-0.138	-0.044	-0.226	-0.203	-0.013	-0.022	-0.031
	(0.166)	(0.417)	(0.389)	(0.142)	(0.347)	(0.327)	(0.144)	(0.32)	(0.305)
Labor market regulations X Ln (industry outsourcing)	0.125**	0.230*	0.223*	0.120**	0.231	0.233*	0.069	0.09	0.075
	(0.057)	(0.122)	(0.117)	(0.060)	(0.141)	(0.132)	(0.080)	(0.200)	(0.193)
Observations	1,973	1,973	1,971	1,948	1,948	1,946	1,295	1,295	1,292
PANEL A: Rural (Tobit)									
Ln (industry outsourcing)	-0.128	-0.214	-0.191	0.233	0.609	0.583	-0.31	-0.881	-0.826
	(0.155)	(0.380)	(0.355)	(0.158)	(0.423)	(0.403)	(0.192)	(0.555)	(0.516)
Labor market regulations X Ln (industry outsourcing)	0.087	0.072	0.104	0.185	0.367	0.367	0.492***	1.560***	1.389***
	(0.097)	(0.208)	(0.218)	(0.124)	(0.319)	(0.303)	(0.161)	(0.405)	(0.387)
Observations	1,973	1,973	1,970	1,948	1,948	1,948	1,295	1,295	1,291
PANEL A: Urban (Tobit)									
Ln (industry outsourcing)	0.001	-0.003	0.018	-0.157	-0.496	-0.453	0.078	0.226	0.195
	(0.152)	(0.384)	(0.361)	(0.166)	(0.416)	(0.393)	(0.172)	(0.404)	(0.389)
Labor market regulations X Ln (industry outsourcing)	0.111**	0.212*	0.208*	0.155***	0.334**	0.331**	0.047	-0.056	-0.035
	(0.056)	(0.117)	(0.112)	(0.055)	(0.157)	(0.147)	(0.102)	(0.271)	(0.258)
Observations	1,973	1,973	1,971	1,948	1,948	1,945	1,295	1,295	1,292

Notes:1) "Labor market regulations" is a dummy variable that equals 1 if a state has relatively flexible labor laws (see Gupta, Hasan, and Kumar 2009). 2) All regressions include 3-digit industry dummies. 3) Errors in parentheses clustered at the 3 digit industry level. 4) *** $p<0.01$, ** $p<0.05$, * $p<0.1$.

Table 3.5B MARGINAL EFFECT OF INDUSTRY OUTSOURCING

Labor Market Regulations and the Relationship between the Formal Sector Outsourcing and the Informal Sector

	(1)	(2)	(3)	(4)	(5)	(6)	(7)	(8)	(9)
	OAME = 1989, 1994, 2000			NDME = 1989, 1994, 2000			DME = 1994, 2000		
Dependent Variable	Ln (Informal Empl.)	Ln (Informal Output)	Ln (Informal VA)	Ln (Informal Empl.)	Ln (Informal Output)	Ln (Informal VA)	Ln (Informal Empl.)	Ln (Informal Output)	Ln (Informal VA)
All regions (Tobit)									
Labor market regulation dummy = 1	0.033	0.05	0.068	0.075	0.005	0.03	0.055	0.067	0.044
	(0.138)	(0.356)	(0.335)	(0.167)	(0.396)	(0.371)	(0.146)	(0.327)	(0.312)
Labor market regulation dummy = 0	-0.06	-0.13	-0.108	-0.043	-0.223	-0.2	-0.013	-0.021	-0.03
	(0.122)	(0.324)	(0.305)	(0.14)	(0.342)	(0.323)	(0.142)	(0.313)	(0.299)
Rural (Tobit)									
Labor market regulation dummy = 1	-0.04	-0.136	-0.083	0.163**	0.424**	0.419**	0.012	0.068	0.054
	(0.155)	(0.357)	(0.34)	(0.072)	(0.215)	(0.207)	(0.015)	(0.06)	(0.054)
Labor market regulation dummy = 0	-0.123	-0.205	-0.184	0.085	0.254	0.246	-0.014	-0.06	0.055
	(0.149)	(0.365)	(0.34)	(0.059)	(0.178)	(0.172)	(0.01)	(0.043)	(0.039)
Urban (Tobit)									
Labor market regulation dummy = 1	0.11	0.204	0.221	-0.002	-0.158	-0.119	0.12	0.161	0.152
	(0.153)	(0.392)	(0.367)	(0.17)	(0.406)	(0.384)	(0.175)	(0.412)	(0.391)
Labor market regulation dummy = 0	0.001	-0.003	0.018	-0.152	-0.482	-0.441	0.075	0.214	0.186
	(0.147)	(0.375)	(0.352)	(0.16)	(0.403)	(0.383)	(0.166)	(0.382)	(0.37)

Notes: 1) Marginal effects are for the year 1994 for the median industry and state by informal sector employment (see Appendix A1). 2) All continuous variables are set at their mean value for the relevant enterprise type. 3) Standard errors of the marginal effects are calculated using the delta method.

Table 3.6A TRADE LIBERALIZATION AND THE RELATIONSHIP BETWEEN THE FORMAL AND THE INFORMAL SECTOR

Dependent Variable	(1)	(2)	(3)	(4)	(5)	(6)	(7)	(8)	(9)
	OAME = 1989, 1994, 2000			NDME = 1989, 1994, 2000			DME = 1994, 2000		
	Ln (Informal Empl.)	Ln (Informal Output)	Ln (Informal VA)	Ln (Informal Empl.)	Ln (Informal Output)	Ln (Informal VA)	Ln (Informal Empl.)	Ln (Informal Output)	Ln (Informal VA)
PANEL A: All regions (Tobit)									
Ln (corresponding formal sector variable)	0.276***	0.302**	0.282**	0.451***	0.712***	0.631***	0.695***	1.266***	1.059***
	(0.093)	(0.152)	(0.130)	(0.078)	(0.170)	(0.138)	(0.073)	(0.188)	(0.102)
Ln (tariff – all regions)	-4.000***	-10.871***	-9.732***	-0.271	-4.294	-2.923	-1.971	-9.22	-6.037
	(0.875)	(2.748)	(2.295)	(1.037)	(2.652)	(2.439)	(3.825)	(11.279)	(10.112)
Ln (tariff – all regions) XLabor market	-0.045	-0.278	-0.256	-0.166	-0.423	-0.496	0.409	1.443*	1.499**
Regulation	(0.145)	(0.314)	(0.293)	(0.169)	(0.414)	(0.378)	(0.267)	(0.77)	(0.71)
Observations	1,951	1,951	1,923	1,951	1,951	1,921	1,307	1,307	1,286
PANEL A: Rural (Tobit)									
Ln (corresponding formal sector variable)	0.350***	0.529***	0.546***	0.542***	0.982***	0.858***	0.620***	1.487***	1.384***
	(0.088)	(0.177)	(0.138)	(0.091)	(0.219)	(0.170)	(0.136)	(0.360)	(0.305)
Ln (tariff – rural) lagged	-2.267***	-7.243***	-6.402***	-0.781	-5.505**	-4.317	9.733***	26.296***	28.405***
	(0.639)	(1.415)	(1.282)	(1.158)	(2.705)	(2.676)	(2.412)	(7.249)	(7.239)
Ln (tariff – rural) XLabor market	0.075	0.033	0.157	-0.511*	-1.415**	-1.369**	-0.532	-2.549	-2.082
Regulation	(0.27)	(0.739)	(0.698)	(0.283)	(0.713)	(0.627)	(0.537)	(1.667)	(1.614)
Observations	1,951	1,951	1,922	1,951	1,951	1,924	1,307	1,307	1,285
PANEL A: Urban (Tobit)									

Ln (corresponding formal sector variable)	0.273***	0.382**	0.314**	0.384***	0.681***	0.596***	0.689***	1.325***	0.946***
	(0.102)	(0.167)	(0.154)	(0.086)	(0.195)	(0.161)	(0.071)	(0.166)	(0.100)
Ln (tariff –urban) lagged	−0.495	−3.935	−3.952	3.527	5.292	6.203	−9.778***	−28.201***	−24.544***
	(2.312)	(6.964)	(6.821)	(2.213)	(5.387)	(5.820)	(3.541)	(10.432)	(9.148)
Ln (Tariff –urban) XLabor market Regulation	0.06	−0.149	−0.225	−0.127	−0.339	−0.451	0.462	2.090*	1.907*
	(0.219)	(0.546)	(0.522)	(0.191)	(0.473)	(0.421)	(0.386)	(1.141)	(1.046)
Observations	1,951	1,951	1,922	1,951	1,951	1,920	1,307	1,307	1,287

Notes: 1) "Labor market regulations" is a dummy variable that equals 1 if a state has relatively flexible labor laws (see Gupta, Hasan, and Kumar 2009). "Tariff" is defined as employment weighted nominal rate of protection. 2) All regressions include 3-digit industry, state, and year effects. 3) Robust standard errors in parentheses clustered at the state level. 4) *** $p < 0.01$, ** $p < 0.05$, * $p < 0.1$.

with rigid labor regulation. For NDMEs, trade liberalization is associated with greater activity in the informal sector in rural areas, especially in states with more flexible labor laws—again consistent with outsourcing.

For DMEs, we observe differences between rural and urban enterprises. In the rural sector, trade liberalization is associated with lower informal sector activity. However, in the urban sector, greater formal sector activity is associated with greater informal sector activity in DMEs, very slightly more so in states with rigid labor laws. Table 3.6B presents marginal effects and reports the impact of the tariff for a state and industry with median informal employment with flexible labor laws, and with rigid labor laws. As an example, for OAMEs in the overall sector, we find that a 1 percent decrease in tariffs is associated with a 3.36 percent increase in informal employment in states with flexible labor laws and a 3.40 percent increase in informal employment in states with rigid labor laws. Similarly, for DMEs in the urban sector, we find that a 1 percent decrease in tariffs is associated with a 9.3 percent increase in informal employment in a state with flexible labor laws, but a 9.8 percent increase in a state with rigid labor laws. These look like large effects. However, the reasons for such large effects might be several other policy changes accompanying trade liberalization, making the precise identification of the effects of the latter somewhat difficult.

Overall, our analysis of trade liberalization suggests stronger positive association between trade exposure and informal activity for the smaller OAMEs and NDMEs in rural areas, and for the larger DMEs in the urban areas. In rural areas, trade liberalization is associated with lower activity in DMEs, probably indicative of possible competition between DMEs and formal firms. This is a result that is not easily explained by an increase in foreign competition. Results also suggest heterogeneity in the role of labor market institutions in either augmenting or mitigating trade exposure effects, over firm size distribution and across rural and urban sectors.

In Tables 3.7A and 3.7B, we investigate the interaction between industry outsourcing and trade liberalization to see if the positive impact of trade liberalization on formal sector output is greater in industries where there is a stronger outsourcing relationship between the formal and informal sectors. We do not find such a relationship. However, on the whole, the evidence still points toward a positive effect of trade liberalization on informal sector activity.

Evidence on Informal Sector Outsourcing

Finally, we pursue further direct evidence on outsourcing activity in the informal sector. Results from table 3.8A show that greater formal sector employment, output, and value-added are associated with a greater proportion of informal enterprises selling their output to other enterprises and contractors

Table 3.6B MARGINAL EFFECT OF TARIFF

Trade Liberalization and the Relationship between the Formal and the Informal Sector

Dependent Variable	-1	-2	-3	-4	-5	-6	-7	-8	-9
	OAME = 1989, 1994, 2000			NDME = 1989, 1994, 2000			DME = 1994, 2000		
	Ln (Informal Empl.)	Ln (Informal Output)	Ln (Informal VA)	Ln (Informal Empl.)	Ln (Informal Output)	Ln (Informal VA)	Ln (Informal Empl.)	Ln (Informal Output)	Ln (Informal VA)
All regions (Tobit)									
Labor market regulation dummy = 1	-3.356***	-8.987***	-8.075***	-0.42	-4.627*	-3.343	-1.561	-7.775	-4.536
	(0.784)	(2.309)	(1.957)	(0.997)	(2.615)	(2.443)	(3.733)	(10.936)	(9.891)
Labor market regulation dummy = 0	-3.395***	-9.309***	-8.338***	-0.266	-4.254	-2.896	-1.964	-9.194	-6.007
	(0.743)	(2.341)	(1.964)	(1.016)	(2.626)	(2.417)	(3.811)	(11.244)	(10.057)
Rural (Tobit)									
Labor market regulation dummy = 1	-2.127***	-7.024***	-6.083***	-0.416	-2.482**	-1.87*	0.009	0.028	0.021
	(0.555)	(1.381)	(1.321)	(0.421)	(1.107)	(1.014)	(0.006)	(0.019)	(0.015)
Labor market regulation dummy = 0	-2.184***	-7.048***	-6.199***	-0.444	-3.396**	-2.559	0.046*	0.386**	0.237**
	(0.614)	(1.369)	(1.237)	(0.657)	(1.664)	(1.584)	(0.025)	(0.176)	(0.115)
Urban (Tobit)									
Labor market regulation dummy = 1	-0.422	-3.966	-4.061	3.214	4.761	5.463	-9.314***	-26.112**	-22.636**
	(2.308)	(6.885)	(6.744)	(2.092)	(5.215)	(5.541)	(3.573)	(10.442)	(9.205)
Labor market regulation dummy = 0	-0.476	-3.847	-3.879	3.411	5.17	6.052	-9.764***	-28.176***	-24.516***
	(2.223)	(6.81)	(6.696)	(2.135)	(5.259)	(5.672)	(3.534)	(10.42)	(9.133)

Notes: 1) Marginal effects are for the year 1994 for the median industry and state by informal sector employment (see Appendix A1). 2) All continuous variables are set at their mean value for the relevant enterprise type. 3) Standard errors of the marginal effects are calculated using the delta method.

Table 3.7A TRADE LIBERALIZATION AND THE RELATIONSHIP BETWEEN FORMAL OUTSOURCING AND THE INFORMAL SECTOR

	(1)	(2)	(3)	(4)	(5)	(6)	(7)	(8)	(9)
	OAME = 1989, 1994, 2000			NDME = 1989, 1994, 2000			DME = 1994, 2000		
Dependent variable	Ln (Informal Empl.)	Ln (Informal Output)	Ln (Informal VA)	Ln (Informal Empl.)	Ln (Informal Output)	Ln (Informal VA)	Ln (Informal Empl.)	Ln (Informal Output)	Ln (Informal VA)
PANEL A: All regions (Tobit)									
Ln (industry outsourcing)	-0.332	-0.682	-0.622	0.188	0.988	0.973	1.141	3.177	2.954
	(0.435)	(0.988)	(0.955)	(0.450)	(1.019)	(0.960)	(1.028)	(2.218)	(2.101)
Ln (industry outsourcing) X	0.089	0.18	0.169	-0.059	-0.351	-0.339	-0.356	-0.999	-0.933
Tariff	(0.106)	(0.221)	(0.220)	(0.123)	(0.278)	(0.261)	(0.316)	(0.678)	(0.642)
Ln (tariff – all regions) lagged	-3.849**	-9.931**	-9.256**	-0.739	-4.485	-4.275	-0.627	-4.747	-4.692
	(1.553)	(4.017)	(3.842)	(1.261)	(3.541)	(3.357)	(4.211)	(11.220)	(10.499)
Observations	1,973	1,973	1,971	1,948	1,948	1,946	1,295	1,295	1,292
PANEL A: Rural (Tobit)									
Ln (industry outsourcing)	-0.44	-0.495	-0.346	0.319	1.494	1.272	1.433	5.938	5.268
	(0.558)	(1.351)	(1.243)	(0.723)	(1.832)	(1.726)	(1.888)	(4.840)	(4.591)
Ln (industry outsourcing) X	0.106	0.094	0.058	-0.008	-0.238	-0.177	-0.501	-2.004	-1.792
Tariff	(0.155)	(0.367)	(0.339)	(0.203)	(0.501)	(0.470)	(0.608)	(1.548)	(1.470)
Ln (tariff – rural) lagged	-2.181	-6.126*	-5.815*	-0.48	-3.709	-3.726	12.704**	39.010**	35.891**
	(1.438)	(3.487)	(3.416)	(1.540)	(3.940)	(3.727)	(6.160)	(17.052)	(16.124)
Observations	1,973	1,973	1,970	1,948	1,948	1,948	1,295	1,295	1,291
PANEL A: Urban (Tobit)									
Ln (industry outsourcing)	0.06	-0.094	-0.091	0.476	1.125	1.203	1.461	2.94	2.834
	(0.539)	(1.251)	(1.217)	(0.564)	(1.219)	(1.154)	(1.686)	(3.947)	(3.770)

Ln (industry outsourcing) X	-0.007	0.041	0.046	-0.158	-0.411	-0.421	-0.384	-0.771	-0.749
	(0.128)	(0.293)	(0.287)	(0.137)	(0.292)	(0.275)	(0.455)	(1.066)	(1.019)
Tariff									
Ln (tariff – urban) lagged	-3.745*	-10.133*	-10.019*	3.664*	5.272	4.487	-7.185	-22.502	-21.444
	(2.268)	(5.649)	(5.408)	(2.141)	(6.023)	(5.777)	(5.203)	(14.484)	(13.471)
Observations	1,973	1,973	1,971	1,948	1,948	1,945	1,295	1,295	1,292

Notes: 1) "Labor market regulations" is a dummy variable that equals 1 if a state has relatively flexible labor laws (see Gupta, Hasan, and Kumar 2009). "Tariff" is defined as employment weighted nominal rate of protection. 2) All regressions include 3-digit industry, state, and year effects. 3) Robust standard errors in parentheses clustered at the 3-digit industry level. 4) *** $p < 0.01$, ** $p < 0.05$, * $p < 0.1$.

Table 3.7B MARGINAL EFFECTS OF LEVELS AND THE INTERACTION

Trade Liberalization and the Relationship between Formal Outsourcing and the Informal Sector

	(1)	(2)	(3)	(4)	(5)	(6)	(7)	(8)	(9)
	OAME = 1989, 1994, 2000			NDME = 1989, 1994, 2000			DME = 1994, 2000		
Dependent Variable	Ln (Informal Empl.)	Ln (Informal Output)	Ln (Informal VA)	Ln (Informal Empl.)	Ln (Informal Output)	Ln (Informal VA)	Ln (Informal Empl.)	Ln (Informal Output)	Ln (Informal VA)
All regions (Tobit)									
Ln (industry outsourcing) XLn	0.21	0.414	0.374	−0.061	−0.365	−0.351	−0.364	−1.065	−0.99
(tariff – all regions)	(0.274)	(0.577)	(0.547)	(0.126)	(0.295)	(0.275)	(0.317)	(0.714)	(0.675)
Ln (tariff – all regions)	−3.121**	−8.456**	−7.891**	−0.791	−4.814	−4.598	−1.139	−6.144	−6.004
	(1.259)	(3.388)	(3.251)	(1.241)	(3.513)	(3.334)	(4.042)	(10.867)	(10.193)
Ln (industry outsourcing)	0.02	0.03	0.047	−0.048	−0.409	−0.376	−0.184	−0.537	−0.516
	(0.133)	(0.328)	(0.31)	(0.159)	(0.385)	(0.359)	(0.202)	(0.426)	(0.404)
Rural (Tobit)									
Ln (industry outsourcing) XLn	0.12	0.115	0.073	−0.021	−0.371	−0.317	0.01	0.042	0.039
(tariff – rural)	(0.171)	(0.419)	(0.387)	(0.129)	(0.611)	(0.581)	(0.018)	(0.064)	(0.06)
Ln (tariff – rural)	−2.019	−5.872	−5.604*	−0.184	−1.762	−1.776	0.008	0.024	0.023
	(1.406)	(3.398)	(3.328)	(0.574)	(1.75)	(1.688)	(0.007)	(0.025)	(0.024)
Ln (industry outsourcing)	−0.023	−0.122	−0.116	0.108*	0.248	0.261	−0.0003	−0.001	−0.001
	(0.157)	(0.357)	(0.338)	(0.064)	(0.188)	(0.18)	(0.0004)	(0.001)	(0.001)
Urban (Tobit)									
Ln (industry outsourcing) XLn	−0.01	0.045	0.049	−0.056	−0.315	−0.337	−0.42	−0.856	−0.819
(tariff – urban)	(0.151)	(0.339)	(0.331)	(0.058)	(0.204)	(0.209)	(0.499)	(1.184)	(1.117)

Ln (tariff – urban)	-3.71*	-9.999*	-9.888*	3.266*	4.632	3.89	-7.723	-23.555	-22.479*
	(2.24)	(5.573)	(5.34)	(1.966)	(5.699)	(5.501)	(5.113)	(14.347)	(13.344)
Ln (industry outsourcing)	0.03	0.084	0.107	-0.194	-0.63	-0.6	-0.102	-0.201	-0.215
	(0.144)	(0.368)	(0.347)	(0.159)	(0.394)	(0.371)	(0.234)	(0.553)	(0.529)

Notes: 1) Marginal effects are for the year 1994 for the median industry and state by informal sector employment (see Appendix A1). 2) All continuous variables are set at their mean value for the relevant enterprise type. 3) Standard errors of the marginal effects are calculated using the delta method.

Table 3.8A THE RELATIONSHIP BETWEEN INFORMAL SECTOR OUTSOURCING AND FORMAL SECTOR ACTIVITY: TOBIT REGRESSION

Dependent Variable: Proportion of Enterprises Selling to Another Enterprise/Middleman

	(1)	(2)	(3)	(4)	(5)	(6)	(7)	(8)	(9)
	OAME = 2000			NDME = 2000			DME = 2000		
Activity Variable (Right-hand side)	Ln (Formal Empl.)	Ln (Formal Output)	Ln (Formal VA)	Ln (Formal Empl.)	Ln (Formal Output)	Ln (Formal VA)	Ln (Formal Empl.)	Ln (Formal Output)	Ln (Formal VA)
All regions (Tobit)									
Ln (activity variable)	0.039**	0.033**	0.028**	0.071***	0.058***	0.051***	0.074***	0.057***	0.048***
	(0.015)	(0.013)	(0.012)	(0.017)	(0.014)	(0.012)	(0.017)	(0.014)	(0.013)
Observations	654	654	648	654	654	648	654	654	648
Rural (Tobit)									
Ln (activity variable)	0.053***	0.031*	0.042***	0.041	0.043*	0.027	0.047	0.035	0.031
	(0.02)	(0.018)	(0.015)	(0.026)	(0.023)	(0.022)	(0.033)	(0.028)	(0.027)
Observations	654	654	648	654	654	648	654	654	648
Urban (Tobit)									
Ln (activity variable)	0.028*	0.031**	0.022*	0.076***	0.065***	0.057***	0.078***	0.067***	0.054***
	(0.017)	(0.015)	(0.013)	(0.016)	(0.014)	(0.012)	(0.018)	(0.015)	(0.014)
Observations	654	654	648	654	654	648	654	654	648

Notes: 1) All regressions include 3-digit industry-state effects. 2) Robust standard errors in parentheses. 3) *** $p < 0.01$, ** $p < 0.05$, * $p < 0.1$

in the year 2000. Coefficients are precisely estimated for the urban sector and overall, while in the rural sector they are precisely estimated for all enterprises except DMEs. Again, these results support our hypothesis of linkages between the formal and informal manufacturing sectors through outsourcing. Table 3.8B presents marginal effects of formal sector activity for the year 2000. Magnitudes show that a 1 percent increase in formal sector activity is associated with a 2–7 percent increase in informal enterprises selling or contracting to sell to another enterprise or middleman.

CONCLUSIONS

In this chapter, we have investigated the relationship between the formal and informal manufacturing sectors in India. We find that there is strong complementarity between these two sectors. Across industries, we find that the employment, output, and value added of the informal part of each of these industries are strongly positively correlated with the corresponding variables for the formal part of the respective industry. Several alternative explanations seem plausible. First, there could be agglomeration externalities arising from the growth of formal manufacturing. These externalities could arise from labor-market pooling, location of input supplies where firms in an industry are concentrated, and other linkage effects, as well as outsourcing by formal sector firms. While our results support the existence of complementarities between formal and informal manufacturing—arising possibly from both agglomeration and outsourcing—and while we provide some evidence of the formal manufacturing sector's role in outsourcing, we do not have the data to identify the relative importance of these channels. We do find fairly strong support for the role of labor market flexibility in enabling this complementarity between formal and informal manufacturing. Trade liberalization also turns out to have an important role.

APPENDIX A1

MARGINAL EFFECTS

Due to the nonlinear nature of the Tobit analysis we use in our estimation, the marginal effects of our variables of interest vary at different values of our right-hand side variables. Hence, we compute marginal effects for each table for key level and interaction terms in our regressions. Marginal effects are calculated for a state and industry with median informal sector employment in the year 1994, where medians are for each enterprise type (medians are reported in table 3.A1 and are calculated for each enterprise type separately by

Table 3.8B MARGINAL EFFECT OF FORMAL SECTOR ACTIVITY

The Relationship between Formal Sector Activity and Informal Sector Outsourcing

	(1)	(2)	(3)	(4)	(5)	(6)	(7)	(8)	(9)
	OAME = 2000			NDME = 2000			DME = 2000		
Activity Variable (Right-hand side)	Ln (Formal Empl.)	Ln (Formal Output)	Ln (Formal VA)	Ln (Formal Empl.)	Ln (Formal Output)	Ln (Formal VA)	Ln (Formal Empl.)	Ln (Formal Output)	Ln (Formal VA)
All regions (Tobit)									
Ln (activity variable)	0.035**	0.030**	0.026**	0.067***	0.055***	0.048***	0.062***	0.048***	0.041***
	(0.015)	(0.013)	(0.011)	(0.015)	(0.012)	(0.011)	(0.015)	(0.013)	(0.012)
Rural (Tobit)									
Ln (activity variable)	0.041**	0.025*	0.033***	0.01	0.011	0.006	0.006	0.003	0.003
	(0.016)	(0.014)	(0.012)	(0.012)	(0.012)	(0.008)	(0.007)	(0.006)	(0.005)
Urban (Tobit)									
Ln (activity variable)	0.021*	0.022**	0.016*	0.065***	0.058***	0.049***	0.053***	0.048***	0.039***
	(0.012)	(0.011)	(0.009)	(0.016)	(0.014)	(0.012)	(0.014)	(0.013)	(0.011)

Notes: 1) Marginal effects are for the median industry and state by informal sector employment in 1994 (see Appendix A1). 2) All continuous variables are set at their mean value for the relevant enterprise type for the year 2000. 3) Standard errors of the marginal effects are calculated using the delta method.

Table 3.A1 LIST OF THE MEDIAN INDUSTRY AND STATE BY INFORMAL EMPLOYMENT FOR 1994

		OAME	NDME	DME
All Regions	State Code	19	7	8
	State	Orissa	Gujarat	Haryana
	3-digit NIC 98 Code	331	341	181
	Industry	Medical equipment	Motor vehicles	Apparel
Rural	State Code	25	14	5
	State	UP	Maharashtra	Bihar
	4-digit NIC 98 Code	252	332	352
	Industry	Plastic	Optical	Locomotives
Urban	State Code	14	4	5
	State	Maharashtra	Assam	Bihar
	5-digit NIC 98 Code	359	192	269
	Industry	Transport	Footwear	Non-metallic minerals

Source: NSS data on unorganized manufacturing (1994) and authors' calculations.

urban, rural, and overall sectors). We fix our continuous right-hand side variables, namely formal sector activity, tariffs and outsourcing, at their sample means (see table 3.A1 for details). We next present the details of the calculations of the marginal effects.

McDonald and Moffitt (1980) show that the unconditional expectation of the dependent variable in the Tobit model is:

$$E(y) = X\beta F(z) + \sigma f(z),$$

where F is the cumulative normal distribution function and f is the normal density function. $z = X\beta/\sigma$.

Let the regression model with interaction terms be:

$$y = \beta_0 + \beta_1 x_1 + \beta_2 x_2 + \beta_{12} x_1 x_2 + u.$$

The marginal effects are calculated as follows:

1) Level Terms: The marginal effect of x_1 is

$$((\partial E(y))/(\partial x_1)) = [\beta_1 + \beta_{12} x_2] F[z] + X\beta f(z)[((\beta_1 + \beta_{12} x_2)/\sigma)] + \sigma f'(z) [((\beta_1 + \beta_{12} x_2)/\sigma)].$$

But $f'(z) = -zf(z)$ for the standard normal density. Hence the third term is:

$$-X\beta f(z)[((\beta_1 + \beta_{12} x_2)/\sigma)]$$

Therefore, we have $((\partial E(y))/(\partial x_1)) = [\beta_1 + \beta_{12} x_2] F[z].$

2) Interaction Terms: We examine two cases.

Case 1: Both interactions are continuous variables. Now the total marginal effect of the interaction term that we want is:

$$((\partial E(y))/(\partial x_1 \partial x_2)) = F(z)\beta_{12} + [\beta_1 + \beta_{12}x_2]f(z)[\beta_2/\sigma].$$

Case 2: Given $((\partial E(y))/(\partial x_1))$, if x_2 is a dummy variable, then the marginal effect of the interaction is a discrete change. In this case, we evaluate both $[\beta_1 + \beta_{12}]F[z_1]$ and $[\beta_1]F[z_0]$, where z_1 is evaluated with the dummy set to 1 and z_0 is evaluated with the dummy set to 0.

We calculate these marginal effects and standard errors using STATA's nlcom command. This is because Norton, Wang, and Ai (2004) show that statistical packages like STATA do not accurately compute marginal effects of interaction terms for nonlinear models like the probit.

APPENDIX A2

DATA SOURCES, CONSTRUCTION, AND CLEANING UNORGANIZED ENTERPRISE DATA

For unorganized manufacturing, our data come from the surveys conducted by the NSSO in 1989–90 (OAMEs and NDMEs only), 1994–95, and 2000–01.

Output and value added: These are, respectively, the value of output and gross value added in nominal rupees deflated by an industry wholesale price index. We drop enterprises reporting zero or negative total employment, negative value of materials, negative fixed assets, negative gross output, or employment exceeding twenty.

Labor: Our measure of employment is the average number of workers, both household and hired, working full time and part time, in the last month of the year.

Outsourcing: A dummy variable which takes the value of 1 if an informal enterprise sells to another enterprise or to a contractor/middleman.

FORMAL SECTOR DATA ON FACTOR PRICES

We rely on the ASI 1989–90, 1994–95, and 2000–01 for the following variables.

Output: Value of total output and gross value added are deflated by an industry wholesale price index.

Labor: Total number of persons employed, both directly and through contractors, is our measure of formal sector employment.

Labor intensity at three-digit level: It is the ratio of wage bill to value added.

ADDITIONAL SOURCES

Prowess Database, Center for Monitoring the Indian Economy (CMIE)

Outsourcing: We use total manufacturing outsourcing reported by the firm.

Output Tariff Data at the State Level for Rural, Urban, and Overall Sectors:

Lagged Tariff: Industry-level tariff rates and non-tariff barrier (NTB) coverage rates for agricultural, mining, and manufacturing industries are weighted by state and sector-specific employment shares as follows:

$$(2) \quad Tariff_{it}^{j} = \sum_{k} \gamma_{ik,1993}^{j} * Ind\_Tariff_{kt}$$

$$(3) \quad NTB_{it}^{j} = \sum_{k} \gamma_{ik,1993}^{j} * Ind\_NTB_{kt}$$

Here, $\gamma_{ik,1993}^{j}$ is the employment share of industry k in broad sector j of state i derived from the 1993 employment–unemployment survey.[3] Ind_Tariff_{kt} and Ind_NTB_{kt} are industry-specific tariff rates and non-tariff coverage rates that are measured at the two-digit industry level for each year t. $\sum_{k} \gamma_{ik,1993}^{j} = 1$ where k represents tradable two-digit industries (comprising agricultural, mining, and manufacturing industries). Non-tradable industries were excluded from the calculations. For each observation used in our regression analysis, we use state-level protection data from the year closest to the year corresponding to our informal and formal sector activity. Our state-level protection data are for the years 1986, 1992, and 1998, on average resulting in a two-year lag in protection relative to our formal and informal sector variables on employment, output, and value added.

Labor Regulation Dummy Variable (Gupta, Hasan, and Kumar 2009)

The dummy takes the value of one for states with flexible labor laws and zero otherwise. Table 3.A2 provides a list of our fifteen states and their classification.

TABLE 3.A2

State	Labor Regulation Dummy
Andhra Pradesh	1
Assam	0
Bihar	0
Gujarat	0
Haryana	0
Karnataka	1
Kerala	0
Madhya Pradesh	0
Maharashtra	0
Orissa	0
Punjab	0
Rajasthan	1
Tamil Nadu	1
Uttar Pradesh	1
West Bengal	0

Source: Gupta, Hasan, and Kumar (2009)

Missing Observations:

In the NSS data for the unorganized sector, we observe missing economic activity in our state-industry-sector-year cells. Given the NSS survey design, this suggests that no enterprises reported activity in these state-industry-sector-year cells. We exploit the information in these observations by coding them to zero and employing a Tobit analysis. We also observe missing observations in a few cells in our formal sector activity variable on our right-hand side. We drop these observations due to measurement error concerns.

ACKNOWLEDGMENT

We thank Arvind Panagariya for several very useful conversations on this topic. Work on this paper has been supported by Columbia University's Program on Indian Economic Policies, funded by a generous grant from the John Templeton Foundation. In addition, Reshad N. Ahsan gratefully acknowledges financial support from the Australia-India Institute. The opinions expressed in the paper are those of the authors and do not necessarily reflect the views of the John Templeton Foundation or of the Australia-India Institute.

NOTES

1. See Appendix A1 for details on the computations of marginal effects. These are more important for our later regressions that have interaction terms.
2. See Appendix A1 for details on the median entries and Appendix A2 for the lists of states falling in the two separate categories of labor-market regulations.
3. The year 1993–94 is one of the middle years in the data and is thus treated as the base (reference) year in the construction of state-level openness index. As in the case of any good index, the weights therefore are not allowed to change from one year to another.

REFERENCES

Anant, T. C. A. (2000). "Reforming the Labour Market." In S. Gangopadhyay and W. Wadhwa, eds., *Economic Reforms for the Poor*. New Delhi: Konark.

Besley, T., and R. Burgess. (2004). "Can Labor Regulation Hinder Economic Performance? Evidence from India." *Quarterly Journal of Economics* 19(1):91–134.

Bhattacharjea, A. (2006). "Labour Market Regulation and Industrial Performance in India: A Critical Review of Empirical Evidence." *The Indian Journal of Labour Economics* 49(2):211–32.

Bhattacharjea, A. (2008). "How do Indian Firms Respond to Employment Protection Legislation?" Unpublished paper, University of Delhi.

Datta-Chaudhuri, M. (1996). "Labor Markets as Social Institutions in India." IRIS-India Working Paper no. 10. University of Maryland at College Park.

Gupta, P., R. Hasan, and U. Kumar. (2009). "Big Reforms but Small Payoffs: Explaining the Weak Record of Growth in Indian Manufacturing." *India Policy Forum* 5, 59–123.

Hasan, R., D. Mitra, and B. Ural. (2006). "Trade Liberalization, Labor Market Institutions, and Poverty Reduction: Evidence from Indian States." *India Policy Forum* 3(1), 71–122.

McDonald, J. F., and Robert A. Moffitt. (1980). "The Uses of Tobit Analysis." *The Review of Economics and Statistics* 62(2):318–21.

Mitra, D., and B. Ural. (2007). "Indian Manufacturing: A Slow Sector in a Rapidly Growing Economy." *Journal of International Trade and Economic Development* 17(4):525–60.

Norton, E. C., H. Wang, and C. Ai. (2004). "Computing Interaction Effects and Standard Errors in Logit and Probit Models." *The Stata Journal* 4(2):154–67.

OECD. (2007). *OECD Economic Surveys: India*. Volume 2007, Issue no. 14.

Panagariya, Arvind. (2001). "Rigid Labor Laws: A Minor Barrier to Growth?" *The Economic Times*. September 26.

Panagariya, Arvind. (2008). *India: The Emerging Giant*. New York: Oxford University Press.

Topalova, P. (2010). "Factor Immobility and Regional Impacts of Trade Liberalization: Evidence on Poverty from India." *American Economic Journal: Applied Economics* 2(4), 1–41.

Topalova, P. and Khandelwal, A. (2011). "Trade Liberalization and Firm Productivity: The Case of India." *The Review of Economics and Statistics* 93(3), 995–1009.

CHAPTER 4
Services Growth in India

A Look Inside the Black Box

RAJEEV DEHEJIA AND ARVIND PANAGARIYA

INTRODUCTION

It is now widely recognized that the pattern of growth in India in recent years has been an unconventional one. Virtually all labor-abundant developing countries—such as Taiwan, South Korea, and China—saw the shares of manufacturing in GDP and employment rise and those of agriculture fall during their high-growth phases. In contrast, during its recent high-growth phase, India has witnessed the share of manufacturing in GDP stagnate despite a decline in the share of agriculture. Moreover, the movement of workers out of the agricultural sector has been extremely piecemeal, with the absolute number of workers in agriculture still rising due to the rising size of the workforce. An additional difference between the experiences of countries like Taiwan, South Korea, and China and that of India has been with respect to labor-intensive manufacturing. While the former set of countries saw these products' share of GDP and employment rapidly rise, India has experienced no such change during the high-growth phase. In India, services have grown more rapidly than manufacturing.

The somewhat exceptional pattern of growth in India poses several puzzles. First, why have manufactured goods in general and labor-intensive products in particular responded sluggishly to the liberalizing reforms since 1991? Second, why have services grown more rapidly in the post-reform period? And finally, why has the transition from a primarily agrarian and rural to an urban and modern structure been slower in India? Specifically, why has the movement of labor out of agriculture into industry been slower than in other fast-growing developing countries?

To be sure, economic reforms, including opening to trade and foreign investment and freeing up domestic controls, have helped improve the performance of both industry and services. In particular, capital-intensive manufacturing sectors (automobiles, auto parts, and petroleum refining) and skilled labor-intensive service sectors (the software industry, telecommunications, pharmaceuticals, and banking and finance) have grown very rapidly during the high-growth phase. These sectors have been impacted directly by increased openness to trade and foreign investment and relaxed domestic entry conditions.

The key to the first puzzle lies in explaining why the abolition of investment licensing, the massive trade reforms, and foreign investment liberalization failed to stimulate rapid growth of unskilled labor-intensive manufactured goods such as apparel, footwear, and light consumer goods—products in which India has a clear comparative advantage. Until recently, the poor performance of these sectors was to be attributed to the policy of small-scale industries (SSI) reservation. This policy required virtually all labor-intensive manufactures to be produced exclusively by small enterprises whose total investment remained capped below $100,000 initially and later $250,000. This left the labor-intensive manufacturing sector in India populated by very small enterprises, largely catering to highly localized markets. Smallness of the enterprises combined with the absence of foreign competition due to prohibitive trade barriers also resulted in poor product quality.

Though the SSI reservation was effectively eliminated and international trade considerably liberalized by the early 2000s, truly large-scale firms in labor-intensive sectors such as apparel and footwear have not emerged. In all likelihood, the reason for this is the existence of other regulations that have come to bind since the effective relaxation of the SSI reservation: stringent labor laws that asymmetrically punish large-scale manufacturing firms in labor-intensive sectors. With labor costs accounting for less than 10 percent of their total costs, large firms in capital-intensive sectors (such as automobiles) are able to absorb the costs of stringent labor laws without undue impact on profitability. In contrast, for sectors such as apparel, whose labor costs could be as high as 80 percent of total costs, the extra cost of satisfying these laws renders large-scale operation unprofitable.[1]

The slow growth of labor-intensive manufacturing also explains to some degree the sector's slow growth in general. Labor-abundant countries can typically expand manufacturing at a rapid pace by capturing the vast world markets for labor-intensive products. It is more difficult to rely on this strategy by expanding capital- and skilled-labor-intensive products because of the at best limited cost advantage developing countries enjoy over developed countries in these products. Therefore, growth in these products is often bottled by the growth in the domestic market. For example, automobiles and two- and three-wheeler vehicles have grown rapidly in India in the post-liberalization phase, but so far these products have had limited success in world markets. In addition, the limited availability of skilled labor required to produce these goods can quickly exhaust the country's cost advantage in them. As the sectors producing these products expand, wages for skilled workers are rapidly bid up, thus dissipating the cost advantage—a phenomenon India has witnessed in recent years.

Turning to the second puzzle, the rapid growth of services is to be partially explained by the liberalizing reforms themselves. For example, the end of public monopoly in the telecommunications and airline industries introduced new dynamism in these sectors as they were opened to private entrepreneurs. India went from having just five million telephones at the end of 1990 to adding more than fifteen million phones per month in 2010. The financial sector received a similar boost by the easing of regulations governing the entry of private and foreign banks.

But this explanation is insufficient to account for the acceleration in growth in services that had no direct connection to liberalization. For example, transport services other than air transport, education, and health services were subject to no major direct liberalizing measures. Indeed, the same also applies to software services that are exported and were therefore not impacted by import protection in a direct way. How do we explain the growth acceleration in these services in the post-reform era? We conjecture that two factors are behind this acceleration.

First, slow growth in the goods and services that directly benefited from liberalization kept the demand for non-traded services low. Many non-traded services are bought by enterprises in traded sectors so that the growth in the latter has a direct bearing on the growth of the former. Equally, the demand for non-traded services bought by individuals depends on the level of expenditures incurred by them. For example, demands for passenger travel, telecommunications, fax and courier services, tourism, restaurant food, real estate activity, beauty parlors, education, medical services, nursing and veterinary services, and garbage collection rise with consumer expenditures. Low growth in the economy in general means low growth in the demand for these non-traded services as well.

The second reason why non-traded and export-oriented services did not take off prior to the reforms is that the efficiency of production crucially depends on the availability of quality tools and equipment. For example, the information technology industry needs access to state-of-the-art hardware and software. Similarly, firms in the transport sector need access to high-quality cars, buses, and trucks. Taxi services cannot grow without access to high-quality cars in the necessary quantities. Courier services require high-quality motorcycles and other means of transportation. Travel agencies, stock brokers, and independent accountants need computers and access to the Internet. Even small shops providing phone, fax, and photocopying services require proper equipment that provides high-quality output without frequent breakdowns. Those in the communications industry need telephones, fax machines, and computers. Those engaged in repair jobs need top-quality tools. Restrictions on international trade and domestic economic activity greatly limit the access to top-quality tools and equipment in adequate quantities—with adverse effects on productivity.

Our hypothesis is that the reforms helped release both constraints. Growth in traded goods and services increased the demand for non-traded services directly as well as through increased incomes. External and internal deregulation also opened the door to state-of-the-art equipment in adequate volume through imports as well as improved quality of domestic output. For instance, high-quality automobiles, buses, trucks, motorcycles, computers, cell phones, and equipment of all kinds are more easily available today than in the pre-reform era. Increased demand allowed fuller use of workers' time, while the availability of high-quality equipment helped raise the efficiency of the work performed. Both factors contributed to productivity growth.

Finally, we turn to the third puzzle relating to the slow movement of the workforce from agricultural to non-agricultural sectors. At one level, the slow growth of labor-intensive manufactures explains this phenomenon. But one must also answer why the rapid growth in services has not delivered rapid growth in employment as well. Our conjecture here is that the services sector in India operated like a subsistence economy in the nineteenth century in the sense that it had large volumes of underutilized labor. Workers were hired because they were needed for certain tasks but were underemployed due to either insufficient demand or unavailability of proper equipment. The slack in labor use was perhaps even more pronounced among the self-employed. This situation allowed many services sectors to grow rapidly by employing underemployed workers more fully. Some indirect evidence favoring this hypothesis can be found in the rapid expansion of services output without a commensurate expansion in labor employment.

To date, formal analyses of economic reforms in India using detailed enterprise-level data have remained confined principally to manufacturing. Scientific analyses of services, mainly by Poonam Gupta with various coauthors, have relied exclusively on sectoral data provided by the National Accounts Statistics.[2] While this is a good starting point for developing an understanding of the growth and transformation underway in India's services sector, it is extremely limiting. Firms providing services vary considerably in size, ranging from those that employ no workers to very large ones with tens of thousands of workers. They also vary considerably in ownership structure, ranging from proprietorship to cooperative to partnership to corporate. To understand the sources of growth impulses, we need to study services at the level of the firm.

Until recently, data at the level of the firm in the services sector that would allow analysis over time were not available. Such data have recently become available, however. The National Sample Survey Organization (NSSO) of the

Central Statistical Organization (CSO) has produced two very large surveys covering a substantial subset of services for 2001–02 (July 1–June 30) and 2006–07. These surveys provide systematic data on 244,376 enterprises in 2001–02 and 190,282 enterprises (including 438 very large enterprises under the list frame as detailed below) in 2006–07. With one possible exception, discussed later, the surveys follow a uniform sample design and the questionnaires are comparable across rounds. Geographically, the surveys cover the entire country, with rural and urban enterprises separately identified. They also distinguish among own-account enterprises (OAEs) which hire no regular workers, those that hire workers but nevertheless remain small, and those with a formal corporate structure.

Although India had begun to grow at a 5–6 percent annual rate in the late 1980s, the shift to the 8–9 percent range took place in fiscal year 2003–04 (April 1–March 31). This latter shift followed the reforms during 1998–2003 under the National Democratic Alliance. Those reforms were wide-ranging; they touched virtually every aspect of the economy, except labor laws and higher education. Therefore, the two surveys give us observations from the pre- and post-reform eras that also coincide with pre- and post-growth-acceleration periods.

In this chapter, we present the first analysis of the services sector that uses these enterprise-level surveys. The data allow us to study not just growth in output but also in employment and enterprises by sectors and by states. While we touch on some of the themes discussed above in this chapter, we address some others in our future work. For example, in a forthcoming paper, we propose to formally test the two hypotheses relating to the growth of non-traded services that may not have directly benefited from the liberalization since 1991. In Chapter 10 of this volume, we go further and discuss entrepreneurship among the socially disadvantaged groups vis-à-vis the better-off groups.

The chapter is organized as follows. In the next section, we describe the broad contours of the two surveys on which this chapter is based. In the third section, we situate within the broad economic context both the services in general and those covered by the two surveys in particular. In the fourth section, we set out the distinction between formal and informal sector firms within the services sector. In the fifth section, we describe the characteristics of enterprises as revealed by the surveys. A key finding here is that while output is concentrated in larger urban enterprises, more than half of the workforce is employed in tiny OAEs that employ no hired workers on a regular basis. This pattern translates into much higher per-worker and per-enterprise output in the large enterprises than in the smaller ones. In the sixth section, we summarize the pattern of growth across enterprises, states, and different service sectors. We show that though growth can be seen in all enterprises, sectors, and states, it is heavily concentrated in the largest enterprises, some key services sectors such as communications and business services, and some key states such as Maharashtra and Karnataka. Uneven growth that usually characterizes rapid growth across broad sectors and regions of the economy also characterizes the growth within services. In the seventh section, we estimate productivity growth. Consistent with our conjecture that the opening up of the economy has led to fuller use of previously underutilized labor, our results here show very substantial growth in productivity. In some states, it reaches as high as 5 percent per year. In the final section, we conclude the chapter.

SOME PRELIMINARY OBSERVATIONS ON THE SURVEYS

To explain the broad contours of the two surveys we analyze, it is best to begin with an introduction to the National Industrial Classification (NIC) 2004, which serves as the basis of identification of various sectors of the economy.[3] This classification initially divides the economy into seventeen "sections" identified by alphabetical letters A, B, . . . , Q. Table 4.1 lists these sections. On the one hand, these sections can be combined into a smaller number of broader sectors, while on the other, they may be disaggregated into much narrower categories referred to as "divisions" in the NIC 2004. The broader sectors are frequently called agriculture, industry, and services such that agriculture includes sectors A and B; industry includes sectors C, D, E, and F; and services includes sectors G thru Q. The narrower "divisions" in the classification are defined using two- or higher-digit numerical codes. Appendix table 4.A1 exhaustively lists all two-digit divisions within each alphabetical section.

The 2006–07 services survey, the second of the two surveys we analyze in this chapter, covered Sections H thru O (minus L), with some narrower divisions within these broad sections excluded. A full listing of the two- or higher-digit divisions covered and a detailed description of the services within each of the latter can be found in NSSO (2009, 7–10).[4] Within the divisions covered, the following enterprises were excluded from the survey: (i) all government and public sector enterprises, (ii) government-aided educational institutions defined as institutions in which the entire salary of all teaching and non-teaching staff was borne by the government, and (iii) service enterprises registered under the Factories Act of 1948 and covered by the latest (2004–05) Annual Survey of Industries frame. The 2001–02 survey covered the same sectors as the 2006–07 survey with two exceptions: (i) it did not cover the financial intermediation sector (NIC Section J), and (ii) it did include divisions with codes 601 (non-mechanized transport activities related to transport via railways) of Section I and 911 (community activities of business, employers and professional organizations) of Section O, which the 2006–07 survey did not cover. Throughout this chapter, our analysis excludes Section J to make the two surveys comparable. The differences between the surveys due to the exclusion of divisions 601 and 911 in the 2006–07 surveys are tiny.

Table 4.1 BROAD SECTORS IN NATIONAL INDUSTRIAL
CLASSIFICATION (NIC) 2004

Section	Description
Agriculture:	
A	Agriculture, hunting, and forestry
B	Fishing
Industry:	
C	Mining and quarrying
D	Manufacturing
E	Electricity, gas, and water supply
F	Construction
Services:	
G	Wholesale and retail trade; repair of motor vehicles, motorcycles and personal and household goods
H	Hotels and restaurants
I	Transport, storage, and communications
J	Financial intermediation
K	Real estate, renting, and business activities
L	Public administration and defense; compulsory social security
M	Education
N	Health and social work
O	Other community, social and personal service activities
P	Activities of private households as employers and undifferentiated production activities of private households
Q	Extraterritorial organizations and bodies

Source: Ministry of Statistics and Program Implementation

The surveys cover all twenty-nine states (including Delhi as a state) and six union territories in the country.[5] The sample is highly stratified, with rural and urban areas clearly distinguished. The first stage units (FSUs) are villages in rural areas and urban frame survey blocks in urban areas. These units are first identified and the ultimate stage units, called enterprises, sampled out of them. Enterprises are divided into two types: OAEs, which do not employ any hired workers on a regular basis, and establishment enterprises, which employ one or more hired workers on a regular basis.

One important difference exists between the 2001–02 and 2006–07 survey designs. The former includes all establishment enterprises, whether large or small, in the area frame. The latter takes the view that this approach results in under-representation of the large enterprises, which account for a disproportionately large volume of gross value added (GVA) and assets. It therefore introduces a separate "list frame" for the largest enterprises in the private corporate sector. It identified 998 large service sector companies distributed throughout India for this frame but, after excluding some of them for reasons of public ownership and registration under the Factories Act of 1948, narrowed down the relevant universe of eligible list frame enterprises to 626. For a variety of reasons, the survey was able to sample only 438 of the 626 enterprises. When estimating GVA, the number of workers, assets, and other variables, it imputed the values based on the enterprises actually sampled. This is the only substantive difference in the sample design between the 2001–02 and 2006–07 surveys. While its likely effect is to correct for the under-representation of large enterprises in the 2001–02 survey, it may also lead to an upward bias in the growth of variables such as GVA and assets of establishment enterprises. We comment on this issue in greater detail later.

The 2001–02 survey selected a total of 15,869 FSUs, of which 41 percent were rural and the remainder urban. Altogether, 244,376 enterprises within these FSUs were surveyed—37.85 percent in rural areas and 62.15 percent in urban areas. The 2006–07 survey selected 13,271 FSUs, of which 42 percent were in rural and 58 percent in urban areas. It surveyed 189,844 enterprises (not counting the 438 list frame units), with 43.82 percent in rural and 56.18 percent in urban areas. The union territory of Lakshadweep accounted for the minimum number of enterprises covered in each survey: 171 in the 2001–02 survey and 187 in the 2006–07 survey. State- or union-territory-level estimates of variables such as value added, workers employed, and assets are likely to be associated with large standard errors when the number of sampled enterprises is small.

Before considering further details of the surveys, it is now useful to situate the services sectors covered by them within the overall economy.

SITUATING THE SERVICES COVERED BY THE SURVEYS WITHIN THE ECONOMY

Table 4.2 reports the breakdown of GDP and employment among three broad sectors of the economy: agriculture, industry, and services. As noted in the previous section, the first of these sectors includes agriculture, forestry, and fisheries (Sections A and B of NIC 2004). Industry is defined to include mining and quarrying; manufacturing; gas, electricity, and water supply; and construction (Sections C through F). Services include Sections G thru Q. The data on GDP shares in table 4.2 are from the National Accounts Statistics (NAS), and those on employment are from the NSSO Employment-Unemployment Surveys.

Recall that the two service-firm surveys we propose to analyze were conducted in 2001–02 and 2006–07. Accordingly, we report the output shares of the three sectors in these two years and their growth rates over the five-year

Table 4.2 SHARES OF BROAD SECTORS IN THE GDP AND EMPLOYMENT

Sector	Share in GDP (2001–02)	Share in GDP (2006–07)	Growth (2001–02 to 2006–07)	Employment Share (2001–02)	Employment Share (2007–08)
(1)	(2)	(3)	(4)	(5)	(6)
Agriculture and allied activities	24	18.5	2.5	60.8	57.3
Industry	25	26.7	9.2	17	18.7
Services	51	54.7	9.3	22.1	24
Services covered by the surveys	24	27.3	10.6	9.9	11.9
GDP in billion rupees (columns 2 and 3) or total workers in million (columns 5 and 6)	19726	28643	7.8	417	408
Absolute number of workers in services covered by the surveys (million)				41	48

Source: Authors' calculations using the data from the CSO and NSS

period in columns 2, 3, and 4 of table 4.2. The employment-unemployment survey is available for 2001–02 but not 2006–07. Therefore, for the latter year, we substitute the employment shares from the survey report for 2007–08. To give the reader an idea of the approximate relative size of the services covered by our surveys, we report in the fourth row of table 4.2 the approximate output and employment shares of these services as reported in the NAS GDP data and NSSO employment-unemployment survey reports. As previously noted, most but not all NIC divisions and enterprises within these categories are covered by the surveys. In particular, any public sector enterprises—including the railways, the largest single employer in the world—are not included in the surveys. Therefore, the true GDP and employment shares of the sectors covered in the surveys are slightly below those reported in the fourth row of table 4.2.

Though agriculture and allied activities accounted for just 24 percent of the GDP in 2001–02, they employed 60.8 percent of the workforce. An examination of the shifts in the output and employment shares of agriculture over time shows that the former has evolved much faster than the latter. Migration of workers out of agriculture in India has been painfully slow despite rapid economic growth.

Industry accounted for a quarter of the GDP but employed only 17 percent of the workforce in 2001–02. Services accounted for 51 percent of the GDP in the same year and employed just 22.1 percent of the workforce. Even at the highly aggregated level of table 4.2, it is evident that the services sector has a higher average output per worker than both industry and agriculture. This turns out to be even truer of the services covered by the surveys that are the object of the analysis in this chapter. The ratio of output share to employment share in 2001–02 was 2.5 in these latter services. In comparison, the same ratio was 2.3 in services as a whole, 1.5 in industry, and 0.4 in agriculture. The services in the fourth row of table 4.1 also grew more rapidly than services as a whole between 2001–02 and 2006–07.

We may note that the number of workers employed in the sectors as reported in the surveys themselves were 26.6 million in 2001–02 and 27.7 million in 2006–07. These numbers are smaller than those shown in the last line (columns 5 and 6) of table 4.2 for several reasons. First, the surveys entirely exclude public enterprises, which employ large numbers of workers in sectors such as education and health. Second, the coverage of the surveys across NIC two- or higher-digit divisions within the covered sections and across enterprises is not exhaustive. For example, the surveys entirely exclude the railways from the transportation sector. Finally, some difference may have also resulted from sampling errors. The coverage of the specific sectors we consider here in the employment-unemployment surveys is likely to have been less exhaustive than in the surveys under analysis.

Table 4.3 provides some details on services in terms of the NIC sections. The relevant NIC section code is shown in parentheses following the description of the sector. Several exclusions from the above list in the surveys under analysis may be noted here. First, neither of the surveys includes Section G, which represents retail and wholesale trade and repair services for cars, motorcycles, and household appliances. This is a sizable sector in terms of output as well as employment.

Second, as already noted, while the 2006–07 survey covers banking and insurance (Section J), the 2001–02 survey does not do so. Because one of our key objectives is to analyze the change observed between the two surveys, our analysis excludes this sector.

Third, the surveys also exclude NIC categories L, P, and Q. Category L, which employed 1.8 percent of the workforce in 2007–08, represents public administration and defense and is part of the public sector. Category P represents activities of private households as employers and accounted for 0.7 percent of the total employment in 2007–08. This category is clearly a part of the private services sector, but the surveys do not cover it. Category Q stands for extraterritorial organizations and bodies and registered zero shares in employment in both 2001–02 and 2007–08 employment-unemployment surveys.

Finally, railway and air transport (NIC 2004 categories 601 and 62) and transport via pipelines (NIC 2004 category 603) are also excluded from the surveys. Railways are in the public sector. Air transport contains both private and public sector firms.

Table 4.3 DETAILED SERVICES SECTORS

Services Sectors	Share in GDP (2001–02)	Share in GDP (2006–07)	Growth (2001–02 to 2006–07)	Employment Share (2001–02)	Employment Share (2007–08)
Trade and auto and household appliance repair (G)	13.6	13.9	8.3	9.4	8.9
Hotels and restaurants (H)	1.3	1.5	10.5	1.2	1.4
Transport, storage, and communication (I)	8.2	11.4	15.3	3.4	4.2
Banking and insurance (J)	5.7	6.7	11.3	0.5	0.7
Real estate, ownership of dwellings, and business services (K)	7.5	7.6	8.2	0.6	1.2
Public administration and defense (L)	6.5	5.6	4.7	2.4	1.8
Other services (education, health, other community services, etc.) (M, N, O, P and Q)	8.2	8	7.1	4.6	5.8
All services	51	54.7	9.3	22.1	24
Services included in both surveys (H, I, K, M, N, O with some exclusions)	24	27.3	10.6	9.9	11.9

Source: Authors' calculations using the CSO and NSS data.

A NOTE ON FORMAL VERSUS INFORMAL SECTOR SERVICES

Defining the informal sector services is always a challenge. In India, the term *informal sector* is often identified with the "unorganized" sector. As we explain immediately below, this is not a bad approximation when it comes to manufacturing. But the issue is more complex when considering services.

In India, the organized sector typically includes all enterprises and employees in the public sector and firms registered under the Factories Act of 1948. All firms engaged in manufacturing must register under the act if they employ ten workers and use power, or if they employ twenty workers regardless of the use of power. This places all private sector manufacturing enterprises with fewer than 10 workers and those with fewer than 20 workers but not using power in the unorganized sector. For most purposes, we can reasonably identify these enterprises with the informal sector. In principle, it is conceivable that a highly automated large-scale plant could escape registration under the Factories Act, but it is unlikely in practice.

The problem in services arises from the fact that firms in this sector are not required to register under the Factories Act unless they also happen to be engaged in manufacturing activity. Therefore, most private sector services enterprises, whether small or large, are officially in the unorganized sector. For instance, large private sector banks such as the ICICI Bank and the HDFC Bank and software export giants such as Infosys, Wipro, and Satyam are officially in the unorganized sector.

In carrying out its "unorganized" sector surveys, the NSSO works with this definition. This means that its unorganized services sector surveys include enterprises of all sizes as long as they are in the private sector. This is true of the two surveys we study. As previously mentioned, the surveys broadly divide enterprises into OAEs and establishment enterprises, with the former referring to enterprises that do not employ any hired workers on a regular basis and the latter referring to those that do. While the OAEs clearly belong to the informal sector, the establishment enterprises include both informal and formal sector enterprises. In principle, it is possible to identify and exclude all limited liability companies or enterprises with workers exceeding a certain threshold to distinguish between formal and informal sector enterprises, but there is some arbitrariness in doing so. Therefore, our analysis categorizes enterprises according to several alternative criteria, which we specify below.

SOME BASIC CHARACTERISTICS
OF THE ENTERPRISES

We are now in a position to report some basic economic characteristics of the enterprises. The sectors common to the two surveys are estimated to have fifteen million enterprises and 27.75 million workers in 2006–07. The vast majority of the enterprises are tiny OAEs that do not hire any outside workers on a regular basis. In other words, the majority of workers are employed in these small enterprises. This makes the separate study of growth and productivity in small and large enterprises important from a social welfare standpoint.

The top part of table 4.4 reports the composition of value added at current prices, workers, and enterprises across OAEs and establishment-type enterprises in rural and urban areas at the national level as per the 2006–07 survey.[6] The lower part of the table reports value added per worker and

Table 4.4 VALUE ADDED AND WORKERS ACROSS ENTERPRISES
AND REGIONS (2006–07)

Enterprise Type	Rural	Urban	All India
Percent shares in total GVA			
OAE	11	10.3	21.2
Establishment	6.9	71.9	78.8
Total	17.8	82.2	100
Percent shares in the total number of workers			
OAE	36	22.7	58.8
Establishment	11.9	29.3	41.2
Total	48	52	100
Percent shares in the total number of enterprises			
OAE	52.3	32.7	85
Establishment	5.4	9.6	15
Total	57.7	42.3	100
GVA per worker in 2006–07 rupees			
OAE	21415	31753.3	25417.2
Establishment	40494.9	172693.7	134440.6
GVA per enterprise in 2006–07 rupees			
OAE	27264.6	40827.6	32494.1
Establishment	166193.6	977715.9	685383.2

Source: Authors' calculations from unit level data in round 63, NSS services survey

value added per enterprise in OAEs and establishment enterprises in rural and urban areas in 2006–07. A key observation that jumps out of the table is that output is heavily concentrated in urban establishment enterprises (71.9 percent), while the majority of the workers (58.8 percent) work in OAEs. This translates into a much higher value added per worker and per enterprise in urban establishment enterprises relative to the remaining categories.

In addition to accounting for a large proportion of output, urban establishment enterprises employ 29.3 percent of the workers. This makes a careful study of urban establishment enterprises crucial. At the same time, because the majority of workers are employed in OAEs, these enterprises require close attention as well. On average, value added per enterprise is 1.3 times the value added per worker in OAEs. On average there are 1.3 workers per OAE; in many cases (indeed modally), the owner is the only worker.

Perhaps the most important conclusion that follows from table 4.4 is that a very large proportion of the services labor force remains employed in enterprises with very low average productivity. The transformation problem India faces with respect to the movement of the vast workforce out of agriculture into more productive activities is also present within services. A majority of

Table 4.5 DISTRIBUTION OF VALUE ADDED AND WORKERS ACROSS
ACTIVITIES (2006–07)

Sector and Approximate NIC Section	GVA	Workers
Hotels and restaurants (H)	14.5	18.5
Transport, storage, and communication (I)	22.4	30.2
Real estate and business services (K)	34.6	11.2
Education and training (M)	12	14
Health and social work (N)	9.3	7.9
Other service activities (O)	7.2	18.3
Total	100	100
Total (GVA in billion rupees and workers in million)	1952	28

Source: Authors' calculations from unit level data in round 63, NSS services survey

the services workforce is in small, informal enterprises with relatively low output per worker. We will see in the next section that smaller enterprises are also subject to relatively low growth. As such, the gap in labor productivity is widening rather than narrowing.

We next consider the composition of services output and workers across various NIC sections. Table 4.5 provides the distribution of value added and workers according to NIC sections for 2006–07. Because different sectors employ various factors of production in different proportions, it is no surprise that employment and value added do not go hand in hand. While transport, storage, and communications (NIC Section I) account for the largest share in employment, real estate, renting, and business activities (NIC Section K) generate the largest share in value added.

Finally, in table 4.6, we show state-by-state shares in nominal GVA and workers for both the fifty-seventh and sixty-third rounds in sectors common to the two surveys. The states are arranged in order of declining share of value added in the sixty-third round conducted in 2006–07. Four observations follow. First, between the two surveys, the concentration in the GVA shares at the top end has risen dramatically. Whereas the top three states in 2001–02 accounted for 31 percent of the GVA, they accounted for 50 percent of the GVA in 2006–07. Second, by 2006–07, the degree of concentration at the top end had reached a very high level. The top three states alone accounted for half the services output of the country in the categories covered. Just two states—Maharashtra and Karnataka—account for as much as 41.3 percent of countrywide GVA. Third, the shares in workers employed in the covered sectors tell a somewhat different story. The shifts between the two surveys are much smaller. And the shares are also far less concentrated. Finally, the state with the largest number of workers by far, Uttar Pradesh, ranks just seventh in terms of the GVA in 2006–07. While it had a 14.1 percent share in the workforce, its share in the GVA was only 5.5 percent that year. Taken together, these facts point to a dualistic structure *within* the covered services whereby more productive firms seem to be concentrated in a very small number of states.

THE PATTERN OF GROWTH: 2001–02 TO 2006–07

We are now in a position to consider the changes between 2001–02 and 2006–07, which can be partially attributed to the reforms that took place in the late 1990s and early 2000s. Because the surveys provide data on all values at current prices, our first task is to convert them into a common base using appropriate deflators. For this, we use the NAS GDP data, which provide values of sectoral outputs in various states for each financial year at both current and constant 1999–2000 prices. The current and constant price magnitudes for a given sector in a given state in a given year implicitly define a deflator that converts the current price magnitude into a constant, 1999–2000 price

Table 4.6 STATE-WISE SHARES IN NOMINAL GVA AND WORKERS

State	Percent share in GVA		Percent share in workers	
	57th round	63rd round	57th round	63rd round
Maharashtra	15.1	23.2	9.8	10.2
Karnataka	7.9	18.1	5.2	5.4
Andhra Pradesh	6.1	8.5	9.6	10
West Bengal	6.8	7.3	8.8	9.7
Tamil Nadu	7.6	5.5	8	7.8
Kerala	5.7	5.5	4.6	5.7
Uttar Pradesh	10.3	5.5	15.7	14.1
Gujarat	7.7	5.4	5	4.2
Chandigarh	0.3	4.4	0.2	0.8
Rajasthan	3.6	2.6	3.9	4.2
Punjab	3	2.1	2.5	2.8
Madhya Pradesh	2.9	1.5	3.6	3.4
Bihar	4.9	1.5	6.7	4.7
Assam	1.7	1.4	2.1	3
Haryana	2.1	1.3	1.7	2.1
Orissa	1.9	1.1	4.3	3.1
Jharkhand	1.2	1	1.6	2.2
Delhi	6.2	0.9	2.3	1.2
Other*	5	4.6	3.2	5.2
Total	100	100	100	100

*These include 12 smaller states and 5 Union Territories.
Source: Authors' calculations from unit-level data, rounds 57 and 63, NSS services surveys

magnitude. This deflator can be used to convert a current price value in a given sector in a given state in a given year into a corresponding value at constant 1999–2000 prices. We follow this procedure as closely as the data allow.

Growth and Composition by Enterprise Type

In table 4.7, we show the total growth over five years and the associated annual compound growth rate in real GVA, the number of workers, and the number of enterprises associated with various enterprise types between 2001–02 and 2006–07. To track the changes in the composition of output produced by this growth, table 4.8 shows the shares in the total national GVA, workers, and enterprises in the relevant sectors in 2001–02 and 2006–07.

Six features of the changes reflected in these tables are noteworthy. First, the overall growth in the services covered by the surveys has been far higher than that observed in the NAS. In current rupees, GVA rose from 747.82 billion

Table 4.7 GROWTH RATES BY ENTERPRISE TYPE

Enterprise Classification	Five-year growth			Annual compound growth		
	GVA	Workers	Enterprises	GVA	Workers	Enterprises
All enterprises	113.5	4.5	3.6	16.4	0.9	0.7
OAE	18.5	2.9	5.5	3.5	0.6	1.1
Establishment	181.3	6.8	−6.1	23	1.3	−1.2
Urban OAE	18.9	6.6	7.8	3.5	1.3	1.5
Rural OAE	18.2	0.8	4.2	3.4	0.2	0.8
Urban establishment	252.2	23.9	7.9	28.6	4.4	1.5
Rural establishment	−3.3	−20.3	−23.6	−0.7	−4.4	−5.2
Fewer than five workers	24.4	1.6	4	4.5	0.3	0.8
Five or more workers	246.8	13	−3.9	28.2	2.5	−0.8
Urban: less than five workers	35	7.4	7.9	6.2	1.4	1.5
Urban: five or more workers	316.3	31.8	7.3	33	5.7	1.4
Establishment: non-corporate	41.6	−1	−5.7	7.2	−0.2	−1.2
Establishment: corporate	540.9	52.2	−11.1	45	8.8	−2.3

Source: Authors' calculations from unit-level data, rounds 57 and 63, NSS services surveys

Table 4.8 SHARES OF VARIOUS ENTERPRISE TYPES IN THE NATIONAL TOTAL

Enterprise classification	GVA		Workers		Enterprises	
	Round 57	Round 63	Round 57	Round 63	Round 57	Round 63
OAE	41.7	23.1	59.6	58.8	83.5	85
Establishment	58.3	76.9	40.4	41.2	16.5	15
Urban OAE	19.6	10.9	22.3	22.7	31.4	32.7
Rural OAE	22	12.2	37.3	36	52.1	52.3
Urban establishment	42.1	69.5	24.7	29.3	9.2	9.6
Rural establishment	16.2	7.3	15.7	11.9	7.3	5.4
Less than five workers	59.9	34.9	74.8	72.8	95.3	95.6
Five or more workers	40.1	65.1	25.2	27.2	4.7	4.4
Urban: Fewer than five workers	30.4	19.2	31	31.8	37.8	39.3
Urban: Five or more workers	31.4	61.3	16	20.2	2.9	3
Establishment: Non-corporate	42	27.9	34.5	32.7	15.6	14.2
Establishment: Corporate	16.3	49	5.9	8.6	0.9	0.8

Source: Authors' calculations from unit-level data, rounds 57 and 63, NSS services surveys

rupees in 2001–02 to 1952.11 billion rupees in 2006–07. This amounted to 161.0 percent growth over the five-year period or a compound growth rate of 21.16 percent per year. Once we apply price deflators to convert the nominal magnitudes into real, the two growth rates come down to 113 and 16.4 percent, respectively. The latter is well above the 10.6 percent growth in the NAS data for the same services.

Second, GVA growth rates are dramatically higher for the larger enterprises, which often operate in the formal sector. OAEs, which employ no hired workers on a regular basis, grew just 3.5 percent annually compared with a much larger 23 percent for establishment enterprises, which include all enterprises hiring one or more workers on a regular basis. Only rural establishment enterprises showed a decline in GVA, but this reflects a decline in their numbers as well as the number of workers they employed. Enterprises with five or more workers grew 28.2 percent annually, while those with four or fewer workers grew 4.5 percent. Both enterprise types grew faster in urban areas. Finally, corporate establishment enterprises grew the fastest, at an annual rate of 45 percent compared with 7.2 percent for non-corporate enterprises.

Third, in relation to the growth in GVA, growth in workers employed has been extremely slow. The annual employment growth in all enterprises has been a negligible 0.9 percent. Only corporate enterprises showed a significant growth in workers at the annual rate of 8.8 percent. The slow growth in workers means that the real GVA per worker has shown very impressive growth. At the aggregate level, GVA per worker grew 15.5 percent per annum. In corporate enterprises, this growth has been a phenomenal 36.2 percent. These observations lend indirect support to the hypothesis that considerable slack in labor use allows for substantial increases in productivity with just a marginal expansion of the workforce through more effective use of existing labor resources.

Fourth, the total number of establishment enterprises declined. In terms of the composition of this decline, two features are of interest. First, taking the four-part split across OAEs and establishment enterprises on the one hand and rural and urban on the other, rural establishment enterprises accounted for the entire decline. And second, within subcategories, it is interesting that even the number of corporate enterprises declined between the two surveys. This suggests some degree of consolidation in the corporate sector.

Fifth, the composition of output shifted considerably in favor of larger enterprises between the two survey years. For example, the share of corporate enterprises rose from 16.3 percent in 2001–02 to 49 percent in 2006–07. Alternatively, the share of urban establishment enterprises with five or more workers jumped from 31.4 to 61.3 percent over the same period. Finally—and rather remarkably, when we consider the four-part division of enterprises into OAEs and establishment on the one hand and rural and urban on the other— the share of urban establishment enterprises gained at the expense of all three remaining categories, rising from 42.1 to 69.5 percent.

Finally, the differences in per-worker output across enterprise types call for a close study of the reasons for these differences. Some differences, no doubt, reflect the differences in skill levels and per-capita capital used. Corporate enterprises are likely to be more capital intensive than their non-corporate counterparts. On average, the same is likely to be true of urban enterprises relative to rural ones. A large proportion of corporate workers is also likely to be among the most skilled. Even so, the differences appear to be too large to be explained by these factors alone and suggest considerable scope for productivity increases as modernization proceeds and the formal sector expands to absorb informal sector workers.

Is GVA Growth Real?

No matter how we look at the data, overall GVA growth—especially in the large enterprises—is extremely high. At the aggregate level, the NAS data show a growth of only 10.6 percent compared to the 16.4 percent implied by the survey data. In the case of corporate enterprises, the growth rate is an astounding 45 percent. Is this growth real or the result of measurement error?

To be sure, some degree of measurement error cannot be ruled out. Recall that the sixty-third round made special effort to capture the contribution of large enterprises through the list frame, which it had not done in the fifty-seventh round. By itself, this would mean that the contribution of large enterprises was undercounted, shrinking the base over which our growth rates are calculated. The particularly high growth rate of corporate enterprises noted above reinforces this point.

Yet, this is not the entire story for at least three reasons. First, the undercount of large enterprises in the fifty-seventh round can be easily overstated. While it is true that this round did not create a separate list frame for those enterprises, it did make a special effort to capture their contribution. This is explicitly brought out in Appendix B of NSSO (2003) report 482 on the fifty-seventh round. Describing the sample design, the appendix notes:

> After determining the boundaries of the sample FSU, all big non-agricultural enterprises having 200 or more workers in the entire FSU and having operated at least one day during the last 365 days preceding the day of survey (here-inafter to be called as big enterprises for brevity) were listed. All the listed big enterprises constituted segment 9 of the selected FSU. All big enterprises under coverage listed in segment 9 were surveyed separately in addition to the required number of smaller enterprises under coverage in the other segments of the selected FSU as per normal procedure. (B6)

Second, going by the numbers in table 4.8, we notice that the number of corporate enterprises fell by 11.1 percent in 2006–07 relative to 2001–02. Ceteris paribus, an undercount in 2001–02 should have led to an increase in the number of enterprises in 2006–07. Because the condition "ceteris paribus" is not valid, this by itself is not compelling evidence against under-count; however, taken in conjunction with the previous point, the sharp decline somewhat undermines the possibility of a large undercount in 2001–02.

Finally, there is some independent evidence of the larger enterprises grow-ing extremely rapidly during these years. While we have not collected this evi-dence systematically, we checked on just one enterprise that we know grew rapidly during the last decade: Infosys. This enterprise had 9,831 employees at the end of 2000–01 (March 31, 2001) and 72,241 by the end of 2006–07. Total nominal revenues rose from 19.6 billion rupees during 2000–01 to 138.9 billion rupees in 2006–07. This revenue growth works out to an annual compound rate of 38.6 percent. Infosys is, of course, not alone in experiencing such growth. Several large companies grew at comparable rates. Therefore, our conclusion is that while the numbers reported in table 4.7 are on the high side, they are indicative of substantial real growth, which probably exceeds that indicated by the NAS numbers.

Growth and Composition by Industry Sections

We next consider growth across NIC sections. Table 4.9 shows the proportionate growth rates over five years and the corresponding annual compound growth rates of GVA, workers, and the number of enterprises. Looking at the fourth column of numbers, we note that except "other service activities," which represent a mixture of activities, GVA in each service section has grown at the annual compound rate of nearly 10 percent or more. The section experiencing the fastest GVA growth is real estate and business services (NIC Section K) followed by transport, storage, and communications (NIC Section I). This is no surprise since communications, real estate, and business services have been known to be very rapidly growing sectors in the economy.

Two of the fastest growing sections in GVA terms also account for the highest growth rates of worker employment—5 percent annualized growth in Section K and 2.8 percent growth in Section I. Other sections show either

Table 4.9 FIVE-YEAR AND ANNUALIZED COMPOUND GROWTH RATES BY NIC SECTIONS

NIC Section	Five-year growth			Annual compound growth		
	GVA	Workers	Enterprises	GVA	Workers	Enterprises
Hotels and restaurants (H)	63.4	0.9	−4.5	10.3	0.2	−0.9
Transport, storage, and communication (I)	88.8	14.6	16.9	13.6	2.8	3.2
Real estate and business services (K)	404.6	27.4	10	38.2	5	1.9
Education and training (M)	77.6	−7.8	−17.8	12.2	−1.6	−3.9
Health and social work (N)	60.4	0.1	−18.6	9.9	0	−4
Other service activities (O)	26.9	−4.9	2.1	4.9	−1	0.4
All Sections	113.5	4.5	3.6	16.4	0.9	0.7

Source: Authors' calculations from unit-level data, rounds 57 and 63, NSS services surveys

Table 4.10 COMPOSITION OF SERVICES ACROSS NIC SECTIONS

NIC Section	GVA		Workers		Enterprises	
	Round 57	Round 63	Round 57	Round 63	Round 57	Round 63
Hotels and restaurants (H)	17.5	13.4	19.2	18.5	14.9	13.7
Transport, storage, and communication (I)	31.8	28.1	27.5	30.2	37.1	41.8
Real estate and business services (K)	13.1	31	9.2	11.2	8.8	9.3
Education and training (M)	13.7	11.4	15.8	14	8.8	6.9
Health and social work (N)	12.1	9.1	8.2	7.9	9.3	7.3
Other service activities (O)	11.8	7	20.1	18.3	21.2	20.9
Total	100	100	100	100	100	100

Source: Authors' calculations from unit-level data, rounds 57 and 63, NSS services surveys

a small growth or decline in worker employment. Enterprise growth follows the same broad pattern; transport storage and communications register the highest growth, followed by real estate and business services.

It is also instructive to consider briefly the composition of the covered services across NIC Sections. This is presented in table 4.10. The pattern here shows heavy and rising concentration: rapid growth in Sections K and I has concentrated GVA, employment, and enterprises in these sections. By 2006–07, these sectors together came to account for 59 percent of GVA, 41 percent of employment, and 51 percent of enterprises in the covered services.

Growth by States

We finally present growth in GVA, workers, and enterprises by states. To economize on space, we exclude eleven smaller states and five union territories, which together account for less than 5 percent of GVA, workers, and enterprises. The five-year and annual compound growth rates of GVA, workers, and enterprises for eighteen states (counting Delhi as a state) and Chandigarh are shown in table 4.11. We arrange the states in a declining order of GVA shares in 2006–07.

Table 4.11 GROWTH BY STATES

State	Five-year growth			Annual compound growth		
	GVA	Workers	Enterprises	GVA	Workers	Enterprises
Maharashtra	228.6	8.7	13	26.9	1.7	2.5
Karnataka	356.4	8.2	–1.8	35.5	1.6	–0.4
Andhra Pradesh	191.3	9.6	4.4	23.8	1.8	0.9
West Bengal	132.1	15.9	23.1	18.3	3	4.2
Kerala	118.3	31.2	28.1	16.9	5.6	5.1
Tamil Nadu	66.2	2.2	–3	10.7	0.4	–0.6
Gujarat	62.6	–11.1	4.2	10.2	–2.3	0.8
Uttar Pradesh	11	–5.7	–11.3	2.1	–1.2	–2.4
Chandigarh	3186.4	376.6	28.7	101.1	36.7	5.2
Rajasthan	63.2	13.2	4	10.3	2.5	0.8
Punjab	53.5	18.8	24.4	8.9	3.5	4.5
Assam	98.2	52.7	43.6	14.7	8.8	7.5
Madhya Pradesh	16.7	0.2	–5.3	3.1	0	–1.1
Bihar	–36.6	–27.1	–27	–8.7	–6.1	–6.1
Haryana	33.6	26	44.2	6	4.7	7.6
Orissa	30.3	–24.9	–19.2	5.4	–5.6	–4.2
Jharkhand	97.8	49.5	51.7	14.6	8.4	8.7
J&K	117.2	28.4	27.1	16.8	5.1	4.9
Delhi	–67.8	–46.9	–40.8	–20.3	–11.9	–9.9
India	113.5	4.5	3.7	16.4	0.9	0.7

Source: Authors' calculations from unit-level data, rounds 57 and 63, NSS services surveys

Two points may be made with respect to the growth rates in the states. First, growth rates in many states have been extremely high. Moreover, the states with the highest level of services GVA, which are in the top part of the table, have also experienced some of the highest growth rates. Leaving aside Chandigarh, which is a small centrally administered city, the five largest states by GVA in the covered services (accounting for 61 percent of the GVA in 2006–07) are also the five fastest growing states. To some degree, the story of growth in services in India may well be the story of growth in Maharashtra, Karnataka, and Andhra Pradesh. Beyond the five biggest states in the covered services and Chandigarh, all other states exhibited growth rates below the national average. The state with the most workers in the covered services—Uttar Pradesh—did poorly, exhibiting just 2.1 percent annual growth rate.

The second point relates to some striking anomalies in the data. Chandigarh shows exceptionally high growth in GVA, workers, and enterprises. While it is true that based on the NAS data, Chandigarh saw annual growth of 11.2 percent during those five years, a growth rate of 101 percent in GVA in the services covered by the surveys is still difficult to explain. In a similar vein, Delhi shows a declining growth rate in GVA of 20.3 percent and correspondingly high declining rates of workers and enterprises. There is no obvious explanation for these declining rates either.

PRODUCTIVITY GROWTH

The analysis in the previous section focuses entirely on growth. The survey data include information on various inputs used by the enterprises and can be used to estimate productivity growth between the two survey years. We caution that, as usual, we must work with some variables in *value* terms rather than physical quantities, which poses an interpretation problem. To make this point explicit, the conventional production function is written:

$$(1)\ X(t) = A(t)[K(t)]^{\alpha}[L(t)]^{\beta}[M(t)]^{\gamma}.$$

Here X stands for output, K for capital, L for labor, M for intermediate inputs, and t for time. Term $A(t)$ measures the level of productivity. Letting P_X, P_K, and P_M stand for the price of X, K, and M, respectively, we can rewrite this equation as:

$$(2)\ P_X(t)X_X(t) = \frac{P_X(t)A(t)}{[P_K(t)]^{\alpha}[P_M(t)]^{\gamma}}[P_K(t)K(t)]^{\alpha}[L(t)]^{\beta}[P_M(t)M(t)]^{\gamma}.$$

Letting V stand for value, this equation can be rewritten as:

$$(3)\ V_X(t) = \frac{P_X(t)A(t)}{[P_K(t)]^{\alpha}[P_M(t)]^{\gamma}}[V_K(t)]^{\alpha}[L(t)]^{\beta}[V_M(t)]^{\gamma}$$

A long-recognized difficulty in estimating equation (3) is that any time-invariant firm-level unobservable input (for example, managerial skill) will be absorbed into $A(t)$. A standard solution is to use longitudinal data: two (or more) observations per firm allow us to difference out the firm fixed effect. Taking logs on both sides and differentiating with respect to time, we obtain:

$$(4)\ \hat{V} = \hat{A} + [\hat{P}_X - (\alpha \hat{P}_K + \gamma \hat{P}_M)] + \alpha \hat{V}_K + \beta \hat{L} + \gamma \hat{V}_M$$

Here we use "^" over a variable to denote the proportionate change in that variable. Because we use output values at constant prices, we can think of P_X as being constant, in other words, $\hat{P}_X = 0$. This means that total factor productivity (TFP) growth, which equals $\hat{A}$, would be underestimated by the weighted sum of the proportionate change in the prices of capital and intermediate input prices. Unfortunately the NSS data provide us with repeated cross sections of firms rather than a panel. Consequently we create a panel of synthetic firms by collapsing the data into cells defined by two-digit NIC, state, and survey round, which yields 560 state × year × two-digit NIC observations. Thus, we are assuming that, within a given state, year, and two-digit industry, firms use identical technology.

A further challenge in estimating the production function is that unobserved productivity shocks are likely to lead to both increased output and input use. A number of solutions to this simultaneity have been proposed in the recent literature. We implement the Levinsohn and Petrin (2003) estimator, which uses intermediate inputs as proxies for productivity shocks. Intermediate inputs are more likely to respond simultaneously and smoothly to unobserved productivity shocks.

Finally, it is important to note that our estimates of total and TFP growth correspond to the average growth in value added at the industry-state level, rather than the growth in total value added across all industries. To the extent that growth is highly skewed across industries, our estimates of average growth at the industry-state level will tend to be lower than the growth in total value added. Our production function estimates are presented in table 4.A2.

In figure 4.1, we break productivity growth down into factor growth and TFP growth, with the sum of the two categories corresponding to total growth. Our numerical estimates on which figure 4.1 is based are reported in table 4.A3. India-wide, TFP growth is 18 percentage points out of a total growth in services of 31 percent; hence, productivity growth explains approximately 60 percent of total growth. The fastest growing states are Maharashtra, Karnataka, Goa, Andhra Pradesh, Gujarat, and Goa, with total growth ranging from over 80 percent to just over 50 percent and TFP accounting for 15 percent or more of growth.

According to figure 4.1, as one would expect, the contribution of TFP growth varies considerably across states. An interesting feature of the numbers is that in states where value added has grown rapidly, the relative contribution of TFP growth is low. In contrast, productivity growth makes a much larger contribution in states such as West Bengal, Orissa, and J&K, where overall growth has been low. One speculative interpretation of these results is that TFP growth tends to be highest in states where the services sector was relatively undeveloped as of 2001–02.

A potentially important element of TFP in India has been the shift within the services sector to the fast-growing industries. In figure 4.1 this would be subsumed within our TFP estimates; this is appropriate in the sense that shifts to more productive activities are a legitimate increase in factor productivity. Nonetheless, it is interesting to consider how factor productivity has increased within industry, as this is more likely to capture actual technological improvements. The results presented in figure 4.2, with the numerical estimates relegated to table 4.A4, show that this predictably reduces the contribution of productivity gains, though it still

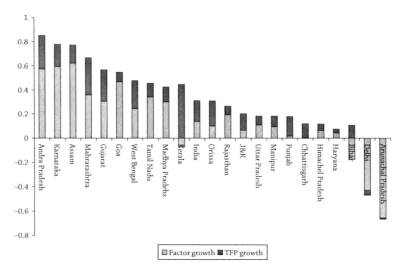

Figure 4.1
Contribution of Productivity Growth to the Total Industry-State Growth in Services in 22 Large States Based on Levinsohn-Petrin Estimator

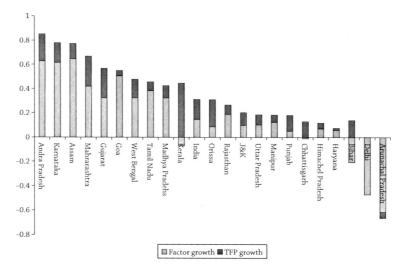

Figure 4.2
Contribution of Productivity Growth to the Total Industry-State Growth in Services in 22 Large States Based on Levinsohn-Petrin Estimator Corrected for Industry Fixed Effects

remains substantial—especially in some of the states—and underlines our view that TFP growth is a significant part of the story of the growth in services.

We conclude this section with the observation that no matter how we estimate it, productivity growth remains a far greater proportion of pre-dicted growth for most states than is commonly observed. This result cannot be attributed to the upward bias in measurement due to the better capture of data for the large, list-frame enterprises. This is because such bias must impact not just output but also input usage. Our own hypothesis is that the large contribution is due to more effective utilization of labor. We noted in the introduction that prior to liberalization, the services sector in India operated like a nineteenth-century subsistence economy in the sense that it had large volumes of underutilized labor. As liberalization proceeded and the demand for services grew, this labor came to be utilized more and more fully.

CONCLUDING REMARKS

In this chapter, we have taken a first stab at analyzing the growth of services in India using firm-level data. For this purpose, we have used the data collected by the NSSO during 2001–02 and 2006–07 employing a broadly comparable sample design. The main variation in the sample design is that the second survey makes a special effort to capture the output of the largest enterprises, which turn out to contribute as much as 38 percent of total services output covered by the survey, despite employing only 2 percent of the workforce. Because the output of these same enterprises may not have been captured as well in the first survey, the absolute growth in services implied by the two surveys is potentially biased upward.

Nevertheless, the surveys offer the first glimpse into the performance of enterprises of different sizes. In these concluding remarks, we wish to emphasize three main findings. First, while services output is heavily concentrated in urban establishment enterprises, more than half of the workers are employed in OAEs, which do not employ any outside workers at all. If we included enterprises with fewer than five workers among smaller enterprises, the contrast between the concentration of output and workers in large and small enterprises becomes even stronger. The smaller enterprises, no matter how we choose to define them, exhibit much lower output per worker, output per enterprise, and growth in output over time than larger enterprises. This means that the transformation to a modern economy would require not just the movement of workers from agriculture to industry—as the second author has emphasized in a number of his writings (for example, see Panagariya 2008a, 2008b)—but also a movement of workers from the smaller to the larger services enterprises or, alternatively and minimally, modernization of OAEs.

Second, services output and growth are highly concentrated in a handful of states. Maharashtra and Karnataka alone account for almost half of the services output covered by the second survey, which includes financial sector services. These same states also account for by far the highest growth in the services common to the two surveys. In contrast, Uttar Pradesh accounts for the most workers in the services covered in the second survey, but it ranks eighth in terms of output value. At first glance, leading states such as Maharashtra and Karnataka exhibit higher output per worker in services than lagging states such as Uttar Pradesh.

Finally, our calculations suggest a very substantial contribution of productivity growth to overall growth in services. This finding is consistent to some degree with that of Bosworth et al. (2006–07), who undertake a growth accounting exercise across agriculture, industry, and services at the national level using macroeconomic data. They find a much larger contribution of productivity growth in services than in industry. Our calculations yield annual compound productivity growth rates of 3 percent or more in a number of states, with Maharashtra, Gujarat, Kerala, and Andhra Pradesh exhibiting rates in excess of 4.5 percent. Given the dominant role of services in India's growth, these findings suggest that its growth has relied less on factor accumulation and more on productivity improvements. We have hypothesized that this productivity growth has resulted at least in part from more effective use of previously underutilized labor.

ACKNOWLEDGMENT

The authors are at New York University and Columbia University, respectively, and can be reached at rajeev@dehejia.net and ap2231@columbia.edu. Work on this chapter has been supported by Columbia University's Program on Indian Economic Policies, funded by a generous grant from the John Templeton Foundation. The opinions expressed in the chapter are those of the authors and do not necessarily reflect the views of the John Templeton Foundation. The authors are grateful to Barry Bosworth, Rupa Chanda, and other participants of the conference held under the auspices of the Columbia Program on Indian Economic Policies in New York on November 4–6, 2010 and that under joint auspices of the Program and the National Council on Applied Economic Research in New Delhi on March 31–April 1, 2011.

APPENDIX

Table 4.A1 NIC 2004 TWO-DIGIT CLASSIFICATION

Sections/ Divisions	Description
Section A	Agriculture, hunting, and forestry
Division 01	Agriculture, hunting, and related service activities
Division 02	Forestry, logging, and related service activities
Section B	Fishing
Division 05	Fishing, aquaculture, and service activities incidental to fishing
Section C	Mining and quarrying
Division 10	Mining of coal and lignite; extraction of peat
Division 11	Extraction of crude petroleum and natural gas; service activities incidental to oil and gas extraction
Division 12	Mining of uranium and thorium ores
Division 13	Mining of metal ores
Division 14	Other mining and quarrying

Table 4.A1 Continued

Sections/ Divisions	Description
Section D	Manufacturing
Division 15	Manufacture of food products and beverages
Division 16	Manufacture of tobacco products
Division 17	Manufacture of textiles
Division 18	Manufacture of wearing apparel; dressing and dyeing of fur
Division 19	Tanning and dressing of leather; manufacture of luggage, handbags, saddlery, harnesses, and footwear
Division 20	Manufacture of wood and of products of wood and cork, except furniture; manufacture of articles of straw and plaiting materials
Division 21	Manufacture of paper and paper products
Division 22	Publishing, printing, and reproduction of recorded media
Division 23	Manufacture of coke, refined petroleum products, and nuclear fuel
Division 24	Manufacture of chemicals and chemical products
Division 25	Manufacture of rubber and plastics products
Division 26	Manufacture of other non-metallic mineral products
Division 27	Manufacture of basic metals
Division 28	Manufacture of fabricated metal products, except machinery and equipment
Division 29	Manufacture of machinery and equipment not elsewhere classified
Division 30	Manufacture of office, accounting, and computing machinery
Division 31	Manufacture of electrical machinery and apparatus not elsewhere classified
Division 32	Manufacture of radio, television, and communication equipment and apparatus
Division 33	Manufacture of medical, precision, and optical instruments, watches and clocks
Division 34	Manufacture of motor vehicles, trailers, and semi-trailers
Division 35	Manufacture of other transport equipment
Division 36	Manufacture of furniture; manufacturing not elsewhere classified
Division 37	Recycling
Section E	Electricity, gas, and water supply
Division 40	Electricity, gas, steam, and hot water supply
Division 41	Collection, purification, and distribution of water
Section F	Construction
Division 45	Construction
Section G	Wholesale and retail trade; repair of motor vehicles, motorcycles, and personal and household goods
Division 50	Sale, maintenance, and repair of motor vehicles and motorcycles; retail sale of automotive fuel
Division 51	Wholesale trade and commission trade, except of motor vehicles and motorcycles
Division 52	Retail trade, except of motor vehicles and motorcycles; repair of personal and household goods

(Continued)

Table 4.A1 Continued

Sections/Divisions	Description
Section H	Hotels and restaurants
Division 55	Hotels and restaurants
Section I	Transport, storage, and communications
Division 60	Land transport; transport via pipelines
Division 61	Water transport
Division 62	Air transport
Division 63	Supporting and auxiliary transport activities; activities of travel agencies
Division 64	Post and telecommunications
Section J	Financial intermediation
Division 65	Financial intermediation, except insurance and pension funding
Division 66	Insurance and pension funding, except compulsory social security
Division 67	Activities auxiliary to financial intermediation
Section K	Real estate, renting, and business activities
Division 70	Real estate activities
Division 71	Renting of machinery and equipment without operator and of personal and household goods
Division 72	Computer and related activities
Division 73	Research and development
Division 74	Other business activities
Section L	Public administration and defense; compulsory social security
Division 75	Public administration and defense; compulsory social security
Section M	Education
Division 80	Education
Section N	Health and social work
Division 85	Health and social work
Section O	Other community, social, and personal service activities
Division 90	Sewage and refuse disposal, sanitation, and similar activities
Division 91	Activities of membership organizations not elsewhere classified
Division 92	Recreational, cultural, and sporting activities
Division 93	Other service activities
Section P	Activities of private households as employers and undifferentiated production activities of private households
Division 95	Activities of private households as employers of domestic staff
Division 96	Undifferentiated goods-producing activities of private households for own use
Division 97	Undifferentiated service-producing activities of private households for own use
Section Q	Extraterritorial organizations and bodies
Division 99	Extraterritorial organizations and bodies

Source: Ministry of Statistics and Program Implementation

Table 4.A2 PRODUCTION FUNCTION ESTIMATES

VARIABLES	OLS Time Fixed Effects	OLS Time Fixed Effects	OLS state x time FE	OLS state x time FE	OLS state x time FE & industry FE	Levinsohn-Petrin GMM Time Fixed Effects	Levinsohn-Petrin GMM Time Fixed Effects	Levinsohn-Petrin GMM Time Fixed Effects & industry Fixed Fffects
Average TFP	11.816*** [0.058]	4.168*** [0.160]						
Average TFP growth	0.312*** [0.081]	0.187*** [0.025]					0.175*** [0.030]	0.165*** [0.028]
log Labor		0.447*** [0.032]		0.455*** [0.033]	0.335*** [0.046]	0.359*** [0.040]	0.370*** [0.035]	0.232*** [0.055]
log Capital		0.080*** [0.014]		0.082*** [0.015]	0.075*** [0.017]	0.108 [0.129]	0.128 [0.085]	0.132 [0.098]
log Intermediate inputs		0.580*** [0.014]		0.559*** [0.014]	0.643*** [0.022]	0.437** [0.187]	0.410** [0.173]	0.425*** [0.157]
Observations	555	555	555	555	555	555	555	555
p value for CRS		0.000025		0.00026	0.13	0.31	0.43	0.017

Standard errors in brackets

*** $p < 0.01$, ** $p < 0.05$, * $p < 0.10$

Table 4.A3 COMPARING TOTAL AND TFP GROWTH IN SERVICES

State/Country	Factor growth	TFP growth	Total growth	Total growth
Andra Pradesh	0.574	0.278	0.852	0.852
Karnataka	0.593	0.186	0.779	0.779
Assam	0.622	0.151	0.773	0.773
Maharashtra	0.358	0.309	0.667	0.667
Gujarat	0.306	0.261	0.567	0.567
Goa	0.469	0.08	0.549	0.549
West Bengal	0.243	0.235	0.478	0.478
Tamil Nadu	0.341	0.116	0.457	0.457
Madhya Pradesh	0.301	0.125	0.426	0.426
Kerala	-0.072	0.447	0.375	0.375
India	0.137	0.175	0.312	0.312
Orissa	0.099	0.211	0.31	0.31
Rajasthan	0.194	0.072	0.266	0.266
J&K	0.065	0.138	0.203	0.203
Uttar Pradesh	0.108	0.076	0.184	0.184
Manipur	0.094	0.089	0.183	0.183
Punjab	0.016	0.164	0.18	0.18
Chhattisgarh	-0.001	0.12	0.119	0.119
Himachel Pradesh	0.063	0.054	0.117	0.117
Haryana	0.042	0.033	0.075	0.075
Bihar	-0.175	0.107	-0.068	-0.068
Delhi	-0.427	-0.042	-0.469	-0.469
Arunachal Pradesh	-0.654	-0.009	-0.663	-0.663

Table 4.A4 COMPARING TOTAL AND TFP GROWTH CONTROLLING FOR
INDSUTRY–FIXED EFFECTS IN SERVICES

State/Country	Factor growth	TFP growth	Total growth
Andra Pradesh	0.627	0.225	0.852
Karnataka	0.615	0.164	0.779
Assam	0.645	0.128	0.773
Mahrarashtra	0.419	0.248	0.667
Gujarat	0.324	0.243	0.567
Goa	0.505	0.044	0.549
West Bengal	0.323	0.155	0.478
Tamil Nadu	0.383	0.074	0.457
Madhya Pradesh	0.323	0.103	0.426
Kerala	−0.071	0.446	0.375
India	0.147	0.165	0.312
Orissa	0.087	0.223	0.31
Rajasthan	0.188	0.078	0.266
J&K	0.098	0.105	0.203
Uttar Pradesh	0.101	0.083	0.184
Manipur	0.123	0.06	0.183
Punjab	0.051	0.129	0.18
Chhattisgarh	−0.01	0.129	0.119
Himachel Pradesh	0.07	0.047	0.117
Haryana	0.058	0.017	0.075
Bihar	−0.206	0.138	−0.068
Delhi	−0.47	0.001	−0.469
Arunachal Pradesh	−0.612	−0.051	−0.663

NOTES

1. To give just one example, the Industrial Dispute Act of 1948 makes it virtually impossible for a manufacturing firm with one hundred or more employees to legally lay off workers under any circumstances. Even if the firm goes bankrupt, it must pay the workers their regular salary. Capital-intensive firms get around this law by giving overly generous packages to workers they want to lay off. Because labor costs are a small proportion of the total costs, these firms can afford to pay such golden shake hands. The same option is not available in sectors where 80 percent or more of the cost is accounted for by labor.
2. See Gordon and Gupta (2004) and Eichengreen and Gupta (2011).
3. Table 4.A1 in the Appendix exhaustively lists two-digit NIC 2004 sectors. Further disaggregation going down to three, four, and five digits can be found at http://mospi.nic.in/Mospi_New/site/inner.aspx?status=2&menu_id=129 (accessed on May 10, 2012). Concordances are available between earlier classifications and NIC 2004. For example, the 2001–02 services survey employed NIC 1998 classification, but it can be readily converted into NIC 2004.

4. The excluded subsectors are: transport by railways (NIC 601), transport via pipeline (NIC 603), and air transport (NIC 62) in Section I; monetary transactions (NIC 651) in Section J; activities of business, employers, and professional organizations (NIC 911), activities of trade unions (NIC 912), and activities of political organizations (9192) in Section O.
5. The only exclusions are the districts of Leh in Ladakh and Kargil, Punch, and Rajauri in Jammu and Kashmir, plus some interior villages in Nagaland and Andaman and Nicobar Islands.
6. Value added is defined as the total revenue minus the costs of intermediate inputs and approximately represents the payments to primary factors of production and taxes, if any.

REFERENCES

Bosworth, Barry, Susan Collins, and Arvind Virmani. 2007. "Sources of Growth in the Indian Economy." *India Policy Forum 2006/07* vol. 3, 1–50. New Delhi: Sage.

Eichengreen, Barry, and Poonam Gupta. 2011. "The Services Sector as Road to India's Economic Growth?" *India Policy Forum*, Volume 7.

Gordon, Jim, and Poonam Gupta. 2004. "Understanding India's Services Revolution." Working Paper no. WP/04/171. International Monetary Fund.

Levinsohn, James, and Amil Petrin. 2003. "Estimating Production Functions Using Inputs to Control for Unobservables." *Review of Economic Studies* 70(2), No. 243, 317–42.

National Sample Survey Organization. 2009. *Service Sector in India (2006–07): Operational Characteristics of Enterprises*. Report No. 528 (63/2.345/1), February.

National Sample Survey Organization. 2003. Unorganized *Service Sector in India— 2001–02: Salient Features*. Report No. 482 (57/2.345/1), August.

Panagariya, Arvind. 2008a. "Transforming India." In Jagdish Bhagwati and Charles Calomiris, eds., *Sustaining India's Growth Miracle*. New York: Columbia University Press, 9–45.

Panagariya, Arvind. 2008b. *India: The Emerging Giant*. New York: Oxford University Press.

CHAPTER 5

Organized Retailing in India

Issues and Outlook

RAJEEV KOHLI AND JAGDISH BHAGWATI

INTRODUCTION

Where India shops in the future is at the center of a vigorous and ongoing debate. On one side of the debate are the millions of street and pushcart vendors and small stores that have dominated Indian retailing for centuries. On the other side are large Indian and multinational corporations seeking new opportunities.

Small retailers claim that large firms, especially multinational retailers, will rob them of their livelihoods. Large businesses say that they can provide better and cheaper products and bring much-needed investment, efficiency, organization, and know-how to retailing.

Policymakers in India believe that they face a difficult dilemma. They do not want to harm small retailers (known in a similar and earlier Japanese debate as "mom-and-pop stores") and are wary of making changes that might harm them and even throw millions of them out of work. But they also seek to promote greater efficiency and productivity *via* the growth of the large retailers, especially as retailing (as we show below) is an important and rapidly growing sector of the economy. We contend, however, that this dilemma is largely illusory. The expansion of the large retailers will not be at the expense of the small ones.

The modernization of Indian industry has traditionally been held up by yet another fear, which is now being extended to the modernization of the retail sector: the fear that the large retailers will lead to monopoly and hence should not be permitted. This fear is implausible. But we argue that anticompetition practices could be minimized in a variety of entry-facilitating ways rather than by shooting oneself in the foot by denying the benefits of a modern retail sector.

SOME SALIENT FACTS

1. *Restricted Foreign Entry*: Retail is presently one of the few sectors in which the Indian government limits the entry of foreign firms. Some retailers have entered the Indian market under a provision allowing them up to 51percent equity ownership in their Indian operations provided that they sell products under a single brand name. Examples of such firms are Louis Vuitton, Cartier, Armani, Reebok, Marks and Spencer, Debenhams, Next, Bodyshop, Oshkosh, and Carter's.

International firms that want to sell multiple brands cannot open retail stores but can own 100 percent equity in wholesale stores. Their customers must be institutional buyers who pay in cash and carry the merchandise from the store shelves. From 2000–10, multinational companies like Walmart and Metro invested about $1.8 billion in such cash-and-carry stores that sell to retailers, cooperatives, hotels, restaurants, caterers, and various food and non-food traders (Department of Industrial Policy and Promotion 2010). They offer lower prices and wider assortments than traditional wholesalers and are open for longer hours. Still, most multinational firms see cash-and-carry wholesaling as a point of entry into India. Their aim is to obtain government approval for 100 percent foreign direct investment (FDI) in multibrand retailing.

2. *Defining "Small" and "Large" Retailers*: Retailers, like manufacturers, are categorized in India as either formal or informal and as organized or unorganized.

(i) The *informal sector* (generally synonymous with "small" retailers) consists of unincorporated businesses that are owned and run by individuals or households. These businesses are not legally distinct from their owners, who raise capital at their own risk and have unlimited personal liability for debts and obligations. Informal businesses typically employ family members and casual labor without formal contracts. The *formal sector*, on the other hand, includes corporations, limited companies, and businesses run by or on behalf of cooperative societies and trusts.

(ii) The *organized sector* comprises incorporated businesses. Information about this sector is available from company budgets and reports. Importantly, partnerships, private and limited companies, and businesses run by cooperative societies and trusts are not considered to be organized businesses in India. Instead, they are classified as part of the *unorganized sector*, which also includes all businesses in the informal sector.

The precise relationship between these two sets of definitions of "small" and "large" retailers is set out in figure 5.1. As seen there, organized retailing includes some large incorporated stores, and all chain stores, supermarkets, hypermarkets, department stores and stores-in-stores. Unorganized retailing includes all informal retailers, including mom-and-pop stores (which are called

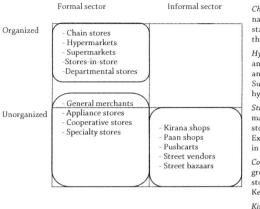

	Formal sector	Informal sector
Organized	- Chain stores - Hypermarkets - Supermarkets - Stores-in-store - Departmental stores	
Unorganized	- General merchants - Appliance stores - Cooperative stores - Specialty stores	- Kirana shops - Paan shops - Pushcarts - Street vendors - Street bazaars

Chain stores are retail outlets that share a brand name and have central management and standardized business practices. Walmart is the world's largest retail chain.

Hypermarkets are combinations of supermarkets and department stores. For example, Big Bazaar and Spencer's Retail are hypermarkets in India; Super Walmart and Super Target are hypermarkets in the United States

Stores-in-store are (typically branded) manufacturers who rent space within a larger store and operate independent businesses. Examples are cosmetics and perfume counters in many departmental stores.

Cooperative stores are owned by a society or groups of individuals. Examples of cooperative stores in India are Super Bazaar and Kendriya Bhandar.

Kirana stores are small, owner-operated, mom-and-pop stores.

Paan shops are small roadside stalls that sell beetle nut wrapped in a leaf, cigarettes, and tobacco.

Figure 5.1
Classification of Retailers in India

"kirana" stores in India), vegetable and fruit stalls, paan shops (which sell beetle nut wrapped in a leaf, cigarettes, and tobacco), pushcarts, street hawkers, and street vendors. It also includes general merchants, chemists, appliance stores, and various specialty stores that are part of the formal sector but that operate as partnerships, private and limited companies, cooperatives, or trusts.

3. *Retail Employment:* Retailing is the second largest employer in India after agriculture. According to the National Survey Sample Organization (round 64), retail businesses employed 33.1 million people—an estimated 7.2 percent of all workers in the country—in 2007–08 (Department of Industrial Policy and Promotion 2010).

The composition of retail sector employment is heavily biased in favor of informal retailing. Thus, informal retailing provides employment to the individuals and families who run the country's twelve million or so kirana stores and to the casual workers such as shop and delivery boys whom they employ. Informal retailing also provides employment to about 3.4 million street vendors and several millionpushcart vendors who sell products door-to-door and on the street.

In contrast, organized retailing, a category that includes supermarkets and hypermarkets, employs only about 500,000 people, almost all in urban areas. Supermarkets and business hubs have grown faster in smaller towns rather than in the traditional large cities like Mumbai and Kolkata (Reardon, Timmer, and Minten 2010).

While the retail sector employment is sizable, its growth is another matter. In fact, retail employment grew at a slower rate than overall employment in India from 2005–06. More recently, the two have grown at about the same rate because retail employment rates have risen and overall employment rates have fallen.

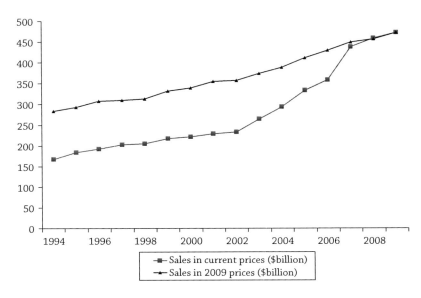

Figure 5.2
Retail Sales in India at Current and Constant Prices: 1994–2009

    This acceleration of retail employment has been predominantly in the rural areas. Between 1999–2000 and 2004–05, retail employment grew by more than 30 percent in rural areas but by less than 3 percent in urban areas.

    4. *Retail Sales:* As for retail sales, the story is somewhat similar but not quite the same. Retail sales, both at current and constant prices, have accelerated since 2002 (see figure 5.2), though they have not grown at the same rate as GDP. As a result, the ratio of retail sales (which is a gross value) to GDP (which is value added) has fallen since the mid-1990s (see figure 5.3), much in line with the relative growth rates in retail and total employment.

    As for the composition of the sales growth, we do not have systematic year-to-year data on the distribution of retail sales between the organized and unorganized retailers. However, recent data for 2005–09 suggest that organized retailers accounted for 3.3 percent of retail sales in 2005 and 4.8 percent in 2009, implying that the growth was biased in favor of the organized sector (see table 5.1).[1]

    Table 5.1 shows the corresponding sales for organized and unorganized retailers in 2005 and 2009, and the average annual growth rates over the five-year period. The most striking conclusion from table 5.1 is that organized retailing grew from 2005–09 four times as fast as unorganized retailing and gained a 1.5 percent share of retail sales. On the other hand, unorganized retailing captured the vast bulk of the increase in retail sales over this time period because it was growing from such a large sales base.

    If organized and unorganized retail sales were to continue to grow at the 2005–09 rate (13.65 percent and 3.07 percent, respectively), then organized

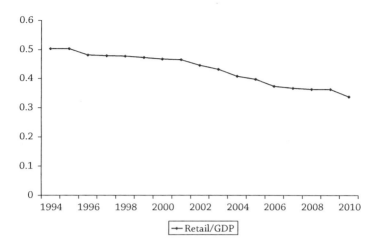

Figure 5.3
Ratio of Retail Sales to GDP in India: 1994–2009

Table 5.1 SHARE OF SALES, DOLLAR SALES, AND AVERAGE GROWTH RATES
FOR ORGANIZED AND UNORGANIZED RETAILERS IN INDIA: 2005–09

	Year	
Share of Retail Sales	2005	2009
Organized retailers	3.30	4.80
Unorganized retailers	96.70	95.20

Retail sales in billions of dollars (US)

	Nominal sales		Sales in constant (2009) prices	
Year	2005	2009	2005	2009
Organized retailing	10.97	22.62	13.56	22.62
Unorganized retailing	321.59	448.65	397.45	448.65
Total retail sales	332.56	471.27	411.01	471.27

Average annual growth rate: 2005–09

	Nominal sales	Sales in constant (2009) prices
Organized retailing	19.82%	13.65%
Unorganized retailing	8.68%	3.07%
All retailing	9.10%	3.50%

Data sources: Malhotra, Agarwalla, and Chaudhry (2010) and Economist Intelligence Unit (2011)/Planet Retail

retailing's share should increase from 4.8 percent in 2009 to 9.1 percent in 2016. But before alarmists conclude that this spells difficulties for the unorganized sector, remember that unorganized retailing would still account for about 76 percent of the US$138 billion increase in retail sales (at constant 2009 prices) from 2009–16.

Are these projections plausible? Our analysis suggests that they are. A time-series model, described in the Appendix, predicts that retail sales (in constant 2009 prices) will be US$574.2 billion in 2016.The confidence interval associated with the prediction includes the US$610 billion in total retail sales if organized and unorganized retailing continue to growth at the observed post-2005 rates.

5. *A Closer Look at Chain Stores*: An important segment of the organized sector is the corporate retail chains. These retail chains sell either or both of food and non-food products. Table 5.2a shows the performance of thirty-three important retail chains, using the data reported by Reardon, Timmer, and Minten (2010). These retail chains have become a substantial part of organized retailing, growing their combined share of organized retail sales from 8.2 percent in 2005 to 22.54 percent in 2009.

Table 5.2b shows that during 2005–09, nominal sales increased by $4.2 billion for these 33 chains, which amounted to a 36.02 percent sales increase for organized retailers and a 3.03 percent increase for all retailers. Overall, these retail chains have grown at a nominal annual rate of nearly 50 percent from 2001–09 and are likely to gain more share of organized retailing.[2] But so far, the growth in total retail sales has been large enough to accommodate these retailers and still allow other unorganized and other organized retailers to garner about 97 percent of the sales increase from 2005–09.

The rapid growth rates for these retail chains are not surprising. Their sales are growing from a small sales base; as sales increase, the same dollar increase represents a smaller percentage growth in sales. Thus, if all $60.26 billion of the increase in real retail sales from 2005–09 were attributed to unorganized retailing, this sector would still have grown at no more than 3.6 percent per year.

Table 5.2 PERFORMANCE OF MODERN RETAIL CHAINS IN INDIA

(a) Performance of 33 modern retail

Sales	2001	2005	2009
33 retail chains (current billion dollars)	0.3	0.9	5.1
Organized retail sales (current billion dolalrs)		10.97	22.63
Total retail sales (current billion dollars)		332.6	471.3
Percent share of 33 retails chains in organized retails sales		8.2	22.54
Percent share of 33 retails chains in total retail sales		0.27	1.08

(b) 2005–2009 increase in nominal retail sales

Change in sales for 33 retail chains ($Billion)	4.2
Change in sales for organized retailing ($Billion)	11.66
Change in sales for all retailing ($Billion)	138.7
Change for 33 chains as percent of change in organized retailing	36.02
Change for 33 chains as percent of change for all retailing	3.03

But we also observe that much of the sales growth for retail chains is a result of new store openings. For example, Reliance Industries launched its first retail store, Reliance Fresh, in November 2006. It had 590 stores across thirteen states by March 2008, and close to 1,000 stores by February 2009 (Knowledge at Wharton 2009). Rapid sales growth is thus neither surprising nor a sign of commercial success. Instead, it is a measure of the investments these firms have made to establish market presence. Eventually, these firms will need to focus on returns on investments, which have so far been difficult for many retail chains to achieve.

It is notable that unsustainable growth was said to be a key reason for the demise of Subhiksa, which was once the second largest retail chain in India with about 1,600 discount food stores. Its annual sales grew by 139 percent in 2006 and 211 percent in 2007, before cash flow and profitability problems led to its closure in 2009. The issue afflicts all forms of organized retailing.

6. *Food and Non-food Retail Sales*: Finally, some observations regarding the relative performance of food and non-food retail sales are in order. In 1994, 75.5 percent of all retail purchases were for food products; by 2009, this percentage had dropped to 65.6 percent (figure 5.4). A time series model (see Appendix) predicts that if the trend continues, food sales will further decline to 60.4 percent of total retail sales by 2016. The model also predicts that retail sales may grow at about 5 percent annually for non-food products but only at about 2 percent annually for food products between 2009–16.[3]

Organized retailers should benefit from this trend because many non-food products require investments that are infeasible for most unorganized retailers. Durable goods, in particular, have high growth rates and low levels of

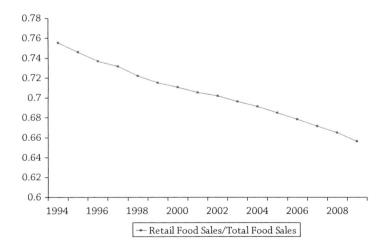

Figure 5.4
Retail Food Sales (f_t) as a Fraction of Total Retail Sales (s_t) in India: 1994–2009

household penetration and represent a significant long-term opportunity for organized retailers.

On the other hand, unorganized retailers should also be able to provide necessary maintenance and repair services and compete in secondhand markets for durable goods, which have long replacement cycles in India. But there are also other reasons why the unorganized retailers will continue to prosper: in many ways, discussed immediately below, they have competitive advantages vis-à-vis the organized retailers.

RELATIVE ADVANTAGES OF LARGE AND SMALL RETAILERS

While our analysis of short-term trends strongly suggests that both the unorganized and unorganized retailers will grow significantly in the near future, the reason why this is so is that each sector enjoys different relative advantages both generally speaking and particularly in the Indian context, so that the organized sector cannot overwhelm the unorganized sector in competition.

1. *Advantages for Unorganized Retailers*: Unorganized retailers in India typically have lower fixed and operating costs and use resources more efficiently than organized retailers.

They convert their homes into shops, use them to store goods, have low overhead and utility costs, hire no managers or sales clerks, use unskilled labor, and have little loss due to stealing and pilferage. In contrast, organized retailers rent or buy stores, incur substantial fixed and overhead costs, pay salaries and benefits to employees, and cannot easily fire workers.

Kirana stores use most of the store space to stock products and use one or two people to fulfill customer orders. On the other hand, chain stores need more space to display products and allow consumers to walk through aisles. Surveys show that self-serve layouts in Indian stores are often poorly managed. In some, products are placed on three or four shelves in each aisle; in others, shelves go to the ceiling, where customers cannot reach them. Fresh produce is often scattered on the floor, and large boxes lie partially opened in the middle of aisles.

Moreover, small retailers can cater to a variety of different needs in ways that organized retailers cannot. Thus, most small stores will accept product returns, exchange damaged goods, and give credit to customers with whom they have longstanding relationships (Vishwanathan, Rosa, and Roth 2010; Martinez and Haddock 2007). They know the likes and dislikes of individual customers, recommend new products to them, and adjust prices for different customers. Organized retailers typically cannot, and indeed do not, provide such services.

Consumers also build routines around and derive pleasure from the many small aspects of shopping: the daily call of a vegetable seller, haggling over prices at the weekly street bazaars, the nightly paan and cigarette, and the chai shop are all part of the rhythm of Indian life. Such rhythms may change, but not quickly.

Unorganized retailers benefit from the fact that most Indian consumers make small but frequent purchases. Over three-quarters of the Indian population still lives on less than US$2 per day. Prahalad (2005) observes that there are millions of consumers at the "bottom of the pyramid" in India who can afford to buy only the quantities they need for their daily needs. This is why sachets of such products as shampoos, beauty creams, detergents, edible oils, and spices are sold widely in India. An added reason for small purchases is that less than 20 percent of Indian homes have refrigerators; most people must limit the perishable goods they purchase to an amount they can consume in a day or two.[4] Moreover, while most Indian homes store supplies of wheat, rice, and lentils, they keep only small quantities of non-perishable goods because they have small homes with limited storage space.

India's high population density (like Japan's, where the expansion of the large retail stores, after the abolition of restrictions on their expansion under US pressure, did not lead to the feared decimation of the mom-and-pop stores) is an added factor that benefits small retailers.[5] They are able to offer—at minuscule or no cost—services like phone orders and free home delivery to nearby customers. Moreover, because there are many consumers in a neighborhood, unorganized retailers can survive by offering a different mix of merchandise, or by catering to a different market segment, than organized retail stores. There is typically a mix of more and less affluent customers in most Indian neighborhoods. Some of them cannot (or choose not to) travel to a more distant chain store in the traffic; others buy from both chain stores and small local stores; and still others prefer buying from a store owner they trust or from a vendor who comes to their doorstep.

2. *Advantages for Organized Retailers*: Proponents of organized retailing often note that these firms can offer wider product assortments and lower prices to consumers than unorganized retailers can.

But among the important benefits obtained by consumers is also the fact that these firms are likely to sell safer products. Food-borne illnesses and contamination are long-standing issues in India. Counterfeit drugs allegedly account for 20–25 percent of total pharmaceutical sales in the country (*Express India* 2009). Multinational retailers have the experience of sourcing products from low-cost countries that meet safety and quality norms in developed countries, and all organized retailers have the incentive to implement product safety standards because they are more likely to face scrutiny and liability than unorganized retailers.

A significant advantage for organized retailers relates also to prices. The organized retailing corporations have the ability to seek out the lowest-cost suppliers around the world. This ability spurs opposition to multinational

retailers and feeds suspicions that firms like Walmart, which has the reputa-
tion of destroying mom-and-pop stores in countries like the United States,
will do the same in India (see, for example, Swamy 2011). But India itself is
one of the low-cost countries from which multinational firms buy products.
Although mom-and-pop stores outside India do not have easy access to these
low-cost producers, unorganized retailers can buy from the same (or similar)
sources, possibly through representative cooperatives like Bhartiya Udyog
Vyapar Mandal. As long as there is competition in supplier markets, efficiency
and scale benefits obtained by organized retailers may be shared with unorganized retailers.

Many organized retailers, especially large multinational firms, also have
deep knowledge and the ability to operate lean distribution systems (see, for
example, Basker 2007). The specifics of the Indian situation promise significant gains, in particular for farmers, from such lean distribution systems.
Thus, the organized retailers can cut distribution costs by working directly
with farmers, and simultaneously improve their incomes. These farmers typically earn a third (instead of the international norm of two-thirds) of the
final price of their produce. Indian farmers earn lower prices partly because
of greater waste and inefficiency in the traditional distribution system and
partly because farmers have been at the mercy of wholesalers, who are allowed
to operate as monopolists by the State Agricultural Produce and Market
Committee (APMC) Acts (Panagariya 2008).

There is evidence now that both domestic and multinational retailers
in the organized sector have begun working with farmers and other rural
workers to improve their growing and harvesting practices (Bajaj 2010).
These retailers now buy directly from farmers and handle all aspects of
distribution, including food processing, transportation, warehousing, storage, and retailing. Multinational firms like Walmart are keen to invest in
farm-to-consumer delivery systems; domestic organized retailers, like
Reliance Industries, are already investing in direct farm-to-store distribution (*Edge Singapore* 2009).

Organized retailers can also achieve lower private and social costs by
building cold storage, warehouses, and processing facilities, which are badly
needed in India. The state of essential cold-storage facilities in particular is
abysmal. A report by the Department of Industrial Policy and Promotion
(2010) notes that that 25–30 percent of fruits and vegetables produced
in the country spoil each year because of the lack of cold-storage facilities. Similarly, the lack of adequate warehousing has resulted in spoilage of
5–7 percent of food grains. Millions of tons of wheat and rice are stored
under tarpaulin or left out to rot in the monsoon (Halarnkar and Randhawa
2010).[6]

Organized retailers can also have lower logistics costs (i.e., transportation,
inventory, warehousing, packing, and handling), which are estimated to be

around 14 percent of GDP in India—compared to 8 percent of GDP in United States (*Technopak Retail Outlook* 2008). Manoj (2008) observes that moving a cargo container one kilometer costs 50 percent more in India than in the United States (even without adjusting for the lower absolute prices in India). Part of the reason is that road transportation, which accounts for the movement of about 77 percent of goods, is largely unorganized and fragmented, and has few economies of scale or scope.[7]

System-wide improvements in logistics and supply-chain operations may be achieved by allowing multinational retailers, who have built substantial expertise in the area, into India.

LONG-TERM PROSPECTS FOR RETAILERS

With real retail sales likely to increase by about a trillion dollars over the next quarter century in India, it is certain that the advantages we have discussed for the unorganized and organized retails sectors will enable both sectors to grow, and that the fear that the unorganized retail sector will shrink with the expansion of the organized sector (voiced, for example, by Swamy 2011) is not justified.

The likely scenario of the growth of the two sectors should reflect certain trends in Indian urbanization that favor the organized sector without entailing the decline of the unorganized sector. India currently has the second largest number of urban dwellers in the world. As in many other developing countries, urbanization has increased in India, from 16 percent in 1950 (Lucas 2004) to 30.9 percent in 2010 (United Nations Department of Economic and Social Affairs Population Division 2012).[8]

A study by McKinsey Global Institute (2010) predicts that India's urban population will increase by 250 million from 2008–30, by which time 40 percent of its people will live in towns and cities. The study predicts that the number of cities will increase from forty-two in 2010 to sixty-eight in 2030, and that six cities will have populations of ten million or more. Mumbai's population is expected to exceed thirty-three million, Delhi's population to exceed twenty-five million, and Kolkata's population to exceed twenty-two million. The McKinsey study estimates that the share of GDP for urban areas will increase from 58 percent in 2008 to 69 percent in 2030, creating about 120 million new jobs.[9]

The forecasted increase in urban markets is likely to favor, at the margin, the organized retailers who are generally seen to focus on urban markets currently. Towns and cities should, however, be able to accommodate both organized and unorganized retailers (since, as we have argued, both sectors have different advantages).

The likely scenario is that of a growing urban-based organized retailing sector that also contributes to the rural economy by investing in rural food-processing facilities, warehouses, and transportation and shipment hubs. Some of these investments are likely to be made in rural areas close to towns and cities (e.g., warehousing), others closer to farmers and suppliers (e.g., food processing, storage), and still others (e.g., trans-shipment points, distribution hubs) at locations that are suitable from a logistics perspective.

Policies to restrict or even prevent the growth of the organized sector, based on the unjustified fear that it would decimate the unorganized retailers and harm the rural communities, would therefore be detrimental. The organized sector offers prospects of better-paid jobs, which also permit the accumulation of skills and offer the workers the opportunity to rise within an organization. It is equally necessary that there be substantial improvements to the inefficient and wasteful distribution system in the country.

YET OTHER CONCERNS

With protectionism, if one set of critiques is refuted, another crops up. The same is true for the opposition to large retailers. The fear that their growth will displace and eliminate the small retailers can be refuted, as we have shown. But the opponents of the large retailers then proceed to claim implausibly that the large retailers will resort to predatory pricing, and this will force out the small retailers. Or some NGOs, reflecting uncritically some Western NGOs' opposition to Walmart, embrace this position to oppose all large retailers.

On the first issue, we may cite a report by the Parliamentary Standing Committee on Commerce (2009), which has expressed concern that organized retailers might use predatory pricing (selling below cost to force out small retailers). Kalhan and Franz (2009) have expressed similar apprehensions about the potential use of predatory pricing by organized retailers to enter new markets.

Predatory pricing can be a concern in markets with high barriers to entry, so that a firm can raise the lowered prices and earn excess profits once its competitors have exited the market. However, unorganized retailers have low entry barriers, which is the reason they are widespread in India. Pricing below cost may succeed temporarily in driving out unorganized retailers from a market, but once prices return to normal levels, the same or other unorganized retailers can reappear. Thus it is difficult, if not impossible, to point to sustainable benefits that an organized retailer can obtain by using predatory pricing.

A related argument is that organized retailers might collude to carve up parts of a larger market into sub-markets, in which they can operate as virtual monopolies (Joseph et al. 2008). This, too, is improbable in the absence of high entry barriers. If there are monopoly profits to be made, there will surely be an incentive for other—organized and unorganized—retailers to enter the market.

Kalhan and Franz (2009) and Singh (2010) have suggested that large retailers can exercise excessive monopsonistic power by extracting better prices from suppliers. But is this credible when there are several large players in the market and farmers cannot be effectively prevented from shifting among them?

Besides, monopsonistic power can be checked by governmental policies that strengthen the functioning of competitive markets. However, policies have tended to do the opposite (just as local monopolies were created in the pre-1991 period by governmental licensing restrictions on entry of domestic and foreign competitors). As noted in a report by the Inter-Ministerial Group (2011), the APMC Act has had the unintended consequence of allowing buyers to set up cartels.

An important alternative policy option that could accompany the freer entry of large retailers and further reduce the low probability of their turning into monopsonies is to facilitate cooperative buying by unorganized retailers. Bhartiya Udyog Vyapar Mandal, the largest national-level association of kirana stores, is leading one such effort. The association negotiates better prices from manufacturers, bypasses middlemen, and obtains financing at terms that are otherwise available only to large organizations (Dave 2008).

Is there any likelihood that, like Standard Oil in nineteenth-century America, the large retailers could acquire monopolistic control over distribution networks to lock out rival firms? However unlikely this scenario is, it makes sense to require the use of common, interoperable standards, creating an effective electronic market that can be accessed at low cost by multiple suppliers and buyers.

It is also important that, as with manufacturing, the Competition Commission of India be able to entertain complaints and cases against the exercise of monopoly and monopsony power by firms in the retail sector as well.

Finally, while the concern about large retailers exercising monopoly and monopsony power is implausible and, in any case, can be effectively laid to rest by the suggested policy actions, the nongovernmental organization (NGO) opposition to the large retail stores is impossible to take seriously. True, the opposition to Walmart in the United States comes from some NGOs. But while the opposition in the US case is to the fact that Walmart brings in cheap *imports*, Indian NGOs should support Walmart because it would enable India to *export*. Unfortunately, much of such agitation proceeds on the principle of "monkey see, monkey do," and works to the disadvantage of India's interests. It should be rejected firmly and summarily.

APPENDIX

A1. Autoregressive Model for Ratio of Retail Sales to GDP

Let $t = 0, \ldots, 14$, correspond to the year $1994, \ldots, 2009$. Let s_t denote the retail sales in year t, and let g_t denote the GDP of India in year t. Let

$$x_t = \ln\left(\frac{s_t}{g_t - s_t}\right),$$

where $g_t - s_t$ is the difference between GDP and retail sales in year t. Note that we can interpret X_t as the logit-transformed value of the ratio of retail sales to GDP:

$$x_t = \ln\left(\frac{s_t}{g_t - s_t}\right) = \ln\left(\frac{s_t / g_t}{1 - (s_t / g_t)}\right).$$

As figure 5.3 shows, the value of s_t/g_t (and thus x_t) decreased from 1994–2009. This is consistent with the observation that consumption (of which retail purchases are a part) has grown at a slower rate than GDP in India.

We consider the first-order autoregressive model:

$$x_t = \alpha_0 + \alpha_1 x_{t-1} + \alpha_2 t + \varepsilon_t,$$

where $|\alpha_1| < 1$. The x_{t-1} term on the right-hand side of the above equation captures the serial dependence in the values of x_t. As the ratio of retail sales to GDP decreases over time, we expect $\alpha_2 < 0$. The value of Durbin's t-statistic is 2.544 ($p = 0.012$), which suggests the presence of first-order autocorrelation in the data.

We use a maximum-likelihood procedure to estimate the model parameters. The estimated model is:

$$\hat{x}_t = 0.7412 x_{t-1} - 0.0425t.$$

$$\text{standard error}\quad (0.1906)\qquad\qquad (0.00349)$$

The intercept term is not statistically significant ($p > 0.10$) and is therefore not included in the above equation. The coefficients α_1 and α_2 are both statistically significant ($p < 0.05$). The estimated model explains almost all of the variance in the data (Total $R^2 = 0.991$).

The model predicts $\hat{x}_t = 0.940$ in 2016; the corresponding 95 percent confidence interval for x_t is ($-1.1413, -0.7384$). The predicted value of s_t/s_t in 2016 is

$$\frac{e^{\hat{x}_t}}{1 + e^{\hat{x}_t}} = \frac{e^{-0.940}}{1 + e^{-0.940}} = 0.281.$$

That is, the model predicts that retail sales will decline to 28.1 percent of GDP in 2016. The corresponding 95 percent confidence interval for s_t/g_t is (0.2421, 0.3234). Figure 5.A1 shows the predicted values and 95 percent confidence intervals for s_t/g_t until 2016.

To estimate the value of predicted retail sales, we use GDP projections from the International Monetary Fund, which forecasts real GDP in India will grow at an average annual rate of 6.67 percent until 2016. This implies that the GDP of India (in constant 2009 prices) will be $2,043.92 billion in 2016. Thus, the model predicts that retail sales in constant 2009 prices will be $\hat{s}_t = \$574.2$ billion (0.281 × 2043.92 billion) in 2016. The corresponding 95 percent confidence range, in billions of dollars, is ($494.78, $660.92).

A2. Autoregressive Model for Ratio of Retail Food Sales to Total Retail Sales

As in the preceding analysis, let $t = 0, \ldots, 14$, correspond to the year 1994, ..., 2009. Let s_t denote the retail sales in year t, and let f_t denote the retail food sales in year t. Let

$$y = \ln\left(\frac{f_t}{s_t - f_t}\right),$$

where s_t-f_t is the difference between total retail sales and food retail sales in year t. We can interpret y_t as the logit-transformed value of the ratio of food retail sales to total retail sales in a year:

$$y_t = \ln\left(\frac{f_t}{s_t - f_t}\right) = \ln\left(\frac{f_t/s_t}{1 - (f_t/s_t)}\right)$$

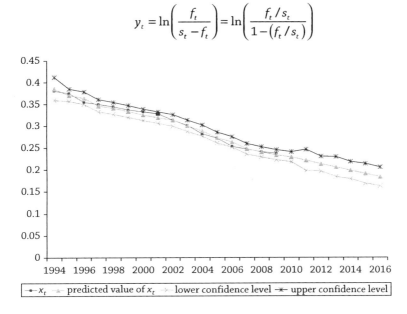

Figure 5.A1
Fit and Predictions from Autoregressive Model of Retail Sales (s_t) as a Fraction of GDP (g_t) in India: 1994–2016

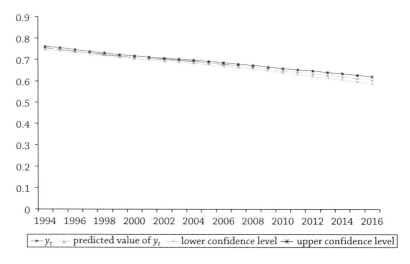

Figure 5.A2
Fit and Predictions from Autoregressive Model of Retail Food Sales (f_t) as a Fraction of Total Retail Sales (s_t) in India: 1994–2016

Figure 5.A2 shows that the value of f_t/s_t (and thus y_t) decreased from 1994–2009.

We consider the first-order autoregressive model:

$$y_t = \beta_0 + \beta_1 y_{t-1} + \beta_2 t + \varepsilon_t,$$

where $|\beta_1| < 1$. The y_{t-1} term on the right-hand side of the above equation captures the serial dependence in the values of y_t. As the ratio of retail food sales to total retail sales (figure 5.4) decreases over time, we expect β_2 Medium 0 The value of Durbin's t-statistic is 2.544 ($p = 0.012$), which suggests the presence of first-order autocorrelation in the data.

We use a maximum-likelihood procedure to estimate the model parameters. The estimated model is:

$$\hat{y}_t = 1.1126 + 0.8257 y_{t-1} - 0.0314t$$

$$\text{standard error} \quad (0.0166) \quad (0.1431) \quad (0.00161)$$

Each of the coefficients is statistically significant (p < 0.0001). The estimated model explains most of the variance in the data (Total $R^2 = 0.996$).

Figure 5.A2 shows the predicted values and 95 percent confidence intervals for f_t/s_t until 2016. The predicted value of f_t/s_t in 2016 is

$$\frac{e^{\hat{y}_t}}{1 + e^{\hat{y}_t}} = 0.604$$

The corresponding 95 percent confidence interval is (0.588–0.620).

Food sales in 2016 can thus be estimated to be $0.604 \times \$574.2$ billion $=$ \$346.82 billion where $\hat{s}_t = \$574.2$ billion is the value of predicted retail sales (in constant 2009 prices) obtained in Section A1 of the Appendix.

ACKNOWLEDGMENT

Work on this chapter has been supported by Columbia University's Program on Indian Economic Policies, funded by a generous grant from the John Templeton Foundation. The opinions expressed in the chapter are those of the authors and do not necessarily reflect the views of the John Templeton Foundation.

NOTES

1. Our major source for the information on market shares is the study by Malhotra, Agarwalla, and Chaudhury (2010). The 4.8 percent share for organized retailing in 2009 that they report is consistent with the figure of about 5 percent share noted in the report by the Parliamentary Standing Committee on Commerce (2009). However, Joseph et. al. (2008) report that organized retailing had 3.3 percent share of retail sales in 2003–04, not in 2005. We use the later date reported by Malhotra, Agarwalla, and Chaudhry (2010) because it is from a more recent study, and because it provides a more conservative assessment of the performance of unorganized retailing, which is the major issue of concern for policymakers.
2. Reardon and Minten (2011) report similar growth rates for twenty-six major national and regional food chains.
3. These average growth rates are estimated as follows: (1) Total retail sales were \$471.271 billion in 2009. Food sales were 65.6 percent (\$301.18 billion), and non-food sales were 34.4 percent (\$162.09 billion) of the total retail sales. (2) As described in the Appendix, total retail sales are projected to be \$574.2 billion in 2016. Food sales are projected to be 60.4 percent (\$346.82 Billion) and non-food sales are projected to be 39.6 percent (\$227.38 billion) of the total retail sales.
4. Data obtained from Euromonitor (2011) show that refrigerator ownership increases with income and over time. However, even among households in the highest income decile, refrigerator penetration was only 55.5 percent in 2009.
5. India is similar to Japan in terms of high population density. It is notable that while US pressure led Japan to lift restrictions on the entry of large retail stores, the growth of the latter did not lead to the feared decimation of mom-and-pop stores in that country. To this day, large and small stores coexist in Japan, in part because high population density affects where and how consumers shop and allows small retailers the opportunities that are not available in countries like the United States.
6. Basu (2010) observes that India needs a redesign of the mechanisms by which the country acquires and releases food to the market.
7. Sriram et al. (2006) report that small business owners do the vast bulk of transportation, and that operators who have twenty or more trucks are responsible for only 6 percent of the traffic.

8. According to census reports, the number of people living in Indian cities grew from 290 million in 2001 to 380 million in 2008, at a growth rate that was 58 percent higher than the country's population growth rate as a whole. About 80 percent of the urban growth resulted from the expansion of city boundaries and the reclassification of rural areas (the rest was due to migration).

9. Their analysis assumes annual GDP growth of 7.4% from 2008–30, with urban GDP growing 8.3% per year and rural GDP growing 5.9% per year. The study also predicts that the number of urban households earning less than Rs. 90,000 per year will fall below 20%, and the number of people earning between Rs. 200,000 and Rs. 1 million per year will increase fourfold from 32 million to 147 million. In contrast, 75% of urban populations today are in the lowest income segment, with average earnings of about Rs. 80 (about $1.80) per day.

REFERENCES

Bajaj, Vikas (2010), "How Wal-Mart's Wooing Indian Farmers," *New York Times,* April 12.

Basker, Emek (2007), "The Causes and Consequences of Wal-Mart's Growth," *Journal of Economic Perspectives*, 21 (3), 177–98.

Basu, Kaushik (2010), "The Economics of Foodgrain Management in India," Report by Ministry of Finance, New Delhi.

Dave, Sachin (2008), "Mom & Pop Shops Eye Cooperatives to Take on Big Retailers,"*Economic Times*, May 16.

Department of Industrial Policy and Promotion (2010), "Foreign Direct Investment (FDI) in Multi-Brand Retail Trading," discussion paper.

Economist Intelligence Unit (2011), "India: Consumer Goods and Retail Report," *Consumer Goods Briefing and Forecast*.

The Edge Singapore (2009), "Manager@Work: Battle Begins for the Wallets of 500 Million Indian Consumers," March 23.

Euromonitor International (2011), "Country Market Insight: Retailing—India," January 2010.

Express India (2009), "Multi-Crore Illicit Drug Industry Thriving in India," July 24.

Halarnkar, Samar and Manpreet Randhawa (2010), "India Lets Grain Rot Instead of Feeding Poor," *Hindustan Times*, July 26.

Inter-Ministerial Group (2011), "Position Paper Number 1 from the IMG on Inflation," working paper 3/2011-DEA, Ministry of Finance, Government of India.

Joseph, Mathew, Nirupama Soundararajan, Manisha Gupta, and Sanghamitra Sahu (2008), "Impact of Organized Retailing on the Unorganized Sector," Indian Council for Research on International Economic Relations, November.

Kalhan, Anuradha and Martin Franz (2009), "Regulation of Retail: Comparative Experience," *Economic and Political Weekly*, 44 (32), 56–64.

Knowledge at Wharton (2009), "Trouble in Store: A Setback for India's Organized Retail Sector," February 26.

Lucas, Robert E., Jr. (2004), "Life Earnings and Rural-Urban Migration," *Journal of Political Economy*, 112 (1), Part 2, S29–S59.

Malhotra, Abhishek, Vikash Agarwalla, and Srishti Chaudhry (2010), "FMCG Roadmap to 2020: The Game Changers," report prepared by Booz and Company for Confederation of Indian Industry.

Manoj, P. (2008), "Rising Transportation and Port Costs Start to Hurt India's Trade," *Livemint*, July 10.

Martinez, Alonso and Ronald Haddock (2007), "The Flatbed Factory," *Strategy + Business*, 46, 66–79.

McKinsey Global Institute (2010), "India's Urban Awakening: Building Inclusive Cities, Sustaining Economic Growth," April.

Panagariya, Arvind (2008), *India: The Emerging Giant*, New York: Oxford University Press.

Parliamentary Standing Committee on Commerce (2009), "Foreign and Domestic Investment in Retail Sector," 90th Report, presented to Lok Sabha and the Rajya Sabha, June 8.

Prahalad, C. K. (2005), *The Fortune at the Bottom of the Pyramid: Eradicating Poverty Through Profit*, Upper Saddle River, NJ: Wharton School Publishing.

Reardon, Thomas and Bart Minten (2011), "Surprised by Supermarkets: Diffusion of Modern Food Retail in India,"*Journal of Agribusiness in Developing and Emerging Economies*, 1 (2), 134–61.

Reardon, Thomas, C. Peter Timmer, and Bart Minten (2010), "Supermarket Revolution in Asia and Emerging Development Strategies to Include Small Farmers," *Proceedings of the National Academy of Sciences*, October 12.

Singh, Sukhpal (2010), "Implications of FDI in Food Supermarkets," *Economics and Political Weekly*, 45 (34), 17–20.

Sriram, S., Anand Venkatesh, Manisha Karne, and Vidya Mohite (2006), "Competition Issues in the Road Goods Transport Industry in India With Special Reference to the Mumbai Metropolitan Region," report for the Competition Commission of India.

Swamy, Shekar (2011), "The Pitfalls of FDI in Multi-Brand Retailing in India," Briefing Paper #3, Madhyam, Delhi.

Technopak Retail Outlook (2008), "Supply Chain Challenges in the Indian Retail Sector," January.

United Nations, Department of Economic and Social Affairs, Population Division (2012), *World Urbanization Prospects: The 2011 Revision*, CD-ROM Edition.

Vishwanathan, Madhu, Jose Antonio Rosa, and Julie A. Roth (2010), "Exchanges in Marketing Systems: The Case of Subsistence Consumer-Merchants in Chennai, India," *Journal of Marketing*, 74 (May), 1–17.

PART TWO

Reforms and the Transformation within and across Enterprises

CHAPTER 6

Selling the Family Silver to Pay the Grocer's Bill?

The Case of Privatization in India

NANDINI GUPTA

INTRODUCTION

Government-owned firms occupy an important position in the Indian economy. Federal-government-owned firms contributed more than 11 percent of GDP in 2005 (Ministry of Finance, 2008), and just forty-seven listed government-owned firms constituted 22 percent of the total market capitalization of the Bombay Stock Exchange as of February 28, 2011 (Bombay Stock Exchange Disinvestments Database 2011). However, government-owned firms are highly inefficient due to surplus employment, rent-seeking activities by politicians, protection from competitive forces, and the absence of market-based incentives for workers. For example, while 158 federal-government-owned firms reported positive profits, another 59 firms reported cumulative losses of approximately Rs. 158 billion in 2009 (Department of Public Enterprises 2009–10).

Following a balance-of-payments crisis in 1991, the Indian government undertook wide-ranging economic reforms to reduce the role of the government in the economy, including delicensing, foreign investment and trade liberalization, financial sector reforms, and privatization. Since 1991, the government has raised approximately Rs. 960 billion from privatization sales (Bombay Stock Exchange Disinvestments Database 2011). The federal government currently owns 249 non-financial firms but has sold partial equity stakes on the stock market without transferring management control in 47 firms, and has sold majority stakes and transferred management control in 14 firms. The two privatization methods adopted by the Indian government (partial and majority sales), offer insight into the long-standing debate over why government-owned firms perform poorly. First, the managerial view, based on agency theory, is that government-owned firms have difficulty monitoring managers because there is neither an individual owner with strong incentives to monitor managers nor a public share price to provide information about manager actions as judged by stock market participants (Laffont and Tirole 1993). Partial privatization, by which the shares of the firm are traded on the stock market while the firm remains under government control and subject to political interference, offers a test of this theory. Using data on all partial privatizations undertaken between 1991 and 1999 in India, Gupta (2005) finds that, consistent with the managerial view, the sale of partial equity stakes increases the sale revenues, profitability, and labor productivity of government-owned firms.[1]

According to the political view of government ownership, governments pursue objectives in addition to and in conflict with profit maximization, and the resulting political interference may distort the objectives and constraints faced by managers (Shleifer and Vishny 1994). For example, Fan, Wong, and Zhang (2007) find that partially privatized Chinese firms with politically connected CEOs are more likely than those without political connections, to underperform and appoint less professionally qualified but politically connected board members. Therefore, only the outright transfer of firms to private owners will lead to performance improvements. India's privatization experience is useful in this regard because the Indian government undertook both partial privatizations as well as the sale of majority stakes with the transfer of management control, which allows us to investigate the political view. In particular, we examine the effect of privatizing majority stakes and transferring management control on the performance of government-owned firms that have been partially privatized and are trading on the stock market.

The literature has shown that governments are likely to selectively choose firms for privatization based on observable and unobservable characteristics. For example, Gupta, Ham, and Svejnar (2008) show that profitable firms are more likely to be privatized, while Dinc and Gupta (2010) find that firm-level characteristics are likely to affect the selection of firms for privatization. To address the potential endogeneity of privatization to firm performance, we estimate a firm fixed effects specification that addresses selection bias that may arise if more profitable or larger firms are selected for privatization. To address dynamic selection bias, which may arise if the government selects firms for privatization based on unobservable time-varying characteristics, we use the approach suggested by Frydman et al. (1999). In particular, they argue that firms that are selected for privatization are likely to share similar characteristics, so comparing privatized firms to a control group of firms that have also been selected for privatization but have not yet been sold should address this selection bias. Since privatization is distributed over several years in our data, in any given year we also observe firms privatized in later years that form the control group. To minimize the possibility of simultaneity between privatization and performance, we use the lagged share of private ownership. The specifications also include firm-specific controls such as firm size and the industry Herfindahl index to control for the effect of industry-level reforms that may affect the performance of firms. Lastly, we include year dummies to control for contemporaneous macroeconomic shocks.

Using data on all privatizations undertaken since the start of the process in 1991 until 2009, we find that performance improvements are significantly and positively related to the fraction of equity sold. For example, comparing privatized firms to firms that have been selected for privatization but have not yet sold any equity, we find that a 10 percentage point increase in the level of private equity would increase annual sales by 3.3 percent, returns to sales by 3.8 percent, and net worth to sales by 17 percent on average. Our results also suggest that privatization is not associated with a decline in employment. The specifications control for firm fixed effects, average firm size, industry characteristics, and contemporaneous reforms at the country level.

Our results also suggest that the sale of majority equity stakes has an economically significant impact on firm performance. Compared to partially privatized firms, sales and returns to sales increase by an average of 23 percent and 21 percent, respectively, when firms sell majority equity stakes and transfer management control to private owners. Moreover, the sale of majority equity stakes is not accompanied by layoffs. In fact, employment appears to increase significantly following privatization.

Despite the inefficiency of government-owned firms, public support for privatization in India remains low, as suggested by the fact that it is officially referred to as "disinvestment."[2] The prevailing argument against privatization is best captured by a recent quote from a member of parliament: "Disinvestment of the public sector is nothing but selling the family silver to meet the grocer's bill" (*Times of India* 2009). However, our results suggest that privatization leads to significant improvements in the performance of previously government-owned firms, and these effects are robust to the pre-privatization characteristics of firms, indicating that profitable firms also benefit from privatization. Examining the role of politics in India's privatization program, Dinc and Gupta (2010) show that firms located in electoral districts where the governing party is in a close race with opposition parties and firms located in the home state of cabinet ministers are much less likely to be privatized.[3]

Acknowledging the political cost of privatization, one prime minister noted, "If you face immediate political problems—elections in four states—it is hard to push ahead...We had to worry about the prospects of unemployment if public sector units faced closure" (*Asia Times* 1997). However, such fears of layoffs following privatization may be exaggerated; our results suggest that government-owned firms that do not privatize reduce workforce size on average compared to privatized firms.

In the next section, I describe the background to government ownership and privatization in India. The third section describes the data, and the fourth the regression results. The final section concludes.

GOVERNMENT-OWNERSHIP AND PRIVATIZATION

Government-owned Firms

The first prime minister of post-independence India, Pandit Jawaharlal Nehru, envisaged the role of government-owned firms as the "commanding heights" of the economy on the grounds that the nascent private sector would not undertake projects requiring large investments and long gestation periods. The Industrial Policy Resolution of 1956 stated, "The State will progressively assume predominance and direct responsibility for setting up new industrial undertakings and for developing transport facilities." While on the eve of the first five-year plan in 1951 there were 5 federal-government-owned firms with a total investment of Rs. 290 million, in 2010 there were 249 firms with a total investment of Rs. 5,799.2 billion and employing 1.5 million non-casual workers (Department of Public Enterprises 2009–10). We focus on firms owned by the central government, which account for about 85 percent of the total assets of all government-owned companies (Gupta 2005) and operate in a large number of manufacturing, service, and infrastructure industries—including steel, cement, and chemicals; capital goods; electricity and gas; and services such as technology, telecommunications, trade, tourism, and warehousing. The banking, insurance, and financial services sectors are also heavily dominated by federal- and state-government-owned firms.

The influence of the government on India's economy was described by Prime Minister Manmohan Singh: "In the initial stages of India's development central planning was a positive factor for development of promoting industrialization, of building industries which would never have [been] built ... But the real problem starts after 15 or 20 years, because the central-planning system that we have evolved and [that] other countries have evolved lacks an effective incentive system to modernize on a progressive basis, to improve productivity, to bring new technology" (PBS 2001).

In 2009, 158 central-government owned firms reported cumulative profits of about Rs. 1,084.4 billion, while 59 firms reported accumulated losses of Rs. 158 billion (Department of Public Enterprises 2009–10). These firms are typically overstaffed, and the average wages of government-firm workers are twice as high as in the private sector (Panagariya 2008), which may explain why government firm workers typically oppose privatization. Describing this opposition a news article reported: "Over 25,000 ONGC [Oil and Natural Gas Commission] staff observed 'black day' and their union leaders went on hunger strike to mark their protest over the privatisation move" (*The Financial Times* 1993).

Central-government-owned firms are also large. As of February 2011, the total market capitalization of the forty-seven firms listed on the country's largest stock exchange, the Bombay Stock Exchange (BSE), was about Rs. 14 trillion, accounting for 22 percent of the total market capitalization of the 4942 listed companies on the BSE. Taking into account government-owned banks and regional-government-owned firms increases the share of market capitalization of all government-owned firms to 28.8 percent of total market capitalization (Bombay Stock Exchange Disinvestments Database 2011).

Evolving Privatization Policy

In response to a balance-of-payments crisis in 1991, India undertook sweeping economic reforms that included deregulation and privatization. Between 1991 and 2004, nearly every government's annual budget declared that the privatization goal is to reduce government ownership to 26 percent of equity—the minimum equity holding necessary for certain voting powers—in all government-owned firms excluding those in the defense, atomic energy, and railway sectors. However, until 1999, successive governments sold only minority stakes, sometimes as little as 0.1 percent, without transferring management control. Partial privatization proved to be a lucrative source of revenues without the accompanying political controversy of transferring control of government-owned assets to private owners.

In table 6.1 we list the number of privatization transactions and the amounts received from privatization sales for each year since the start of the program until 2009. Out of about 250 non-financial firms owned by the federal government, 55 firms have sold partial and majority equity stakes between fiscal years 1991 and 2009, some in multiple tranches. Since 2010, the Indian government has sold minority equity stakes in another six firms, three of which were initial public offerings (Coal India, Manganese Ore India Limited, and Satluj Jal Vidyut Nigam).[4]

The privatization program was initiated by the idealogically center-left Congress government in 1991, and after a brief hiatus was continued by the conservative Bharatiya Janata Party (BJP) government elected in 1999. However, the program stalled when the BJP government was defeated in 2004, until it was resurrected in 2009 by the reelected Congress government, which sold minority equity stakes in five firms. Between 1991 and 2010, total revenues raised from privatization sales were about Rs. 960 billion. In figure 6.1, we describe the annual breakdown of revenues raised from privatization sales in India between 1991 and 2010.

Table 6.1 PRIVATIZATION BY YEAR

Year	Number of Privatization Transactions	Privatization Revenues (Millions of Indian Rupees)
1991	47	30377.4
1992	35	19125.1
1993		
1994	13	48431
1995	5	1684.8
1996	1	3796.7
1997	1	9100
1998	5	53711.4
1999	4	15847.2
2000	4	18712.6
2001	9	32682.8
2002	6	23479.8
2003	10	155474.2
2004	3	27648.7
2005	1	15696.8
2006	0	
2007	3	41813.8
2008	0	
2009	5	233529.6
2010	6	227627.3

Source: Disinvestment Commission of India, Government of India, *Disinvestment until Now.*

Starting in 1991, the Congress government partially privatized thirty-nine firms, some of which sold equity multiple times. Following the defeat of this government in 1996, the privatization program remained in hiatus until 1999. The incoming BJP government continued the practice of minority equity sales on financial markets, but also sold majority stakes and transferred management control in fourteen firms. Although privatization revenues from strategic sales were only a small fraction of the amounts raised through partial privatizations (Department of Disinvestment 2010), this represented a major shift in policy from previous governments. The companies privatized through majority sales are listed in table 6.2, along with the names of the acquiring firms.

Political considerations may explain why so few privatizations were undertaken by the BJP government. In fact, attributing the defeat of the BJP-led National Democratic Alliance government in the 2004 elections to its disinvestment [privatization] program, a major newspaper's editorial opined, "The Indian voters . . . were rejecting the National Democratic Alliance [NDA] government, which, as one poll slogan had it, stood for the 'National Disinvestment Agency'" (*The Hindu* 2004).

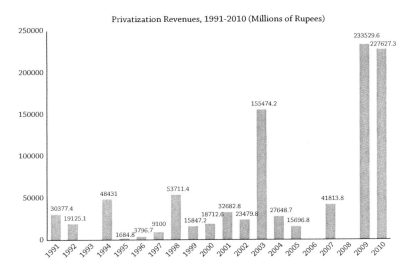

Figure 6.1
Privatization Revenues by Year (Dept. of Disinvestment, Govt. of India)

The privatization program came to a halt after the defeat of the BJP government in 2004, when the Congress party and its coalition partners returned to power. Since 2004, the Congress-led government, which was reelected in 2009, has sold only minority equity stakes in eleven firms. The Economic Survey (Ministry of Finance 2008) describes the current government's policy as follows: (1) Generate at least Rs. 250 billion per year from privatization sales. (2) Sell 5–10 percent equity in previously identified profit-making firms that are not one of the "navratnas," or nine most prestigious firms. (3) List all unlisted firms and sell a minimum of 10 percent of equity to the public. (4) Auction all loss-making firms that cannot be revived.

In February 2010, the government resurrected its stalled privatization program with a secondary offering of shares in National Thermal Power Corporation Limited (NTPC), which owns 20 percent of India's power generation capacity. However, the *Wall Street Journal* noted that the sale of minority equity stakes "makes this a fund-raising exercise rather than a meaningful shift toward less state control" (*Wall Street Journal* 2010). Since then the government has continued the practice of selling minority equity stakes, while retaining majority government ownership and management control of firms.

The lack of meaningful progress in privatization is mainly due to the fact that successive coalition governments have required the support of multiple coalition partners to maintain a parliamentary majority. For example, during the current government's regime, the privatization of Neyveli Lignite located in Tamil Nadu was delayed because of opposition from a coalition member of the DMK party, which is based in Tamil Nadu. And the privatization of firms located in West Bengal has been delayed due to opposition from the West

Table 6.2 MAJORITY SALES TO PRIVATE OWNERS

Company Name	Year of Sale	Name of Buyer	% Stake Sold	% Government Equity
BHARAT ALUMINIUM CO. LTD.	2000–01	STERLITE INDUSTRIES (INDIA) LTD.	51	49
CMC LTD.	2001–02	TATA CONSULTANCY SERVICES LTD.	51	32.31
HINDUSTAN TELEPRINTERS LTD.	2001–02	HIMACHAL FUTURISTIC COMMUNICATION LTD.	74	26
HINDUSTAN ZINC LTD.	2002–03	STERLITE OPPORTUNITIES & VENTURES LTD.	22.07	49.93
HOTEL CORP. OF INDIA LTD.*	2002–03	BATRA HOSPITALITY PVT. LTD.	100	0
"	2001–02	INPAC TRAVELS (INDIA) PVT. LTD.	100	0
"	2001–02	TULIP HOSPITALITY PVT. LTD.	100	0
ICI INDIA LTD.	2003–04	ASIAN PAINTS (INDIA) LTD.	9.2	0
INDIA TOURISM DEVELOPMENT CORP. LTD.*	2002–03	BRIGHT ENTERPRISES PVT. LTD.& CONSORTIUM	89.97	0
"	2002–03	M FAR HOTELS LTD.	89.97	0
"	2002–03	LOKSANGAM HOTELS & RESORTS PVT. LTD. & CONSORTIUM	89.97	0
"	2002–03	AUTO IMPEX LTD.	89.97	0
"	2002–03	BHARAT HOTELS LTD.	89.97	0
"	2002–03	CONSORTIUM OF RAMNATH HOTELS PVT. LTD.	89.97	0
"	2002–03	CONSORTIUM OF UNISON HOTELS LTD. & FORMAX COMMERCIAL PVT. LTD.	89.97	0
"	2002–03	NEHRU PLACE HOTELS LTD.	89.97	0
"	2002–03	MORAL TRADING & INVESTMENT LTD.	89.97	0
"	2002–03	TAJGVK HOTELS & RESORTS LTD.	100	0
"	2001–02	MALNAD HOTELS & RESORTS PVT. LTD.	89.97	0
"	2001–02	LOTUS NIKKO HOTELS	89.97	0

	Year		%	%
"	2001–02	SANGU CHAKRA HOTELS PVT. LTD.	89.97	0
"	2001–02	G.R. THANGA MALIGAI PVT. LTD.	89.97	0
"	2001–02	MOHAN SINGH	89.97	0
"	2001–02	BHARAT HOTELS LTD.	89.97	0
"	2001–02	CONSORTIUM OF SUSHIL GUPTA & OTHERS	89.97	0
"	2001–02	SILVERLINK HOLDINGS LTD. & CONSORTIUM	89.97	0
INDIAN PETROCHEMICALS CORP. LTD.	2002–03	RELIANCE PETRO INVESTMENTS LTD.	26	33.95
JESSOP & CO. LTD.	2003–04	INDO WAGON ENGINEERING LTD.	72	27
KOCHI REFINERIES LTD.	2000–01	BHARAT PETROLEUM CORP. LTD.	55.04	0
LAGAN JUTE MACHINERY CO. LTD.	2000–01	MURALIDHAR RATANLAL EXPORTS LTD.	74	26
MADRAS REFINERIES LTD.	2000–01	INDIAN OIL CORP. LTD.	51.81	0
MARUTI UDYOG LTD.	2003–04		27.51	18.28
MODERN FOOD INDUSTRIES (INDIA) LTD.	1999–00	HINDUSTAN LEVER LTD.	74	26
PARADEEP PHOSPHATES LTD.	2001–02	ZUARI MAROC PHOSPHATES PVT. LTD.	74	26
VIDESH SANCHAR NIGAM LTD.	2001–02	PANATONE FINVEST LTD. (A TATA GROUP CO.)	25	26.12

Notes: * Sale of hotels owned by these companies
Source: Bombay Stock Exchange Disinvestments Database

Bengal-based Trinamool Congress party. As noted in a newspaper editorial, "It is not that the DMK and the Trinamool Congress have any deep ideological opposition to disinvestment . . . these parties' concern over disinvestment will stem from its likely impact on the mood of voters in the next Assembly elections . . . No political party will like to be associated with any proposal that results in obvious job losses or relocation of employees and then lose votes in the elections" (*Business Standard* 2009).

The literature supports the anecdotal evidence. Examining the role of politics in India's privatization program, Dinc and Gupta (2011) find that successive Indian governments have been reluctant to privatize because of a potential electoral backlash. For example, firms located in electoral districts where the governing party is in a close race with opposition parties and firms located in the home state of the cabinet minister are much less likely to be privatized.

DATA

We observe financial data annually for 213 manufacturing and non-financial services sector companies owned by the federal government of India. To avoid attrition bias we do not require the panel to be balanced. The data are collected by the Centre for Monitoring the Indian Economy (CMIE) from company annual reports. The data start in fiscal year 1988, prior to the launch of the economic reforms of 1991, and end in fiscal year 2008. Hence, we include all privatization transactions conducted until the end of 2008–09. Data on privatization transactions were obtained from the Disinvestment Commission of the Government of India and the Disinvestments Database of the BSE.

Comparing the pre-privatization characteristics of privatized firms to firms that remain fully government-owned, we note several differences. In table 6.3 we report that compared to fully government-owned firms, firms selected for partial privatization are nearly four times as large in terms of sales and gross fixed assets, and employ twice as many workers. Firms that are partially privatized are also more profitable and efficient (higher profits, return to sales, and net worth), borrow more, and have lower compensation relative to size. Firms that eventually sell majority equity stakes have higher sales, lower assets, higher returns to sales, fewer employees, and lower levels of employee compensation compared to firms that remain fully government owned. Partially privatized firms are also significantly larger compared to majority-sale firms. In the regression analysis we control for the pre-privatization characteristics of firms.

Table 6.4 presents before–after statistics for selected performance measures for partially privatized firms. Specifically, using the sample of partially privatized firms, we compare average performance in the years following the first public offering to the average performance of firms in the years before

Table 6.3 DESCRIBING GOVERNMENT-OWNED FIRMS

	Fully Government Owned	Partially Privatized	Majority Sale
Sales	708.678	2845.367	960.530
	(2964.530)	(5027.113)	(1534.319)
Observations	3434	184	120
Assets	967.9225	5119.361	388.5783
	5922.774	9644.651	475.1771
	3463	184	119
Profits	188.423	999.779	77.822
	(1018.703)	(1635.273)	(107.370)
Observations	2447	143	107
Return on sales	−0.106	3.629	0.092
	(36.698)	(23.446)	(0.301)
Observations	2303	139	107
Net worth/sales	−98.823	6.200	−0.009
	(2240.821)	(43.549)	(1.734)
Observations	3050	179	119
Total borrowings	552.453	3226.547	191.838
	(2022.717)	(5094.346)	(229.280)
Observations	3463	184	119
Wages/sales	1.549	0.098	0.158
	(16.561)	(0.108)	(0.184)
Observations	3296	180	120
Labor	6933.244	14664.720	4348.369
	(20951.080)	(27568.400)	(5476.173)
Observations	3325	187	111

This table reports the mean and standard deviation for the variables defined in Appendix Table 1 for the fiscal years 1989–2008. Fully government owned are firms that have not privatized any equity; partially privatized are firms that have sold partial equity stakes without transferring management control; majority sale are firms that have sold majority equity stakes and transferred management control. The average values of the variables for the partially and majority privatized firms are calculated for the years prior to privatization.

any equity is sold. We find that firms experience a significant increase in average sales, gross fixed assets, profits, net worth, and cash profits after partial privatization.

In table 6.5 we describe before–after statistics for selected performance measures for firms that have sold majority equity stakes and transferred control to private owners. The average effects suggest that these firms experience a significant increase in sales, asset size, profits, net worth, and cash profits following the sale of majority equity stakes and the transfer of management control to private owners. Unlike partially privatized firms, firms that have transferred control to private owners appear to experience a significant decrease in employment following ownership change. Below we describe the results from the regression analysis.

Table 6.4 COMPARING PARTIALLY PRIVATIZED FIRMS BEFORE AND AFTER
PRIVATIZATION

	Average before Partial Privatization	Average after Partial Privatization	% Change	p-values	
Sales	2845.367	10805.99	279.775	0.000	***
	(5027.113)	(29806.370)			
	184	584			
Assets	5119.361	6811.988	33.063	0.075	*
	9644.651	(14937.440)			
	184	582			
Profits	999.7792	1468.172	46.850	0.069	*
	(1635.273)	(3683.147)			
	143	555			
Net worth	2959.167	3880.826	31.146	0.099	*
	5800.712	(9135.844)			
	184	582			
Cash profits	603.285	1024.316	69.790	0.036	**
	1199.385	(2965.332)			
	170	581			
Total borrowing	3226.547	2247.512	–30.343	0.017	**
	(5094.346)	(5592.648)			
	184	582			
Wages/sales	0.09835	0.13655	38.835	0.005	***
	(0.108)	(0.191)			
	180	582			
Labor	14664.72	15973.35	8.924	0.296	
	(27568.400)	(29615.930)			
	187	584			

This table describes the characteristics of government-owned firms before and after partial privatization for the fiscal years 1989–2008. The variables are described in Appendix Table 1. Partially privatized firms are firms that have sold minority equity stakes without transferring management control.

REGRESSION RESULTS

Effect of Private Ownership

We start out by investigating the average effect of selling partial and majority equity stakes on firm performance, by estimating the following firm fixed effects specification for the years 1989–2008:

$$y_{i,t} = \alpha_i + \alpha_1 \text{Fraction of equity sold}_{i,\,t-1} + \alpha_2 X_{i,t-1} + \alpha_t + \text{Year}_t + \varepsilon_{i,t}, \quad (1)$$

Table 6.5 COMPARING MAJORITY SALE FIRMS BEFORE AND AFTER PRIVATIZATION

	Average before Majority Sales	Average after Majority sales	% Change	p-values	
Sales	1990.199	3527.601	77.249	0.001	***
	(3007.656)	(4910.548)			
	188	89			
Assets	1069.983	1890.675	76.701	0.001	***
	1739.087	(2682.178)			
	187	88			
Profits	275.3154	640.045	132.477	0.000	***
	(474.550)	(1203.438)			
	174	84			
Net worth	702.833	1656.713	135.719	0.000	***
	1255.697	(2863.319)			
	187	87			
Cash profits	166.059	451.923	172.146	0.000	***
	317.7558	(848.587)			
	184	87			
Total borrowing	372.256	450.7316	21.081	0.214	
	(795.576)	(678.146)			
	187	87			
Wages/sales	0.1314	0.1466	11.621	0.293	
	(0.160)	(0.304)			
	188	87			
Labor	4712.59	2369.126	-49.728	0.000	***
	(5178.654)	(3010.993)			
	178	87			

This table describes the characteristics of government-owned firms before and after the sale of majority stakes for the fiscal years 1989–2008. The variables are described in Appendix table 6.A1. Majority sale firms have sold majority equity stakes and have transferred management control to private owners.

where $y_{i,t}$ is the firm performance measure and the $X_{i,t-1}$ variables are firm-specific factors that explain the outcomes. The main variable of interest is fraction of equity sold, which ranges in value from 0 to 100. The control group is restricted to government-owned firms that have been selected for privatization but have not yet been privatized. The specification in equation (1) includes a firm-specific fixed effect, α_i, which reflects differences across firms that are constant but unobserved over time, year dummies that would capture contemporaneous correlation, and a random unobserved component ($\varepsilon_{i,t}$) that reflects unobserved shocks affecting the performance of firms.

To control for other factors that may explain firm performance, we include firm size as measured by gross fixed assets and the Herfindahl index at the three-digit industry level. The latter variable will also control for confounding effects that may arise due to contemporaneous reforms at the industry level that affect firm performance. Firm-level performance measures and all variables used in the analysis are described in table 6.A1. We note that all the level variables, with the exception of fraction of equity sold and the Herfindahl index are in logarithms.

The results from estimating equation (1) are presented in table 6.6. We find that the share of privately owned equity has a positive and statistically significant impact on next period sales, return on sales (ratio of profit before taxes and depreciation to sales), net worth to sales, cash profits to sales, total borrowing, and employment. From the first two columns of table 6.6, we observe that a 10 percentage point increase in the level of private equity would increase annual sales by about 3.3 percent, returns to sales by 3.8 percent, and net worth to sales by 17 percent on average. Firms also experience a significant increase in access to loans, which suggests that privatized firms may be better able to finance growth opportunities compared to firms that remain fully government owned. Further, these results suggest that selling equity to private owners does not cause the government to abandon the political objective of maintaining surplus employment. Average compensation also does not appear to be affected by privatization. The specifications control for average firm size and industry competitiveness.

Prior research suggests that governments are likely to selectively choose firms for privatization based on observable and unobservable characteristics. For example, Gupta, Ham, and Svejnar (2008) show that profitable firms are more likely to be privatized. We take a number of steps to address the potential endogeneity of privatization to firm performance. First, we estimate a firm fixed effects specification that addresses selection bias that may arise if more profitable or larger firms are selected for privatization. However, fixed effects will not address dynamic selection bias, which may arise if the government selects firms for privatization based on unobservable time-varying characteristics. To address this, we use the approach suggested by Frydman et al. (1999), who argue that firms selected for privatization are likely to share similar characteristics. Therefore, comparing privatized firms to a control group of firms that have also been selected for privatization but have not yet been sold should address this potential selection bias. Since privatization is distributed over several years in our data, in any given year we also observe firms privatized in later years that form the control group.

To minimize the possibility of simultaneity between privatization and performance, we use the lagged share of private ownership. The specifications also include firm-specific controls such as firm size and the industry Herfindahl index to control for the effect of industry-level reforms that may affect the performance of firms. Lastly, we include year dummies to control for contemporaneous macroeconomic shocks.

Table 6.6 PRIVATIZATION AND FIRM PERFORMANCE

	Sales	Profits	Return on Sales	PAT/Sales	Net Worth/ Sales	Cash Profits/ Sales	Total Borrowing	Wages/Sales	Labor
Fraction of equity sold (t – 1)	.0033***		.0387*	0.0144*	0.1775***	0.0126*	0.009***	-0.0003	0.0058***
	(0.001)		(0.021)	(0.008)	(0.055)	(0.007)	(0.003)	(0.000)	(0.001)
Assets (t – 1)	.4845***	.4877***	-1.6549***	0.2906	-2.1831	0.2965	0.5439***	-0.0202**	.2831***
	(0.037)		(0.549)	(0.211)	(1.395)	(0.194)	(0.070)	(0.009)	(0.018)
Industry Herfindahl (t – 1)	-0.0897	.3639**	-5.0757***	-0.2852	-16.2715	-0.16944	0.9391	-0.0046	-0.2842***
	(0.119)		(1.739)	(0.666)	(4.483)	(0.601)	(0.674)	(0.0283)	(0.059)
Firm fixed effects	Yes	Yes	Yes	Yes	Yes	Yes	Yes	Yes	Yes
Year fixed effects	Yes	Yes	Yes	Yes	Yes	Yes	Yes	Yes	Yes
Observations	982		907	907	976	958	919	981	857
Number of firms	52		51	51	52	52	51	52	52
R-squared	0.5367		0.0394	0.0289	0.0472	0.0283	0.1026	0.0313	0.4384

Notes: * significant at 10% level; ** significant at 5% level; *** significant at 1% level.
This table reports results from firm-level fixed effects (within) regressions for the fiscal years 1989–2008 to estimate the impact of private ownership with privatized firms as the treatment group and firms that are selected for privatization and sell equity in later years as the control group. The variables are described in Appendix table 6.A1. The firm-specific right-hand side variables are lagged one year. *Annual Sales, Total Borrowing, Labor,* and *Assets* are measured in logs. All regressions include firm and year fixed effects. The standard errors are reported in parentheses.

Effect of Majority Sales

We investigate the marginal effect of selling majority equity stakes with the transfer of management control to private owners by comparing majority sale firms to partially privatized firms. We estimate the following firm fixed effects specification for the years 1989–2008,

$$Y_{i,t} = \alpha_i + \alpha_1 \text{ Majority Sale}_{i,t\text{-}1} + \alpha_2 X_{i,t\text{-}1} + \alpha_t + \text{Year}_t + \varepsilon_{i,t}, \quad (2)$$

where *Majority Sale* is a dummy variable that is equal to 1 when a firm has sold majority equity stakes and transferred management control to a private owner. The control group consists of partially privatized firms that have sold minority equity stakes and are listed on the stock market. The remaining variables are as described in equation (1).

From the first two columns of table 6.7 we note that sales and returns to sales increase by 23 percent and 21 percent respectively on average when firms transfer management control to private owners. Hence, compared to partially privatized firms that are publicly traded on the stock market but are still controlled by the government, the sale of majority equity stakes with the transfer of management control has an economically significant impact on the sales and profitability of government-owned firms. Moreover, this increase in revenues and profits is not accompanied by a decline in employment or wages. While wages are not significantly affected by ownership change, employment appears to increase significantly, perhaps in response to the increase in profitability following privatization.

Despite the small number of majority sales, our results suggest that transferring control to private owners may result in significant performance improvements compared to publicly listed firms that remain under government control. A potential explanation is that firms that have been sold to private owners are no longer subject to political interference, and managers of these firms are given have incentives to align their objectives with those of shareholders. For example, Fan, Wong, and Zhang (2007) show that partially privatized firms in China with politically connected CEOs underperform those without politically connected CEOs, and are more likely to appoint bureaucrats rather than qualified individuals as board members.

Evaluating the Long-run Impact of Privatization

So far, we have considered the effect of privatization on firm performance in the following year. However, the effects of privatization—due to decisions made by new owners in the case of majority sales, or due to improved corporate governance and increased investor scrutiny in the case of public offerings—may

Table 6.7 PRIVATIZING MAJORITY STAKES

	Sales	Return on Sales	PAT/Sales	Net Worth/ Sales	Cash Profits/ Sales	Total Borrowing	Wages/Sales	Labor
Majority Sale (t − 1)	0.2299*	0.2118***	1.1452*	6.7463*	1.0594*	0.1831	-0.0313	0.2811***
	(0.122)	(0.080)	(0.603)	(3.713)	(0.548)	(0.249)	(0.035)	(0.050)
Assets (t − 1)	0.6424***	0.0688*	0.6279**	3.8863**	0.6133**	0.6738***	-0.0153	0.4836***
	(0.062)	(0.040)	(0.302)	(1.882)	(0.278)	(0.130)	(0.018)	(0.024)
Industry	-0.2811**	0.3057***	-1.2637	-9.0424**	-1.1559*	0.9022	0.018	0.0442
	(0.139)	(0.091)	(0.688)	(4.252)	(0.627)	(0.803)	(0.001)	(0.055)
Herfindahl							0.0392	
Firm fixed effects	Yes	Yes	Yes	Yes	Yes	Yes	Yes	Yes
Year fixed effects	Yes	Yes	Yes	Yes	Yes	Yes	Yes	Yes
Observations	733	698	698	729	728	681	732	636
Number of firms	52	51	51	52	52	51	52	49
R-squared	0.4484	0.0762	0.0503	0.0493	0.0515	0.0597	0.0293	0.6027

Notes: * significant at 10% level; ** significant at 5% level; *** significant at 1% level.
This table reports results from firm-level fixed effects (within) regressions for the fiscal years 1989–2008 to estimate the impact of selling majority equity stakes, with firms that sell majority stakes as the treatment group and partially privatized firms that have sold partial equity stakes as the control group. The variables are described in Appendix table 6.A1. The firm-specific right-hand side variables are lagged one year. *Annual Sales, Total Borrowing, Labor,* and *Assets* are measured in logs. All regressions include firm and year fixed effects. The standard errors are reported in parentheses.

not be immediate. Or, it may be the case that some performance effects are not persistent, such as the observed increase in employment following privatization. To capture the long-run effects of privatization, we consider three-year averages of firm performance, including the three years following the year in which the firm was privatized. The results are reported in table 6.8. In panel A of table 6.8, we consider the effect of selling partial and majority equity stakes. The results are similar to those reported in table 6.6. We find that in the three years following privatization, firms that have sold partial and majority equity stakes experience significant improvements in average sales, profitability, net worth, and total borrowing, relative to firms that have not yet privatized. The main difference from the previously reported results is that wages as a fraction of sales appear to decrease in privatized firms, suggesting that average wages do not increase at the same rate as average sales following privatization. We also find that average employment increases significantly in the three years following privatization.

In panel B, we examine the impact of majority equity sales, by which majority ownership and management control is transferred from the government to private owners. We note that the results are substantively similar to those in table 6.7. Firms that sell majority stakes experience a significant increase in sales and profitability, a decline in averages wages as a share of sales, and an increase in employment. The statistical significance of the other dependent variables is slightly lower because of the smaller sample size (sample restricted to firms with at least three years of performance data following privatization). Overall, our results suggest that the effects of privatization are persistent rather than temporary.

Evaluating the Impact of Varying Ownership Stakes

Our results suggest that firm performance is positively related to the fraction of equity sold by government-owned firms. We also find that transferring management control to private owners has an economically significant impact on firm performance. It may however be the case that ownership has a non-linear impact on firm performance. For example, performance improvements may occur only when a sufficiently large share of the firm is privately owned. In table 6.9 we report the results from estimating firm fixed effects specifications that describe the relationship between firm performance and the privatization of 10 percent, 25 percent, and 50 percent or more equity stakes. The results suggest that compared to firms that have not yet been privatized, selling 10 percent or more equity in a firm is associated with a significant increase in sales, net worth, and employment. In comparison, selling majority stakes or 50 percent or more equity is associated with both an increase in sales and net worth, as well as an increase in external borrowings

Table 6.8 LONG-RUN IMPACT OF PRIVATIZATION

Panel A: Partial and Majority Privatization

	Profits Sales	Return on Sales	PAT/Sales	Net Worth/ Sales	Cash Profits/ Sales	Total Borrowing	Wages/ Sales	Labor
Fraction of equity	0.005**	0.002*	0.018***	0.115***	0.015***	0.006***	‑0.001***	0.005***
sold (t − 1)	(0.001)	(0.001)	(0.007)	(0.046)	(0.006)	(0.003)	(0.000)	(0.001)
Assets (t−1)	0.321***	0.005	0.099	-1.036	0.099	0.281***	-0.002	0.334***
	(0.029)	(0.021)	(0.163)	(1.102)	(0.145)	(0.062)	(0.005)	(0.020)
Industry	‑0.555**	0.603***	-0.408	-14.557	-0.617	‑1.143*	‑0.151***	‑0.673***
Herfindahl (t-1)	(0.282)	(0.208)	(1.632)	(10.760)	(1.432)	(0.664)	(0.046)	(0.161)
Firm fixed effects	Yes	Yes	Yes	Yes	Yes	Yes	Yes	Yes
Year fixed effects	Yes	Yes	Yes	Yes	Yes	Yes	Yes	Yes
Observations	875	753	753	863	830	796	872	674
Number of firms	52	51	51	52	52	52	52	52
R-squared	0.6108	0.0424	0.0342	0.0353	0.0353	0.0666	0.1005	0.5302

(Continued)

Panel B: Majority Privatization

Table 6.8 CONTINUED

	Sales	Profits	Return on Sales	PAT/Sales	Net Worth/Sales	Cash Profits/Sales	Total Borrowing	Wages/Sales	Labor
Majority sale (t – 1)	0.241***		0.199***	0.923	5.201	0.831	0.132	−0.033*	0.346***
	(0.095)		(0.050)	(0.685)	(3.966)	(0.577)	(0.219)	(0.018)	(0.058)
Assets (t – 1)	0.499***		0.007	0.434	2.624	0.407	0.347***	0.013	0.429***
	(0.049)		(0.024)	(0.333)	(2.034)	(0.296)	(0.115)	(0.009)	(0.027)
Industry	−0.402		0.620***	−0.539	−8.5731	−0.73	−1.063	−0.176***	−0.195
Herfindahl (t-1)	(0.299)		(0.150)	(2.073)	(12.442)	(1.811)	(0.795)	(0.056)	(0.160)
Firm fixed effects	Yes	Yes	Yes	Yes	Yes	Yes	Yes	Yes	Yes
Year fixed effects	Yes	Yes	Yes	Yes	Yes	Yes	Yes	Yes	Yes
Observations	679		603	603	674	666	619	678	522
Number of firms	50		49	49	50	50	49	50	47
R-squared	0.5601		0.1169	0.0362	0.036	0.0377	0.0368	0.1111	0.6137

Notes: * significant at 10% level; ** significant at 5% level; *** significant at 1% level.
This table reports results from firm-level fixed effects (within) regressions for the fiscal years 1989–2008 to estimate the impact of private ownership with privatized firms as the treatment group and firms that are selected for privatization and sell equity in later years as the control group. The dependent variables are measured as 3-year moving averages over the three years following the year of privatization, or t, t+1, and t+2, where t is the year in which the firm privatizes. The variables are described in Appendix table 6.A1. The firm-specific right-hand side variables are lagged one year. *Annual Sales, Total Borrowing, Labor,* and *Assets* are measured in logs. All regressions include firm and year fixed effects. The standard errors are reported in parentheses.

Table 6.9 EVALUATING THE IMPACT OF VARYING OWNERSHIP STAKES

	Sales			Return on Sales			Net worth/Sales		
Fraction of equity sold >= 10% (t − 1)	0.1897** (0.079)			0.9563 (1.155)			5.9761** (2.959)		
Fraction of equity sold > 25% (t − 1)		0.1461* (0.076)			1.9633* (1.083)			8.2309*** (2.854)	
Fraction of equity sold > 50% (t − 1)			.1690* (0.095)			1.4427 (1.356)			7.5920** (3.578)
Assets (t − 1)	0.4759*** (0.037)	0.4728*** (0.038)	0.4780*** (0.037)	−1.4666*** (0.553)	−1.5662*** (0.556)	−1.4933*** (0.554)	−1.6781 (1.418)	−2.0675 (1.426)	−1.6935 (1.417)
Industry Herfindahl	−0.3912 (0.329)	−0.4673 (0.331)	−0.5269 (0.336)	−6.1603 (4.908)	−6.9287 (4.899)	−7.3177 (4.970)	−22.6779* (12.470)	−26.415** (12.463)	−28.4471** (12.649)
Firm fixed effects	Yes	Yes	Yes	Yes	Yes	Yes	Yes	Yes	Yes
Year fixed effects	Yes	Yes	Yes	Yes	Yes	Yes	Yes	Yes	Yes
Observations	982	982	982	907	907	907	976	976	976
Number of firms	52	52	52	51	51	51	52	52	52
R-squared	0.5379	0.5368	0.5366	0.0308	0.0339	0.0314	0.0355	0.04	0.0359

	Total Borrowing			Labor		
Fraction of equity sold >= 10% (t − 1)	0.0435 (0.147)			0.1658*** (0.041)		
Fraction of equity sold > 25% (t − 1)		0.0441 (0.143)			0.2503*** (0.039)	
Fraction of equity sold > 50% (t − 1)			0.7729*** (0.175)			0.2031*** (0.526)

(Continued)

Table 6.9 (CONTINUED)

	Sales		Return on Sales		Net worth/Sales
Assets (t − 1)	0.5460***	0.5441***	0.2857***	0.2719***	0.2835***
	(0.071)	(0.072)	(0.018)	(0.018)	(0.018)
Industry	1.2857**	1.2534*	0.7335***	-0.8557***	-0.8995***
Herfindahl	(0.658)	(0.661)	(0.162)	(0.160)	(0.165)
Firm fixed effects	Yes	Yes	Yes	Yes	Yes
Year fixed effects	Yes	Yes	Yes	Yes	Yes
Observations	920	920	857	857	857
Number of firms	52	52	52	52	52
R-squared	0.0869	0.1075	0.4215	0.4394	0.4204

Notes: * significant at 10% level; ** significant at 5% level; *** significant at 1% level.
This table reports results from firm-level fixed effects (within) regressions for the fiscal years 1989–2008 to estimate the impact of private ownership with privatized firms as the treatment group and firms that are selected for privatization and sell equity in later years as the control group. The variables are described in Appendix table 6.A1. The firm-specific right-hand side variables are lagged one year. *Annual Sales, Total Borrowing, Labor,* and *Assets* are measured in logs. All regressions include firm and year fixed effects. The standard errors are reported in parentheses.

and employment. The effects also appear to be significant for firms that have sold 25 percent or more equity. In sum, these effects are consistent with our results so far, suggesting that both partial privatization and the sale of majority equity stakes have a significant impact on the performance of government-owned firms.

We also estimate but do not report results using a dummy variable for firms that have sold 5 percent or more equity. The results are less statistically significant. In particular, firms that have sold 5 percent or more equity experience a significant increase in employment relative to firms that are not yet privatized, but there is no significant association with the profitability and other performance measures.

Comparing Privatized Firms to Fully Government-owned Firms

As a robustness check, we also investigate the impact of privatization on firm performance when the control group includes firms that have never been privatized and are fully government-owned. The results reported in table 6.10 are similar to but less statistically significant than what we observe when the control group is restricted to firms that are selected for privatization. In

Table 6.10 COMPARING PRIVATIZED FIRMS TO FULLY GOVERNMENT-OWNED FIRMS

	Sales	Return on Sales	Net Worth/ Sales	Total Borrowing	Wages/ Sales	Labor
Fraction of equity	0.0075***	0.0386	2.5175	0.0044**	–0.0109	0.0055***
sold (t – 1)	(0.002)	(0.062)	(3.742)	(0.002)	(0.026)	(0.001)
Assets (t – 1)	0.4811***	·–2.2011***	125.9256***	0.2972***	–0.2328	0.2638***
	(0.019)	(0.820)	(46.561)	(0.023)	(0.320)	(0.013)
Industry	·–0.6499***	·–9.8313***	17.8529*	0.4240*	1.3355	·–0.1953***
Herfindahl	(0.072)	(3.235)	(182.438)	(0.235)	(1.199)	(0.050)
Firm fixed effects	Yes	Yes	Yes	Yes	Yes	Yes
Year fixed effects	Yes	Yes	Yes	Yes	Yes	Yes
Observations	3937	3039	3706	3688	3935	3180
Number of firms	276	247	275	270	276	253
R-squared	0.3304	0.018	0.009	0.0744	0.007	0.2312

Notes: * significant at 10% level; ** significant at 5% level; *** significant at 1% level.
This table reports results from firm-level fixed effects (within) regressions for the fiscal years 1989–2008 to estimate the impact of private ownership with privatized firms as the treatment group and firms that remain fully government owned as well as firms that sell equity in later years as the control group. The variables are described in Appendix table 6.A1. The firm-specific right-hand side variables are lagged one year. *Annual Sales, Total Borrowings, Labor,* and *Assets* are measured in logs. All regressions include firm and year fixed effects. The standard errors are reported in parentheses.

particular, compared to firms that remain 100 percent government owned, a 10 percentage point decrease in government ownership is associated with an 8 percent increase in sales, 4 percent increase in total borrowing, and 6 percent increase in employment, on average.

CONCLUSION

Privatization in India has encountered numerous roadblocks over the last two decades. Opponents argue that it will lead to widespread layoffs and a redistribution of wealth in favor of the politically connected. It has also been argued that selling profitable firms to raise revenues for general government expenditures does not make economic sense. However, our results suggest that selling both partial and majority equity stakes is associated with significant improvements in the profitability and efficiency of government-owned firms. These effects control for the the pre-privatization characteristics of firms, suggesting that profitable firms also benefit from privatization. Interestingly, privatized firms appear to increase employment compared to firms that have not yet been privatized, yet privatization does not affect average compensation. Hence, the improvement in profitability following privatization is not accompanied by layoffs or a decline in worker compensation.

We find that the sale of majority equity stakes accompanied by the transfer of management control from the government to private ownership has an economically significant impact on performance. This result suggests that full privatization may have a greater impact on the profitability of firms, without requiring layoffs or a decline in worker compensation.

Despite these observed benefits, privatization remains a politically contentious issue in India. Our results suggest that fears regarding employment loss may be exaggerated. Indeed, government-owned firms that do not privatize appear to be reducing average workforce size compared to privatized firms. While there is a potential redistribution of wealth from the government to private investors, this argument ignores the cost of subsidies to government-owned firms. However, since the costs of giving up control will be borne by organized labor and politicians, while the benefits—such as more efficient firms and lower subsidies—are distributed across the population, political economy theory suggests that privatization will continue to generate opposition from organized interests who benefit from maintaining government ownership.

ACKNOWLEDGMENT

Work on this chapter has been supported by Columbia University's Program on Indian Economic Policies, funded by a generous grant from the John Templeton Foundation. The opinions expressed in the chapter are those of the authors and do not necessarily reflect the views of the John Templeton Foundation.

APPENDIX

Table 6.A1 VARIABLE DESCRIPTIONS

Variable	Description	Source
Fraction of equity sold	Percentage of private ownership. Ranges in value from 0% to 100%.	Disinvestment Commission, Government of India and Bombay Stock Exchange
Majority sale	Dummy variable equal to 1 if the firm has sold majority equity stakes and transferred management control to private owners.	Same as above
Fraction of equity sold > 25%	Dummy variable equal to 1 if the firm has privatized more than 25% of equity stake.	Same as above
Fraction of equity sold > 50%	Dummy variable equal to 1 if the firm has privatized more than 50% of equity stake.	Same as above
Assets	Gross fixed assets.	Prowess Database, CMIE
Industry Herfindahl	Herfindahl index.	Same as above
Sales	Revenues received from main activity.	Same as above
Profit	Excess of income over all expenses except tax, depreciation, rent, and interest.	Same as above
Return on sales	Profit/sales.	Same as above
PAT	Excess of income over all expenses.	Same as above
Net worth	Excess of assets over liabilities.	Same as above
Cash profits	Excess of income over all costs, except depreciation and amortization.	Same as above
Total borrowings	All debt, interest bearing and otherwise.	Same as above
Wages	Total expenses incurred by the company on all employees.	Same as above
Labor	Number of workers.	Same as above

NOTES

1. The majority of privatization studies show that privatization has a positive effect on firm performance. For a recent survey see Megginson and Netter (2001).
2. Ahmed and Varshney (2008) note that privatization has been more difficult to implement than other policies such as stock market liberalization: "Within economic policy…some issues are more likely to arouse mass contestation than others. Privatization, a change in labor laws, withdrawal of agricultural subsidies…Either a large number of people are negatively affected in the short run (agriculture), or those so affected, even when not in large numbers, are well organized in unions (privatization and labor laws). It should now be clear why India's decision makers have…achieved limited privatization" (p. 22).
3. There is a growing literature on the political economy of privatization. For example, Jones et al. (1999) show that governments adopt terms of sale that are consistent with political objectives; Clarke and Cull (2002) find that the political affiliation of the government does not have a robust impact on the probability of bank privatization in Argentina; Bortolotti and Pinotti (2008) show that privatization is delayed in democracies with proportional electoral systems; and Dastidar, Fisman, and Khanna (2009) show that there is policy irreversibility in the privatization process in India.
4. The maximum amount raised in any year from privatization through public offerings is Rs. 228 billion in 2010 (Bombay Stock Exchange, Disinvestments Database).

REFERENCES

Ahmed, Sadiq and Ashutosh Varshney, 2008, "Battles Half Won: The Political Economy of India's Growth and Economic Policy since Independence," World Bank Working Paper No. 15.

Asia Times, 1997, "India's Reform Architect Looks on from the Sidelines," April 8.

Bombay Stock Exchange Disinvestments Database, http://www.bsepsu.com.

Bortolotti, Bernardo and Paolo Pinotti, 2008, "Delayed Privatization," Bank of Italy Working Paper No. 663.

Business Standard, 2009, "Disinvestment, There is Many a Slip," June 3.

Clarke, George and Robert Cull, 2002, "Political and Economic Determinants of the Likelihood of Privatizing Argentine Public Banks," *Journal of Law and Economics* 45, 165–97.

Dastidar, Sidhartha, Raymond Fisman, and Tarun Khanna, 2008 "Limits to Policy Reversal: Evidence from Indian Privatizations," *Journal of Financial Economics*, 89, 513–26.

Department of Disinvestment, 2010, "Disinvestment until Now," http://www.divest.nic.in.

Department of Public Enterprises, 2009–10, Public Enterprise Survey, Government of India, New Delhi, India.

Dinc, Serdar and Nandini Gupta, 2010, "The Decision to Privatize: Finance and Politics," *Journal of Finance* 2011, 66(1), 241–69.

Fan, Joseph P. H., T. J. Wong, and Tianyu Zhang, 2007, "Politically Connected CEOs, Corporate Governance, and Post-IPO Performance of China's Newly Partially Privatized Firms," *Journal of Financial Economics* 84, 330–57.

The Financial Times, 1993, "ONGC Staff Fight Change," September 17.

Frydman, Roman, Cheryl Gray, Marek Hessel, and Andrzej Rapaczynski, 1999, "When Does Privatization Work? The Impact of Private Ownership on Corporate Performance in Transition Economies," *Quarterly Journal of Economics* 114, 1153–91.

Gupta, Nandini, 2005, "Partial Privatization and Firm Performance," *Journal of Finance* 60, 987–1015.

Gupta, Nandini, 2008, "Privatization in South Asia," in Gerard Roland (ed.), *Privatization: Successes and Failures* (New York: Columbia University Press), pp. 170–98.

Gupta, Nandini, John Ham, and Jan Svejnar, 2008, "Priorities and Sequencing in Privatization: Evidence from Czech Firm Panel Data," *The European Economic Review* 52, 183–208.

The Hindu, 2004, "Mass Media vs. Mass Reality," May 14.

Jones, Steven, William Megginson, Robert Nash, and Jeffry Netter, 1999, "Share Issue Privatizations as Financial Means to Political and Economic Ends," *Journal of Financial Economics* 53, 217–53.

Laffont, Jean-Jacques, and Jean Tirole, 1993, *A Theory of Incentives in Procurement and Regulation* (Cambridge, MA: MIT Press).

Megginson, William, 2005, *The Financial Economics of Privatization* (New York: Oxford University Press).

Megginson, William and Jeffry Netter, 2001, "From State to Market: A Survey of Empirical Studies on Privatization," *Journal of Economic Literature* 39, 321–89.

Ministry of Finance, 1996, 2008, *Economic Survey of India*, Government of India, New Delhi.

Panagariya, Arvind, 2008, *India: An Emerging Giant* (New York: Oxford University Press).

PBS, 2001, Interview for "Commanding Heights," February 6.

Shleifer, Andrei and Robert Vishny, 1994, "Politicians and Firms," *Quarterly Journal of Economics* 109, 995–1025.

Times of India, 2009, "DMK Puts Spoke in Disinvestment Plans," June 9.

Wall Street Journal, "In India, Offers Fall Well Short of P-word," February 4.

CHAPTER 7

Variety In, Variety Out

Imported Input and Product Scope Expansion in India

PINELOPI GOLDBERG, AMIT KHANDELWAL,
AND NINA PAVCNIK

INTRODUCTION

In 1970, the chairman of the Metal Box Company of India Limited, Bhaskar Mitter, penned an article in *Economic and Political Weekly* reviewing the annual state of the metal containers industry in India. Virtually all aspects of India's complex industrial policies had shackled his company's operations. Controls on sugar and vegetable oils had prevented growth in the confectionary and biscuits markets, which required packing that his company supplied. Upstream suppliers to his company enjoyed a protected market through entry licenses and therefore had little incentive to engage in research and development. As a result, the technology of the firm's primary input, the tinplate, had lagged behind other countries. Moreover, the company faced restrictions on the import of cheaper tinplates from abroad. The unreliability and expense of its tinplates had become the company's major constraint on growth. Mitter wrote:

> For example, while we are ready to introduce containers made from 2CR tinplate, we cannot consider their marketing until Hindustan Steel are equipped to make such a plate or, alternatively, Government can assure continuing imports. In the development of new products such as improved versions of Crown Corks and other sophisticated closures, beer cans, easy opening ends, tinplate aerosol cans, aerosol valves, we have continuous access to the most advanced technology through our technical associates. We can over a reasonably short period equip

ourselves to manufacture all these products, but we need to be certain that raw
material of the right quality and specifications will be available. (Mitter 1970)

Mr. Mitter was not alone. The quote replicates itself across firms operating in
India at the time. Indian firms faced numerous constraints because of India's
economic policies which prevented expansion in capacity, quality, and product scope. In this case, although the Metal Box Company had the technology
to introduce new products for the market, it was unable to do so because of
unreliable access to inputs. This anecdote reveals that constraints on inputs
limited firms' ability to manufacture and market new products, even beyond
constraints due to industrial license policies. Many economists believe that
these frictions led to a great distortion in the allocation of India's scarce
resources and were responsible for the weak 3.2 percent per capita growth
from the mid-1960s to the early 1980s (Panagariya 2008).

In this chapter, we discuss and extend the findings of our recent research
agenda (Goldberg, Khandelwal, Pavcnik, and Topalova [henceforth GKPT]
2010a, 2010b, 2010c) that examines product mix adjustments by Indian
firms during the 1990s. During this period, a large fraction of Indian firms
added products to their product mix, suggesting that the constraints felt
by Mr. Mitter had been to some extent eased twenty years after his article
appeared in print.

This period of firm-level scope expansion coincided with India's large-scale
trade liberalization. Through reforms that began gradually during the
mid-1980s and subsequently picked up speed in 1991, the Indian government
removed many of the constraints that restricted industrial production. The
reforms during the 1980s began to dismantle the licensing requirements, and
the major feature of the 1991 reforms was a massive restructuring of India's
trade policy.

Our research shows that India's trade liberalization substantially increased
firms' access to intermediate inputs from abroad in both volume and variety. Leveraging these new imported inputs, firms subsequently introduced
new products into the domestic market. The lower tariffs on imported inputs
therefore enabled firms to expand their product scope.

There are advantages to studying the relationship between imported inputs
and domestic product scope in the Indian context. First, relative to most developing countries, India has historically provided researchers with relatively
high-quality data, a legacy that dates back to the establishment of large-scale
surveys in the 1950s—and even earlier, to the period of British rule. A unique
firm-level database, Prowess, provides detailed product-level information
for each firm over time. This enables us to track how firms responded to the
trade reforms along a number of typical dimensions, including output and
research and development (R&D), but more interestingly, product scope. This
is the main variable of analysis in our research. Moreover, we complement

these data with detailed product-level import data which record all of India's imports and information from India's plant-level manufacturing database, the Annual Survey of Industries (ASI). Together, these databases allow us to trace how the composition of India's imports at the macro level affected microlevel outcomes inside firms.

The second attractive feature of India's context is the nature of India's trade liberalization. The challenge that empirical researchers face in examining the effects of trade liberalization is that trade policies are frequently subject to endogeneity concerns. For instance, a government may liberalize tariffs for selected industries that are doing well for reasons unrelated to the reform, thus confounding the identification of impacts due to the trade policy. In the case of India, however, the reform was externally mandated and therefore came as a surprise to Indian firms, at least over the initial period of the reform. This setting therefore presents a unique opportunity to isolate the effects of trade reform on firm outcomes.

In response to the trade reform, Indian firms increased their import volumes. The import to GDP ratio increased from 7.6 in 1990 to 11.6 ten years later. The increase in imports featured two important characteristics. Based on GKPT (2010b), we present evidence that growth in imports was driven by a growth in *intermediate inputs*. Second, new types of intermediate inputs—varieties that had not been imported prior to the reform—constituted the majority of the increase in the intermediate inputs. Examples include new products like computer data storage units, automatic data processing machines, and liquefied butane. Moreover, many of these new products were sourced from OECD countries, suggesting that they were likely of relatively high quality. We also present corroborating evidence that large firms in our sample expanded their total imports and industries that enjoyed the largest reductions in tariffs had relatively larger imported input scope after the reform. While the tariff reductions increased competitive pressures for domestic firms, the liberalization also affected firms' cost structures by lower tariffs on intermediate inputs used for production.

As we mentioned above, this period coincided with product scope expansion at the firm level. These new products introduced by the firms had a sizable contribution to manufacturing output growth. GKPT (2010c) show that the product extensive margin—new products introduced by firms following the reform—contributed to 25 percent of overall manufacturing output. More disaggregated analysis in this chapter suggests that new products accounted for more than half of output growth in sectors such as chemicals and fabricated metals.

Using these two attractive features of India's context—detailed data and a plausibly exogenous shock—we demonstrate in GKPT (2010b) that declines in input tariffs had a causal affect on firm scope. Firms added relatively more products to their product mix in industries that experienced relatively larger declines in input tariffs. We provide additional evidence here that lower input tariffs accounted for a wide range of the increase in product scope during this period. Across all industries, lower input tariffs can explain approximately 30 percent of the increases in firm scope. Given that new products accounted for a quarter of India's manufacturing output growth, a conservative estimate suggests that lower input tariffs accounted for 7.8 percent of overall manufacturing growth. Importantly, the input channel continues to hold after accounting for changes in output tariffs and other simultaneous market reforms such as delicensing and foreign direct investment (FDI) liberalization. We also present new evidence investigating heterogeneity in scope response depending on the economic environment in which firms operate.

Our results therefore support the complaints—such as the quote above—made by businesses during India's import substitution era that tariff barriers caused distortions not only within an industry, but also across industries interlinked through supply chains. And as these distortions were removed, increased competitive pressures were offset by beneficial responses to firms' input sourcing.

The remainder of this chapter is organized as follows. In the second section, we document the changes in firm scope during the 1990s. In the third section, we discuss in more detail the trade reform and examine the trade data. In the fourth section, we link the two datasets together to establish how trade affects domestic activity. Finally, we conclude in the fifth section.

NEW PRODUCT GROWTH

In this section, we document the changes in firm scope during the 1990s. The section summarizes the findings from GKPT (2010c) and provides some additional results. We demonstrate that many firms introduced new products during this period, and these new products contributed to a substantial fraction of manufacturing output growth.

Prowess Data

The production information for our analysis comes from the Prowess database. Prowess is collected by the Centre for the Monitoring of the Indian Economy (CMIE), and the database provides detailed firm-level information on India's manufacturing activity. Prowess contains a panel of medium and large firms and accounts for about 60–70 percent of economic activity in India's formal industrial sector.

There are several advantages of these data for our analysis. First, unlike the ASI—India's nationally representative sample of manufacturing plants—the Prowess data is a panel of firms, so we are able to track firms' performance over time. This is a particularly important feature in our context because it enables within-firm comparisons over the course of the reform period. Second, the data span the period of India's trade liberalization from 1989–2003. The third important feature of our database is that we can track firms' product mix over a long time horizon. In contrast, the ASI only reports product-level information for a few years after the major reforms had already occurred. The ability to peer inside the activity of firms is relatively rare in empirical work, and this gives us a unique opportunity to document product-level adjustments in response to changes in the economic environment.

We are able to track firms' product mix over time because Indian firms are required by the 1956 Companies Act to disclose product-level information on capacities, production, and sales in their annual reports. In our earlier work, we have documented several features of the database that give us confidence in its quality. Specifically, we found that product-level information is available for 85 percent of the manufacturing firms, who collectively account for more than 90 percent of Prowess's manufacturing output and exports. More important, product-level sales comprise 99 percent of the (independently) reported manufacturing sales. Prowess is therefore particularly well suited for understanding how firms adjust their product lines over time in response to increased access to intermediate inputs.

Our final sample after cleaning the data leaves us with 4,216 firms that manufacture 1,886 products for the period from 1989–2003. While the level of detail varies across countries depending on the industrial classification, we note that similar data for the United States contain approximately 1,500 products (Bernard et al. 2010). As we show in GKPT (2010c), 47 percent of the firms in Prowess report manufacturing more than one product; these firms account for 80 percent of the total output. We compared these statistics with product-level information for manufacturing plants in the 1997/98, 1999/2000 and 2001/02 ASI rounds. The ASI data indicate that 51 percent of plants manufacture multiple products and these plants account for 78 percent of manufacturing output. Thus, the figures from the ASI data are remarkably similar to Prowess along the scope dimension. The average multiproduct firm in our sample manufactures 3 products compared to 3.5 products in ASI (and 3.3 products per multiproduct plant in ASI).

For an international comparison, 39 percent of US firms manufacture multiple products, and these firms account for 87 percent of total output. This suggests that Indian firms tend to span more product lines but are smaller than US firms. The diversification across product lines is consistent with observations by Kochhar et al. (2006) that India's economic policies have led firms to diversify their portfolios but operate at a smaller scale compared to other similar countries.

Product Addition

In this chapter, we focus mainly on a time series analysis of a firm's manufacturing activity, and in particular, changes to its product mix.[1] We begin by
plotting the average number of products per firm in figure 7.1. The solid curve
plots the coefficients on year indicators from a regression of number of products per firm on year and firm fixed effects. That is, the figure reports average
within-firm changes in the average products during the sample period. There
is a very clear linear and positive relationship indicating a steady increase
in the number of products manufactured per firm during the period of the
reform. Across all firms, firms manufactured about 1.5 products in 1989 and
this increased to about 2.25 by 2003, an increase of around 50 percent. Since
firms enter the database over this period, the dashed curve performs the same
analysis on a constant set of firms that appear in the beginning and end of
the sample. Not surprisingly, these firms are larger and thus manufacture
more products. Moreover, they exhibit the same overall pattern of a general
increase in the number of manufactured products.

The figure indicates growth in the number of products manufactured by
firms. This figure, however, reflects the net change in firms' product mixes. In
principle, firms could be adding and dropping a large number of products while
on net growing their product lines. In order to uncover the dynamics of firm
activity, we followed changes in firms' scope between 1989 and 2003 (GKPT
2010c). We classify firms into four mutually exclusive activity groups: no product mix changes, add products only, drop products only, and both add and drop
products. A product is added in 2003 if it was produced that year but not in

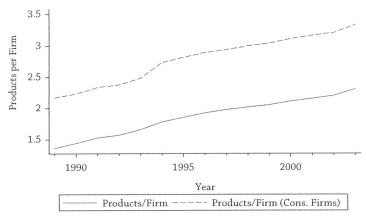

Solid line: Year coefficients of regression of product/firm on year and firm fixed effects

Figure 7.1
Products per Firm, 1989–2003

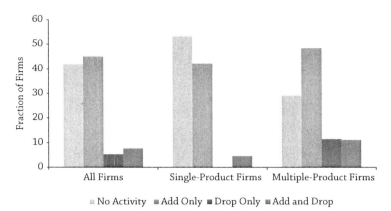

Figure 7.2
Firm Activity, 1989–2003

1989. A product is dropped in 2003 if it was produced in period 1989 but not in 2003. This analysis of product mix changes focuses on incumbent firms.

We graphically summarize the findings from GKPT (2010c) in figure 7.2. The figure indicates several interesting patterns. First, 53 percent of firms report adding a product over the sample period. This figure is mostly made up of the firms that only added a product (45 percent) as opposed to firms that both added and dropped products (8 percent). Thus, a majority of firms added products during the 1990s. Moreover, this finding is not driven by the activity of (initial) multiple-product firms. While 59 percent of multiple-product firms added at least one product, 47 percent of single-product firms also added a product between 1989 and 2003.

The second striking feature of Figure 7.2 is that very few firms report dropping products. So while the majority of firms report adding a product, only 13 percent (5 percent that drop only, and 8 percent that add and drop) dropped a product during the sample.

The prevalence of product additions and lack of product deletions stand in sharp contrast to the activity of US firms. According to Bernard et al. (2010), 39 percent of US firms report adding a product between 1987 and 1997, while 40 percent report dropping a product. The numbers for the United States suggest significant product churning. The numbers for India, however, suggest a much greater likelihood that firms added to their production line but only rarely removed products. Thus, there was far less product churning in India during roughly the same time period.

The lack of product dropping may seem puzzling in light of recent open-economy multiple-product firm models (Bernard et al. 2006, Eckel and Neary 2010). In these models, trade liberalization causes firms to rationalize their product scope and focus on their "core competencies." Here we observe a substantial fraction of firms adding products, with little product dropping, during a period that coincides with the trade reform. We note that these models are not necessarily inconsistent with our findings. In these models, trade liberalization does not provide a beneficial shock to firms in the form of cheaper inputs which could offset the competitive effects of tariffs. In the next section, we provide convincing evidence that intermediate inputs were a prominent feature of India's trade reform.[2]

The products that firms added greatly contributed to their overall output growth and are therefore important to understanding the dynamics of firm behavior over this period. To understand how products contributed to firm growth, we separated total output growth (across a constant set of firms) according to growth on incumbent products (intensive margin) and growth from new products added during the period (extensive margin). This division

Table 7.1 PRODUCT EXTENSIVE MARGIN CONTRIBUTION

NIC Sector	Output Growth (%)	Extensive Margin Contribution
15 Food products and beverages	56	63%
16 Tobacco products	54	17%
17 Textiles	75	43%
18 Wearing apparel	337	0%
19 Tanning and dressing of leather	−2	0%
20 Wood and products of wood	−49	9%
21 Paper and paper products	41	45%
22 Publishing/printing	−59	2%
23 Coke, refined petroleum products	230	1%
24 Chemicals	256	72%
25 Rubber and plastic	208	9%
26 Non-metallic mineral products	68	17%
27 Basic metal	342	17%
28 Fabricated metal products	107	56%
29 Machinery/equipment n.e.c.	115	23%
30 Office, accounting, and computing machines	183	17%
31 Electrical machinery and apparatus	152	85%
32 Radio, TV, and communication	424	19%
33 Medical, precision, and optical instruments	588	71%
34 Motor vehicles, trailers	185	4%
35 Other transport	280	21%
36 Furniture	291	18%
Total	198	25%

Notes: Table decomposes aggregate sales growth into contribution of the extensive and intensive product margin within Prowess from 1989–2003. The table reports the output growth of continuing firms. The final row reports aggregate output growth across all industries. The first column reports sales growth and the second column reports the contribution of the product extensive margin. Values are deflated by sector-specific wholesale price indices.
Source: Authors' calculations from the Prowess database.

illustrates the relative contribution of each margin.[3] The last row of table 7.1 reports the results across all industries (GKPT 2010c). Manufacturing output among these firms grew approximately 200 percent over the sample. About 25 percent of this growth is attributed to new products introduced at the firm level, while the remaining 75 percent can be explained by growth among existing products.[4] Thus, the new products added by firms accounted for nearly one-quarter of manufacturing output growth. This is a sizable contribution of the product extensive margin.

Of course, the overall figures mask heterogeneity across industries. We extend the analysis from GKPT (2010c) and explore the importance of the product extensive margin by sector. The top rows of table 7.1 provide the product extensive margin contribution by sector. The industries in which new products contributed the most to growth were electrical machinery, chemicals, medical instruments, food, and fabricated metal products. In each of these industries, new products contributed to *more than half* of the output growth. It is intuitive that these industries would experience rapid growth in product expansion because India's industrial policy sought to protect capital-intensive industries, an approach that often leads to deficient quality and supply shortages of intermediate inputs. This was precisely Mr. Mitter's complaint. His firm was unable to introduce new types of fabricated metals, such as beer cans and tinplate aerosol cans, simply because of constraints on input supplies. The results here suggest that impediments to introducing new products were alleviated during the 1990s, particularly in certain industries. In subsequent sections, we demonstrate that the trade reform is an important reason why product scope expanded during this period.

In sum, the raw data highlight extensive product additions during the period of the reform, and these new products were an important contribution to overall growth during this period.

INDIA'S TRADE LIBERALIZATION AND IMPORTED PRODUCTION INPUTS

Trade Liberalization Background

In this section, we briefly discuss the events surrounding India's liberalization of foreign trade. For a comprehensive discussion, as well as an extensive discussion of India's other market reforms (e.g., delicensing, privatization, and foreign direct investment), we refer the reader to comprehensive analysis by Panagariya (2008).

After achieving political independence in 1947, India instituted a series of policies designed to achieve economic "independence." Central planners used a series of instruments to allocate resources to targeted sectors and prevent unnecessary redundancies in production. Reflecting the attitude of the time, India's first prime minster, Jawaharlal Nehru, once quipped, "Why do we need nineteen brands of toothpaste?" (Khandelwal 2009). The government instruments included controls on credit provision, prices, and foreign exchange, as well as a system of government monopolies, licensing restriction (often referred to as the "License Raj"), and trade barriers.

India's trade regime was among the most restrictive in Asia, with high nominal tariffs and non-tariff barriers (NTBs) (Aksoy 1992) Not only were imports of final goods restricted, but there were high tariffs on imported inputs. Certain intermediate goods were banned outright, restricted by import licenses controlled by the government. India's tariffs on intermediates were also much larger than other economies at similar lels of economic development at the time (*The Economist* 1991).

In the aftermath of a balance-of-payments crisis in 1991, India launched a liberalization of the economy as part of an International Monetary Fund (IMF) adjustment program. An important part of this reform was to abandon the extremely restrictive trade policies.[5] Average tariffs fell from more than 87 percent in 1990 to 35 percent by 1997, and input tariffs fell 24 percentage points to 10 percent; NTBs also fell from 87 percent in 1987 to 45 percent in 1994 (Topalova and Khandelwal 2011). The extent of the liberalization varied according to final and intermediate industries; tariffs and NTBs for consumer goods declined at a later stage.[6] In the fourth section, we discuss in detail features of the trade reform that are important for our analysis.

Trade Liberalization and Imported Inputs

In this subsection, we document the changes in import levels over the course of the reform period and discuss the key sources of import growth. The discussion, which summarizes the analysis conducted in GKPT (2010b), will highlight that a significant fraction of the growth in imports was concentrated in products classified as production inputs.[7] Moreover, within the production input trade surge, new types of products (mostly originating from OECD countries) drove the growth. The underlying analysis relies on Harmonized System (HS)-level import data obtained from Tips Software Services.[8]

In GKPT (2010b), we document the growth of total (real) imports into India during the late 1980s and 1990s. The results of that analysis are graphically depicted in figure 7.3. The first column depicts the growth in overall imports between 1987 and 2000 and shows that real imports grew 130 percent.[9] Given our focus on the importance of imported inputs for Indian firms, we differentiate imported products by their end use. The total import growth is a weighted average of the growth in final products and products that Indian firms use as production inputs, consisting of basic, capital, and intermediate

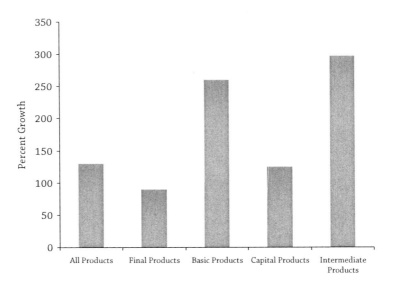

Figure 7.3
Import Growth by End Use, 1987–2000

products. We divide products into these end-use groups using classification from Nouroz (2001).[10] Columns 2–5 depict the growth in imports of these subgroups. Interestingly, the overall import growth was dominated by increased imports of inputs rather than products for final consumption. While imports of final products increased substantially (by 90 percent), increases in production inputs were even more drastic: imports of basic products expanded by 260 percent, imports of capital goods by 125 percent, and imports of intermediate products by 297 percent. These numbers highlight that India's import growth during the 1990s was driven predominantly by imports of components required for production as opposed to final goods.

Further analysis suggests that the vast majority of this import expansion can be attributed to increased trade in products that India did not previously import. We define a product as a six-digit category in the Harmonized System (HS6) and decompose the growth in imports into contribution of two margins: growth in HS6 products that were previously imported (intensive margin) and growth in products that India did not import in the previous period (extensive margin). We further decompose the product-extensive margin by OECD and non-OECD countries, so that the total effect of the product-extensive margin is obtained by adding up the OECD and non-OECD components.[11] The results of this decomposition are graphically depicted in figure 7.4. We normalize each of three margins' contribution by the total growth from figure 7.3, so the three margins sum to 100 percent.

The first feature that emerges from figure 7.4 is that the relative contribution of the extensive margin accounted for almost 64 percent of the overall

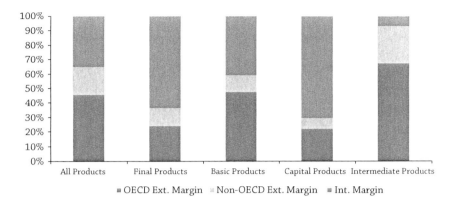

Figure 7.4
Import Growth Decomposition by End Use

import growth (column 1). In our earlier work, we have shown that during this period India started importing previously non-traded products, but did not stop importing many existing foreign products (see GKPT 2010b). The lack of product dropping likely reflects India's restrictive trade regime, which hindered the ability of India's firms and consumers to import products. Once restrictions were lifted, previously unavailable products flooded India's domestic market. The second feature that emerges from figure 7.4 is that the role of the extensive margin was substantially larger in imported inputs than in final consumer goods. New imported products accounted for about 59 percent of import growth in basic products, 30 percent in capital products, and 93 percent in intermediate products.[12] Notice also that the relative importance of the extensive margin is smaller in final goods; the extensive margin accounted for 37 percent of the growth in imports, while the intensive margin contributed 63 percent of the growth. This difference could in part be due to the fact that NTBs on final goods were liberalized later.

The third feature that emerges from figure 7.4 is that the new products were predominately sourced from OECD countries. In a developing country context, there is often a belief that imported inputs are of higher quality than domestic inputs. We have indirect evidence that supports this hypothesis. Kugler and Verhoogen (2008) show that within narrowly defined product categories, imported inputs tend to have higher unit values than their domestically produced counterparts. This claim might be most defensible for imports from OECD countries: inputs produced in OECD countries tend to be R&D intensive and of higher quality. Eaton and Kortum (1995), for example, show that seven OECD countries account for a vast majority of all R&D-intensive goods that are then exported worldwide. Schott (2004) and Khandelwal (2010) further show that within narrowly defined product categories, imports from high-income and capital-abundant countries tend be associated with higher unit values and higher quality. This could in part reflect higher quality of imported inputs. Within each product category, we differentiate between imports stemming from OECD and non-OECD countries (e.g., country-product pairs). All columns of figure 7.4 illustrate that the majority of the growth in new imported products was driven by imports from OECD countries, which—given the evidence—suggests imports of relatively higher quality.

The analysis of import patterns indicates that while Indian firms faced more competition from imported goods (e.g., Krishna and Mitra 1998), Indian firms appear to have had easier access to imported inputs in the period after India's trade liberalization. This easing occurred through higher volumes, new varieties, and probably higher-quality goods.

The decomposition figures are useful for illustrating broad patterns in the underlying sources of Indian import growth. While suggestive, the analysis does not establish a causal link between declines in import tariffs and the sources of import growth. GKPT (2010b) conduct a detailed regression analysis after linking the import data with India's tariff schedule at the HS6 classification. Trade theory predicts that declining import tariffs should increase the total volume of imports and reduce the price of imported goods. The study further shows the usual benefits of trade liberalization in lowering domestic prices of imported goods. Lower tariffs are associated with declining unit values of existing product lines. Finally, lower tariffs were also associated with increased imports of new products. Consistent with the findings in figures 3 and 4, these results were especially pronounced for imported inputs, providing direct evidence that trade liberalization eased access of Indian firms to important production components.

Firm-level Intermediate Input Use

The above discussion illustrates that after trade liberalization, Indian firms purchased imported inputs at a cheaper price and expanded the range of imported inputs in production. In principle, these aggregate figures should be observed in the micro firm-level data as well. However, there are caveats to analyzing firm-level import usage in India. There are four main reasons why analyzing product-level import data, as opposed to firm-level data, is appropriate for documenting firms' access to new imported inputs in our setting.

First, we are limited by data constraints on our ability to analyze the range of imported inputs in firm-level datasets for India. Custom-level transaction data by firm and product are not available during the period of India's trade reform. Neither Prowess nor ASI contains comprehensive information on imported inputs during this period either. Second, firm-level total imports (which we do observe) confound price and quantity information. Third, many firms do not directly import inputs on their own; instead, they rely on intermediaries. Finally, there is potential measurement error in any firm's reported imported input usage, since this requires that the firm know the origin of its inputs. This last point may be particularly problematic in industries where firms do not require highly specialized inputs for production, but rather production inputs such as computers, power looms, or communication devices.

Nonetheless, we use this section to document firm-level imported input usage using several sources of data. For each data source, we offer caveats to interpreting the results and this serves to reinforce our strategy of identifying the expansion of imported inputs at a more aggregate level, as we did in the previous section.

Prowess records some firm-level information on total imports that we can analyze. A measure of total spending on imports is less than ideal in this context because, as we discussed in the third section, imported input prices fell. Total cost of imports could conceivably drop even if firms started to import more. It would be more ideal if we could separately observe prices and quantities of product-level imports, but this information is either unavailable or of poor quality in Prowess.[13]

Our measure for imports is firms' spending on foreign exchange. This is an imperfect measure because it includes any expense incurred by the firm in a foreign currency (e.g., interest payments, royalties, traveling expenses). In 1995, 81 percent of the firms reported imports; this figure is high because the category includes many types of foreign expenses (and because Prowess contains relatively large firms).[14] However, the median import share of sales is only 4.7 percent for all firms and the median import share of sales is only 8 percent for firms that import. Despite this imperfect measure of total firm-level imports, we examine the relationship between firm-level imports and input tariffs. We regress (the log of) imports on input tariffs, input tariff interacted with an indicator for whether a firm size is above the size of the median firm, firm fixed effects, and year fixed effects.[15] The results are reported in columns 1 and 2 of table 7.2. For relatively larger firms, total imports expand relatively more in industries that experienced larger declines in input tariffs. The coefficient for small firms is positive. This is counterintuitive, but recall that the total import measure includes any expense in foreign currency. In columns 3 and 4, we report the same regression results using foreign spending on raw materials as the dependent variable. Here, we observe no statistical relationship for small firms, but large firms increased their direct imports of raw materials in response to lower input tariffs.

One shortcoming of Prowess is that we do not comprehensively observe how the range of inputs changed; that is, we cannot separate the extensive and intensive margins of firms' imported product use as we were able to do using the product-level data in the third section. We therefore complement our firm-level analysis with information from the ASI. The ASI began

Table 7.2 IMPORT VALUES AND INPUT TARIFFS

	(1)		(2)		(3)	(4)	
Input Tariff	−0.060		1.524	***	−0.623	0.727	
	0.487		0.486		0.618	0.602	
Input Tariff X Large Firm	−0.323	**	−2.036	***		−1.734	***
	0.139		0.204			0.186	
Year Effects	yes		yes		yes	yes	
Firm FEs	yes		yes		yes	yes	
R-squared	0.88		0.88		0.86	0.86	
Observations	14,233		14,233		14,233	14,233	

Notes: The dependent variable in columns 1–2 is log (one plus total foreign exchange spending by the firm). The dependent variable in columns 3–4 is log (one plus total spending on raw materials). The large firm dummy takes a value of one if the firm averages above median sales over the sample period. All regressions include firm and year fixed effects and are run from 1989–1997. Standard errors clustered at the industry level. Significance: * 10 percent, ** 5 percent, *** 1 percent.

Table 7.3 NUMBER OF INPUTS AND INPUT TARIFFS

Change in Input Tariffs	−6.464	***	−1.351	***
	(1.790)		(0.348)	
R-squared	0.03		0.01	
Observations	27,970		27,970	

Notes: Table uses information from the 1999–2000 ASI on inputs. The first column regresses plant-level number of inputs on the industry change in input tariffs from 1989–1997. The second column uses average imported inputs per plant. Each column clusters standard errors by industry and uses the sampling weights provided by the ASI. Significance: * 10 percent, ** 5 percent, *** 1 percent.

collecting data on usage of imported inputs after 1997, so we cannot observe firm-level information on the range of inputs during the main period of the reform. We also cannot track input changes over time because the ASI is not a panel. However, since we directly observe comprehensive information on input scope in these data, we can compare the relationship between declines in input tariffs and input scope across industries. Only 10 percent of ASI plants report positive imported input use in this period; this figure is similar to Chilean firms (Kasahara and Rodrigue 2008).

Table 7.3 illustrates the results of running a plant-level regression of the number of inputs and imported inputs on the industry changes in input tariffs between 1997 and 1989. The regression clusters by industry and uses the sampling weights. We observe a very strong, statistically significant negative relationship between input tariff changes and average inputs per firm. This implies that in industries with larger declines in input tariffs, plants were using more inputs, especially imported inputs, in 1999. That is, the plants that experienced the largest input tariff cuts had the largest extensive margin of inputs. Since these correlations are based on a levels-on-change specification, we are cautious about their interpretation. However, we feel that they are suggestive that the input tariff liberalization led firms to use a broader range of inputs. This is not surprising, given that we observe such a large expansion of imports of previously unavailable products in the customs data.

Despite the evidence from these two datasets on increased imports, we believe the product-level analysis in the third section, which determines the intensive and extensive product margins of imports, is the correct level of disaggregation for India's context. The reason, quite simply, is that because the trade regime was previously so restrictive, we observe a large fraction of new products entering the economy during this period. Our data clearly show that many products or varieties were not imported by *any* firm prior to the reform. Thus, we can say with confidence that the large increase in the extensive margin reflects firms using new inputs as opposed to new firms adopting imported inputs that other Indian firms already used in their production process. These new inputs must have been imported by *someone*, be it directly by a firm in our sample or by an intermediary/wholesaler.

Another advantage is that our data capture *all* imports, not just imports that firms directly obtain from abroad. Imports by wholesalers cannot be identified in conventional data sources such as Prowess and ASI. While customs data that record firm-product transactions provide information on the intermediary/wholesaler that imports, they do not identify the final firm that uses the product.[16] Given that firms use intermediaries, conventional firm-level surveys will undercount the total value and fraction of firms that use imported inputs, as well as the timing of when firms begin to import.

We attempt to provide some evidence that Indian firms make use of these intermediaries to source inputs. To our knowledge, the World Bank Enterprise Survey is the only database that provides firm-level information on the use of intermediaries. The survey asks firms about the channel through which they obtain imported inputs. A firm can either directly import the input or *indirectly* import the input through an intermediary. Specifically, the survey asks: "What percentage of your establishment's material inputs and supplies are i) purchased from domestic sources, ii) imported directly, iii) imported indirectly (through a distributor)." Out of 2,037 (manufacturing) firms, 12 percent import materials. Of the firms that import materials, 56 percent import directly, 40 percent import through a distributor, and the remaining 4 percent obtain imported materials through both channels.

Ahn et al. (2010) provide theoretical and empirical evidence that less-productive firms are likely to use intermediaries because it allows these firms to avoid directly paying the costs of trade. We look for this pattern in the Indian data by plotting the share of indirect and direct imports of inputs—conditional on the use of imported inputs—against firm size (measured as the log of total reported sales). The figure therefore illustrates the relationship

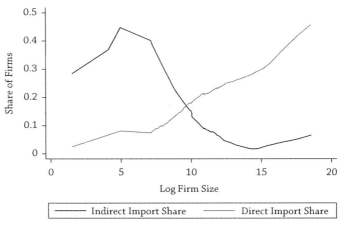

Figure 7.5
Direct and Indirect Imported Input Usage

between mode of import and firm size. The results are presented in figure 7.5. The blue line denotes indirect shares; red indicates direct imports. The reliance on direct imports increases with firm size relatively monotonically, while the indirect imports increase with firm size up to a point and then decline. This suggests that smaller and potentially less-productive firms are more likely to use intermediaries and is consistent with the findings of Ahn et al. (2010).

The findings across these three datasets offer evidence that there was an expansion of imports in terms of scope and value (for large firms) for firms in industries that experience the largest tariff cuts. This is consistent with the findings based on the analysis of total product-level imports in the third section. However, there are caveats to interpreting each of the firm-level results because of data limitations (for instance, not having a panel of firms that report its imported input scope). Firms, especially small and less-productive firms, often use intermediaries to source their inputs, and this will not show up in conventional datasets. For instance, it will not show up as a foreign exchange expense if the firm pays the intermediary in local currency. Perhaps most important, it could easily be that firms themselves do not know which of their inputs are foreign. This will depend on the firm and the industry, but for many inputs, such as computer machines and peripherals, firms may not recognize whether the input itself is an import. Thus, unlike output, firms may have a fuzzier idea of their input scope.

This discussion of data limitations with firm-level imported inputs for the case of India justifies our reliance on product-level imports that aggregate across firms' imports to understand the growth and composition of India's imports following the reform.

VARIETY IN, VARIETY OUT

Imports and Domestic Product Growth

We can easily summarize the facts generated from the previous two sections: variety in, variety out. That is, from the viewpoint of the external economy, the 1990s were characterized by increased access to intermediate inputs. Inputs became cheaper as tariffs fell, but firms also started to import new types of inputs that were previously unavailable under the restrictive trade regime. As the tariff barriers fell, new varieties of inputs entered the economy. Second, the domestic production data indicate that a large fraction of firms began to introduce new products during this period. More than half of the firms introduced at least one new product, and these products contributed to nearly a quarter of the manufacturing output growth. In some industries, the contribution of the extensive margin exceeded 50 percent. So in addition to the flood of varieties entering the economy, there was simultaneous expansion of domestic manufacturing.

In this section, we examine if the two facts are connected. That is, did increased access to intermediate inputs lead to the introduction of new varieties at the firm level? Endogenous growth models have long proposed this variety in, variety out story of economic development. While neoclassical trade models predict a one-time gain from trade as a country moves from autarky to trade, endogenous growth models predict that trade could also affect the steady-state growth rate of any economy. This occurs when international trade expands the range of intermediate inputs, and these new inputs are used in the creation of new products.

Reduction in India's input tariffs can affect a firm's decision to introduce a new product in two ways. First, the input tariff reductions lower the prices of existing imported inputs. Second, liberalization leads to the import of new varieties. Lower prices imply higher variable profits and raise the likelihood that a firm can manufacture previously unprofitable products. The significance of this second channel will depend on the particular form of production technology. In particular, it depends on substitutability between domestic and imported inputs and substitutability across imported varieties. Take an extreme example of Leontief production technology in which a certain intermediate input is essential. Output falls to zero if this input is unavailable. In this case, trade liberalization has large impacts on product scope because it relaxes technological constraints facing domestic firms. At the other extreme, if new imported inputs are perfect substitutes for domestic inputs (or previously imported inputs), there will be no effect on the extensive margin of imports.[17]

The overall effect of trade reform on product scope is therefore ultimately an empirical question. However, isolating the microeconomic mechanisms in the endogenous growth models is challenging. First, it requires very detailed data. As we discussed earlier, we have precisely the data on firm scope required to test the predictions of the model during the relevant time period. Second, one can easily imagine finding a correlation between imported inputs and domestic product growth if other factors, such as productivity or demand shocks, cause firms to introduce new products. Firms could subsequently start to import inputs to sustain their production. This reverse causality concern is difficult to disentangle without a source of exogeneity that can isolate which phenomenon occurs first.

Fortunately, India's trade liberalization provides an unusually clear lens to test the theory that imported inputs lead to domestic product growth. India's trade liberalization came as a response to the balance of payments crisis and was therefore a sudden shock. The conditions of the trade reform were mandated by the IMF in return for loans (Hasan et al. 2007). Moreover, to avoid the inevitable political opposition, the reforms were passed quickly with little debate or analysis (Goyal 1996). This means that the tariff liberalization can be viewed as exogenous from the perspective of the firms and alleviates potential endogeneity of the trade reforms. For instance, industries that were growing rapidly in terms of output, product scope, productivity, and so on may have had less of an incentive to keep tariffs high. However, GKPT (2010b) and Topalova and Khandelwal (2011) demonstrate that this was not the case. The changes in tariffs were uncorrelated with many measures of firm and industry outcomes prior to the reform. As discussed in Topalova and Khandelwal (2011), a guiding feature of the tariff reduction was a harmonization of tariff lines across industries: industries with the highest tariffs received the largest tariff cuts. This also implies that some industries received larger tariff cuts than others, and we exploit this heterogeneity in tariff declines across industries.

Following the 1997 election Topalova and Khandelwal (2011) find evidence that tariffs changed in ways that were correlated with firm and industry performance in the previous years. This indicates that, unlike the initial tariff changes following the reform, the post-1997 tariff changes were subject to political influence. This concern leads us to restrict our analysis in this chapter to the sample period that spans 1989–97.

Main Results

In GKPT (2010b), we estimate the overall impact of the trade liberalization on product scope by relating the changes in product scope, at the firm level, to changes in input tariffs. We estimate the following equation:

$$\ln\left(n_{it}^{q}\right) = \alpha_{i} + \alpha_{t} + \beta\tau_{qt}^{inp} + \varepsilon_{it} \quad (1),$$

where n_{it}^q is the number of products manufactured by firm i operating in industry q at time t, and τ_{qt}^{inp} is the input tariff that corresponds to the main industry in which firm i operates.[18] This regression also includes firm fixed effects to control for time-invariant firm characteristics, and year fixed effects to capture unobserved aggregate shocks. The coefficient of interest is β, which captures the semi-elasticity of firm scope with respect to tariffs on intermediate inputs. Standard errors are clustered at the industry level.

Table 7.4, which is reproduced from GKPT (2010b), presents the main results in column 1. The coefficient on the input tariff is negative and statistically significant: declining input tariffs are associated with an increase in the scope of production by domestic firms. The point estimate implies that a 10 percentage point drop in tariffs results in a 3.2 percent expansion of a firm's product scope. During the period of our analysis, input tariffs declined on average by 24 percentage points, implying that within-firm product scope expanded 7.7 percent. Firms increased their product scope on average by 25 percent between 1989 and 1997, so our estimates therefore imply that declines in input tariffs accounted for 31 percent of the observed expansion in firms' product scope.

Table 7.1 reported that the product extensive margin accounted for 25 percent of India's manufacturing output growth during our sample. If India's trade liberalization impacted growth only through the increase in product scope, our estimates imply that the lower input tariffs contributed 7.8 percent (0.25x0.31) to the overall manufacturing growth. This back-of-the-envelope

Table 7.4 PRODUCT SCOPE AND INPUT TARIFFS

	(1)		(2)		(3)		(4)	
Input tariff	−0.323	**	−0.310	**	−0.327	**	−0.281	**
	0.139		0.150		0.150		0.125	
Output tariff			−0.013		−0.014		−0.010	
			0.043		0.041		0.041	
Delicensed					−0.032		−0.026	
					0.023		0.021	
FDI liberalized							0.037	
							0.024	
Year effects	yes		yes		yes		yes	
Firm FEs	yes		yes		yes		yes	
R-squared	0.90		0.90		0.90		0.90	
Observations	14,882		14,864		13,435		11,135	

Notes: This table is reproduced from GKPT (2010b). The dependent variable in each regression is (log) number of products manufactured by the firm. The delicenced variable is an indicator variable obtained from Aghion et al (2008) which switches to one in the year that the industry becomes delicensed. The FDI variable is a continuous variabled obtained from Topalova and Khandelwal (2011) with higher values indicating a more liberal FDI policy. As with the tariffs, delicensed and FDI policy variables are lagged. All regressions include firm and year fixed effects and are run from 1989–1997. Standard errors clustered at the industry level. Significance: * 10 percent, ** 5 percent, *** 1 percent.

calculation suggests a sizable effect of increased access to imported inputs for manufacturing output growth. Moreover, it is likely to be a lower bound, as input tariffs are likely to have affected the intensive margin as well.

Readers familiar with India's economic policies during this time period are aware that the trade liberalization coincided with additional market reforms. In the remaining columns of table 7.4, we control for these additional policy variables so that we can isolate the effects of tariffs vis-à-vis other policies. Column 2 includes output tariffs to control for pro-competitive effects associated with the tariff reduction. The idea behind this control is related to recent models of how trade liberalization affects multiple-product firms (Bernard et al. 2006, Eckel and Neary 2010) that we discussed above. The coefficient on output tariffs is not statistically significant, while the input tariff coefficient hardly changes and remains negative and statistically significant.[19]

In column 3, we include a dummy variable for industries delicensed (obtained from Aghion et al. 2008) during our sample, and the input tariff coefficient remains robust. Finally, column 4 includes a measure of FDI liberalization from Topalova and Khandelwal (2011). The coefficient implies that firms in industries with FDI liberalization increased scope, but the coefficient is not statistically significant. The input tariff remains negative and significant, indicating that even after controlling for other market reforms during this period, input tariff declines led to an expansion of firm product scope.

We can use these estimates to compare the predicted change in firm scope due to the input tariffs with actual changes by sector. In table 7.5, we report the average change in product scope in the raw data for a constant set of firms in 1989 and 1997. As we saw earlier, there is heterogeneity across industries, but the average increase in firm scope was on the order of 42 percent (this is lower than growth in figure 7.1 since that figure reports firm scope through 2003). In column 2, we report the average change in input tariffs by sector. Average input tariffs declined about 23 percent between 1989 and 1997. Again, this ranged across sectors: input tariffs fell only 10.5 percent for tobacco products but nearly 34 percent for apparel. The third column multiplies the change in input tariffs in column 2 with the point estimate in column 1 of table 7.4. This provides the average change in firm scope exclusively due to the decline in input tariffs. Column 4 divides column 3 by column 1 to show the percentage of the overall scope change that can be attributed to input tariffs alone. We can see that input tariffs accounted for about 15–20 percent of the growth in firm scope for chemicals, fabricated metal products, and electrical machinery, but a lower fraction for medical equipment. The remaining fraction of overall growth can be attributed to general economic growth, which picks up during this period, and factors unexplained by either input tariffs or year fixed effects.

These results indicate that input tariffs causally increased firm product scope, as predicted by endogenous growth models. We demonstrate that the relationship is robust by controlling for additional industrial policies, and in

Sector	Change in Product Scope (1)	Change in Input Tariffs (2)	Predicted Change in Product Scope (3)	Percentage Explained by Input Tariffs (4)
15 Food products and beverages	43%	-18.1%	5.8%	14%
16 Tobacco products	6%	-10.5%	3.4%	61%
17 Textiles	21%	-23.1%	7.5%	35%
18 Wearing apparel	-25%	-33.9%	11.0%	-44%
19 Tanning and dressing of leather	-33%	-28.3%	9.1%	-27%
20 Wood and products of wood	60%	-12.8%	4.1%	7%
21 Paper and paper products	40%	-25.5%	8.2%	21%
22 Publishing/printing	0%	-24.1%	7.8%	na
23 Coke, refined petroleum products	10%	-19.9%	6.4%	64%
24 Chemicals	46%	-28.5%	9.2%	20%
25 Rubber and plastic	41%	-31.0%	10.0%	25%
26 Non-metallic mineral products	44%	-15.7%	5.1%	12%
27 Basic metal	46%	-29.0%	9.4%	20%
28 Fabricated metal products	61%	-27.3%	8.8%	15%
29 Machinery/equipment n.e.c.	46%	-25.3%	8.2%	18%
30 Office, accounting, and computing machines	20%	-19.4%	6.3%	31%
31 Electrical machinery and apparatus	69%	-27.4%	8.8%	13%
32 Radio, TV, and communication	37%	-29.0%	9.4%	25%
33 Medical, precision, and optical instruments	143%	-25.0%	8.1%	6%
34 Motor vehicles, trailers	45%	-24.8%	8.0%	18%
35 Other transport	22%	-25.8%	8.3%	38%
36 Furniture	100%	-18.4%	5.9%	6%

Notes: Table compares the actual change in product scope for firms in 1989 and 1997 with the predicted change due to input tariffs. The first column reports the average change in actual product scope across firms within the sector. The second column reports the average change in input tariffs by sector. The third column multiplies column 2 by -.323, the point estimates input tariffs from equation (1). Column 4 divides column 3 by column 1.

GKPT (2010b) we perform a number of sensitivity results that control for various types of preexisting trends. The fact that the results are robust reinforces the fact that India's trade liberalization came as a surprise to Indian firms. Once the tariffs were slashed, firms re-adjusted their product mixes to reflect the new economic environment. Moreover, we also show that lower input tariffs affected firm total factor productivity (TFP) (Khandelwal and Topalova 2011) and firm-level research and development expenditure. In addition to firm scope, these two findings are also consistent with endogenous growth theory.

One implication of the variety in, variety out model is that firms actually increase the range of inputs used in response to tariff cuts. Unfortunately, as discussed in the third section, due to data limitations we cannot check this prediction with Prowess data nor in a time series with ASI data. The product-level information on inputs within Prowess is only available for a small subsample of firms, only covers information on imported raw materials (and not all intermediate inputs), and is very incomplete. The ASI started collecting comprehensive information on products after 1997, so we do not observe the firm-level information on the range of inputs during the period of our study. ASI is also not a panel, so we cannot track product changes over time. Nontheless, as we discuss in the third section, when we relate the number of imported products used by ASI firms in 1999–2000 to input tariff changes between 1997 and 1989, we find a very strong, statistically significant negative relationship between input tariff changes and average inputs per firm. Industries that experienced the largest input tariff declines during the reform had a large input extensive margin in 1999. We observe a similar relationship for imported input usage. Since these correlations are based on a levels-on-change specification, we are cautious about their interpretation. However, they suggest that tariff liberalization led firms to use a broader range of inputs. Again, this is not surprising given that we observe such a large expansion of imported products in the customs data.

We note that while this framework provides an overall assessment of the relationship between input tariffs and scope, it cannot disentangle the price and variety channels discussed above. This decomposition requires far more assumptions about the structure of firms' production functions and is beyond the scope of this chapter, but we note that in previous work (GKPT 2010b), we conducted an extensive analysis of this issue and found that the input variety channel was the dominant source for the increase in firm scope.[20] This further lends support for the variety in, variety out theory.

Heterogeneous Effects of Input Liberalization

Studies have documented large differences in output growth across Indian states (Kochhar et al. 2006), and these differences have been in part explained by differences in institutions that govern labor relations, finances, and infra-structure across Indian states. For example, Besley and Burgess (2004) find lower output and investment in registered manufacturing in Indian states that passed pro-worker amendments to the Industrial Disputes Act.

These institutional differences might also affect how firms adjust to dereg-ulation or trade policy. For example, Aghion et al. (2008) find that in response to the dismantling of the License Raj, industries improved productivity more in states with pro-worker amendments to the Industrial Disputes Act. Hasan et al. (2007) find that trade reform increased the sensitivity of industry employment to price shocks more in states with more flexible labor laws. It is possible that differences in local insitutions also affect a firm's ability to incor-porate cheaper and more varied imported inputs into its production process and expand its product scope. For example, a firm located in a state where labor market regulations preclude it from reorganizing its production lines, or where low financial development makes it difficult to secure financing, might be less likely to introduce a new product that takes advantage of the increased access to cheaper and more varied imported inputs.

In order to investigate this issue, we replicate the analysis from column 1 of table 7.4 to examine the benefits of lower input tariffs across industries or states. We augment the specification in equation (1) by interacting input tar-iffs with state-level investment climate measures. We consider four measures: level of financial development, geography, road networks, and labor market regulations. Table 7.6 presents the results. We first look for heterogeneous impacts depending on whether or not the industry had been delicensed by 1988. Our assumption is that industries that were delicensed earlier are more likely to benefit from input tariffs. Column 1 reports a negative coefficient on the interaction, suggesting that firms in industries that were deregulated earlier increased product scope more than industries that were delicensed after 1991. However, the coefficient is not statistically significant. Column 2 considers differences between states according to their level of financial development.[21] We identify the state where the headquarter office is located to determine the location of the firm. Again, while firms in financially devel-oped states are more likely to add products, these effects are not statistically significant. In columns 3 and 4 we consider the role of infrastructure. Firms in coastal states might be better positioned to gain access to imported inputs. However, we find no evidence that this matters in column 3. In column 4, we use a (normalized) measure of road networks defined as the percentage of roads that were surfaced (these are taken from Fisman and Khanna 2004). While the negative coefficient on the interaction of roads with input tariffs is negative, suggesting that firms in states with more roads increase product scope by more, this effect is again not statistically significant.

Finally, to explore the potential role of labor market regulations, we clas-sify states according to the strength of their labor market regulations following

Table 7.6 PRODUCT SCOPE AND INPUT TARIFFS, HETEROGENOUS EFFECTS

	License	Financial Development	Coastal	Road Networks	Labor Regulation (Small Firms)	Labor Regulation (Large Firms)
	(1)	(2)	(3)	(4)	(5)	(6)
Input tariff	-0.324 ** (0.155)	-0.327 * (0.188)	-0.352 ** (0.145)	-0.284 * (0.161)	-0.346 (0.249)	-0.358 ** (0.181)
Input tariff X delicensed by 1998	-0.109 (0.122)					
Input tariff X financial development		0.009 (0.143)				
Input tariff X coastal state			0.048 (0.078)			
Input tariff X road network				-0.056 (0.092)		
Input tariff X neutral labor regulation					0.140 (0.219)	0.086 (0.141)

	Column 1	Column 2	Column 3	Column 4	Column 5	Column 6
Input tariff X pro-worker labor regulation					0.257 (0.181)	-0.020 (0.121)
Year effects	yes	yes	yes	yes	yes	yes
Firm FEs	yes	yes	yes	yes	yes	yes
R-Squared	0.90	0.90	0.90	0.90	0.89	0.90
Observations	13,435	14,873	14,873	13,802	5,457	9,416

Notes: This table reports heterogenous impacts of input tariffs across different state and industry characteristics. The dependent variable in each regression is the (log) number of products manufactured by the firm. Column 1 reports the interaction of a dummy that equals 1 if the industry was delicensed by 1988. Column 2 interacts input tariffs with a measure of financial development which takes an indicator of 1 if the state is above the median credit per capita in 1992. Column 3 identifies states that are on the coast. Column 4 uses a measure of road networks from Fisman and Khanna (1998). Column 5 reports the interaction with labor market regulations, taken from Besley and Burgess (2004), for (initially) small firms (below median sales). Column 6 uses initially large firms in the regression. The left out category in these regressions are pro-business states. All regressions include firm and year fixed effects and are run from 1989–1997. Standard errors clustered at the industry level. Significance: * 10 percent, ** 5 percent, *** 1 percent.

Besley and Burgess (2004).[22] Note that our measure of labor market regulation is time invariant. We also find that firms (especially smaller ones) in states with neutral or pro-labor labor market regulation are less likely to add products in response to lower input tariffs, but these results are very imprecisely estimated.

Overall, these results do not provide precise evidence that state-level investment climate affects the ability of firms to introduce products. However, one should be cautious about interpreting these results. Recall that Prowess is more representative of medium and large enterprises. These firms might be better positioned to overcome the location-specific investment climate concerns. Identifying the location of the firm based on its headquarters may also be imprecise if firms have plants in multiple states. Finally, there may not be enough states within each classification, and this could explain why our results are imprecise.

DISCUSSION AND CONCLUSION

This chapter seeks to explain the rise in the number of products manufactured by Indian firms during a period which spans trade reforms. A large fraction of domestic Indian firms added new products during this period, and these products contributed a sizable amount of manufacturing output growth. A key driving force of this phenomenon was imported intermediate inputs. When tariffs fell, firms increased their imports of intermediate goods by expanding the range of inputs, as well as capitalizing on cheaper prices. Together, this increased access to imported inputs enabled firms to expand their production lines. Interestingly, we do not find precise evidence that state-level investment climate affects the ability of firms to introduce products in response to input tariff cuts. As we discuss in the chapter, this last result could simply reflect that medium and large enterprises, which are overrepresented in our data, are better positioned to overcome business climate hurdles.

While our work has focused on a seemingly narrow response—product scope—our results have broader implications for the link between trade reform and economic development. Previous studies have analyzed the impact of lower input tariffs on firm productivity (e.g., Amiti and Konings 2007, Topalova and Khandelwal 2011). Estimating firm productivity is difficult given the data that researchers typically have access to. By focusing on product scope, we can directly identify one margin of adjustment to lower input tariffs. Moreover, we demonstrate that new products had a sizable contribution to overall economic output growth. We therefore view our analysis as peering inside the black box of firm productivity and investigating how one component adjusts with trade reform.

The introduction of new products suggests that India's trade reform might have led to dynamic gains as these new products fed into the domestic economy. In addition to providing a window on the adjustment process within firms, our results might have broader implications that relate to the literature on trade and growth. Neoclassical trade models emphasize static gains from trade. In the Ricardo and Heckscher-Ohlin models, a country that moves from autarky to trade will experience a one-time gain from trade. The endogenous growth literature has hypothesized, however, that trade could also lead to dynamic gains. For instance, Romer (1987, 1990) and Rivera-Batiz and Romer (1991) emphasize that importing new of productscan deliver two gains to an economy: access to imported varieties will lead to productivity gains initially, and the resulting growth fosters the creation of new domestic varieties which further contributes to growth. Our results here provide microeconomic evidence consistent with these channels, although we do not explicitly test for changes in steady-state growth.[23] A more detailed study of dynamic gains from trade associated with Indian trade reform remains a topic for future research.

DATA APPENDIX

HS-level import data are obtained from Tips Software Services. The data record HS8-level imports from 160 countries between 1987 and 2000.

The tariff data, originally reported at the HS6-level, are taken from Topalova and Khandelwal (2011). We use a concordance by Debroy and Santhanam (1993) to aggregate tariffs to the National Industrial Classification (NIC) level, which we use to trace out the impact of changes in tariffs on firm activity.

We obtain India's input-output matrix for 1993/94 from the Ministry of Statistics and Programme Implementation. For each industry, we create an input tariff for that industry as the weighted average of tariffs on inputs used in the production of the final output of that industry. The weights are constructed as the input industry's share of the output industry's total output value. Formally, input tariffs are defined as $\tau_{qt}^{inp} = \sum_i \alpha_{iq} \tau_{it}$, where α_{iq} is the value share of input i in industry q.[24] The weights in the IO table are also used to construct the components of the input exact price index.

ACKNOWLEDGMENT

Work on this chapter has been supported by Columbia University's Program on Indian Economic Policies, funded by a generous grant from the John Templeton Foundation. The opinions expressed in the chapter are those of the authors and do not necessarily reflect the views of the John Templeton Foundation.

NOTES

1. GKPT (2010c) provides an extensive analysis of the cross-sectional properties of these firms, such as the skewness of the distribution of sales within firms and correlations between intensive and extensive margins.
2. We refer the reader to GKPT (2010c) for a more detailed discussion of the reasons that India is characterized by a lack of product dropping compared to the United States.
3. We could also include the contribution of firm entry and exit by focusing on all firms rather than the firms that existed in 1989 and 2003. However, Prowess is not well suited for measuring the firm extensive margin because firm entry into the database is not an indication that the firm is new.
4. It is important to remember that the product extensive margin is a firm-level concept. So a new product is a product that is new to the firm, not necessarily to the entire economy. If we include entering firms into this calculation, total output grew approximately 350 percent. This number is similar to the overall growth in output according to the ASI between 1989 and 2001, which is about 318 percent.
5. The structural reforms of the early 1990s also included a stepped-up dismantling of the License Raj, the extensive system of licensing requirements for establishing and expanding capacity in the manufacturing sector, which had been the corner-stone of India's regulatory regime.
6. See Panagariya (2004) for a more information on final goods liberalization.
7. Mukerji (2009) has also documented the growth of the import extensive margin in the case of India. Her analysis is likely to underestimate the importance of new varieties since she documents the extensive margin at the industry level rather than at product level.
8. Please see Data Appendix for details.
9. Nominal imports, inclusive of tariffs, grew 516 percent over this period. Excluding tariffs, real and nominal import growth was 228 and 781 percent, respectively. The reason the growth numbers excluding tariffs are higher is because tariffs were very high prior to the reform.
10. Nouroz (2001) assigns each code of India's input-output(IO) matrix into one of these groups and then links these codes to the four-digit product codes of the Harmonized System (HS4). While some products can obviously be used simul-taneously as production inputs and final outputs (for example, computers), the most common use of many products often justifies this end-use distinction.
11. The group of countries that we call OECD includes all OECD members as well as Hong Kong, Taiwan, and Singapore.
12. See GKPT (2010a) for decompositions of specific input sectors.
13. In 1995, product-level information on inputs is missing for 1,472 out of 1,934 firms. Of the 462 firms for which information exists, it poorly matches the firm-level raw material information that exists in a separate module in Prowess. On average, the sum of the product-level raw material values only accounts for 69 percent of the reported expenditure on raw materials. This poor quality is in stark contrast to the quality of the product-level production data (see GKPT 2010c).
14. Sixty-one percent of firms report imports of raw materials and 42 percent report imports of capital goods.
15. We use information from the first year of the sample to compute a measure of firm size and median.

16. While we do not have the figures for India, Ahn, Khandelwal, and Wei (2010) report that about one quarter of China's imports were through intermediaries in 2000.
17. Intermediate inputs could also lower the fixed costs of production.
18. Please see Data Appendix for the details on how input tariffs were constructed.
19. We refer the reader to GKPT 2010c for a more extensive discussion of this finding and its relationship to trade models with multiple-product firms.
20. Our methodology to decompose these channels is based on Feenstra (1994) and Broda and Weinstein (2004).
21. We compute credit per capita in 1992 and classify states above and below the median level.
22. The labor measure is a time-invariant variable that classifies states according the cumulative amendments to labor market laws up to 1991. See Topalova and Khandelwal (2011) for this list.
23. Related papers by Feenstra, Madani, Yang, and Liang (1999) and Broda, Greenfield, and Weinstein (2006) provide evidence that more import varieties lead to more export varieties. In our work, however, we focus on production data, rather than exports, and make use of a trade liberalization for our identification strategy. Related papers by Feenstra (1994); Broda and Weinstein (2006); Arkolakis, Demidova, Klenow, and Rodriguez-Clare (2008); and Klenow and Rodriguez-Clare (1997) also document overall welfare gains from imported varieties.
24. The IO table includes weights for manufacturing and non-tradeables (e.g., labor, electricity, utilities, labor, etc.), but tariffs, of course, only exist for manufacturing. Therefore, the calculation of input tariffs implicitly assumes a zero tariff for non-tradeables. All of our regressions rely on changes in tariffs over time and not cross-sectional comparisons.

REFERENCES

Aghion, Philippe, Robin Burgess, Stephen Redding, and Fabrizio Zilibotti, "The Unequal Effects of Liberalization: Evidence from Dismantling the License Raj in India," *American Economic Review*, 98(4), 2008, 1397–1412.

Ahn, JaeBin, Amit Khandelwal, and Shang-Jin Wei, "The Role of Intermediaries in Facilitating Trade," *Journal of International Economics*, 84(1), 2010, 73–85.

Aksoy, M. Ataman, "The Indian Trade Regime," World Bank Working Paper Series, No. 989, 1992.

Amiti, Mary and Jozef Konings, "Trade Liberalization, Intermediate Inputs and Productivity," *American Economic Review*, 97(5), 2007, 1611–1638.

Arkolakis, Costas, Svetlana Demidova, Peter J. Klenow, and Andres Rodriguez-Clare, "Endogenous Variety and the Gains from Trade," *American Economic Review Papers and Proceedings*, 98(2), 2008, 444–50.

Bernard, Andrew B., Stephen J. Redding, and Peter K. Schott, "Multi-product Firms and Product Switching," *American Economic Review*, 100(1), 2010, 70–97.

Bernard, Andrew B., Stephen J. Redding, and Peter K. Schott, "Multi-product Firms and Trade Liberalization," NBER Working Paper No. w12782, 2006.

Besley, Timothy and R. Burgess, "Can Labor Regulation Hinder Economic Performance? Evidence from India," *The Quarterly Journal of Economics*, 119(1), 2004, 91–134.

Broda, Christian and David E. Weinstein, "Globalization and the Gains from Variety," *Quarterly Journal of Economics*, 121(2), 2006, 541–85.

Broda, Christian, Joshua Greenfield, and David E. Weinstein, "From Groundnuts to Globalization: A Structural Estimate of Trade and Growth," NBER Working Paper No. w12512, 2006.

Debroy, Bibek and A. T. Santhanam, "Matching Trade Codes with Industrial Codes," *Foreign Trade Bulletin*, Indian Institute of Foreign Trade, New Delhi, 1993.

Eaton, J. and S. Kortum, "Trade in Capital Goods," *European Economic Review* 45(7), 2001, 1195–1235.

Eckel, Carsten and J. Peter Neary, "Multi-product Firms and Flexible Manufacturing in the Global Economy," *Review of Economic Studies*, 77(1), 2010, 188–217.

Feenstra, Robert C., "New Product Varieties and the Measurement of International Prices," *American Economic Review*, 84(1), 1994, 157–77.

Feenstra, Robert C., Dorsati Madani, Tzu-Han Yang, and Chi-Yuan Liang, "Testing Endogenous Growth in South Korea and Taiwan," *Journal of Development Economics*, 60(2), 1999, 317–41.

Fisman, Raymond and T. Khanna, "Facilitating Development: The Role of Business Groups," *World Development*, 32(4), 2004, 609–28.

Goldberg, Pinelopi K., Amit K. Khandelwal, Nina Pavcnik, and Petia Topalova, "Trade Liberalization and New Imported Inputs," *American Economic* Review, 99(2), 2010a, 494–500.

Goldberg, Pinelopi K., Amit K. Khandelwal, Nina Pavcnik, and Petia Topalova, "Imported Intermediate Inputs and Domestic Product Growth: Evidence From India," *Quarterly Journal of Economics*, 125(4), 2010b, 1727–67.

Goldberg, Pinelopi K., Amit K. Khandelwal, Nina Pavcnik, and Petia Topalova, "Multi-product Firms and Product Turnover in the Developing World: Evidence from India," *Review of Economics and Statistics*, 92(4), 2010c, 1042–49.

Goyal, S. K., "Political Economy of India's Economic Reforms," Institute for Studies in Industrial Development (ISID) Working Paper, 1996.

Hasan, Rana, Devashish Mitra, and K. V. Ramaswamy, "Trade Reforms, Labor Regulations and Labor Market Elasticities: Empirical Evidence from India," *Review of Economics and Statistics*, 89, 2007, 466–81.

Kasahara, Hiroyuki and Joel Rodrigue, "Does the Use of Imported Intermediates Increase Productivity? Plant-level Evidence," *Journal of Development Economics*, 87(1), 2008, 106–18.

Khandelwal, Amit, "The Long and Short (of) Quality Ladders," *Review of Economic Studies*, 77(4), 2010, 1450–76.

Khandelwal, Amit, "Research Brief—Trade Liberalizations: Evidence from India," *Columbia CaseWorks*, 090315, 2009.

Klenow, Peter J. and Andres Rodriguez-Clare, "Quantifying Variety Gains from Trade Liberalization," Penn State University, unpublished manuscript, 1997.

Kochhar, Kalpana, Utsav Kumar, Raghuram Rajan, Arvind Subramanian, and Ioannis Tokatlidis, "India's Pattern of Development: What Happened, What Follows," *Journal of Monetary Economics*, 53(5), 2006, 981–1019.

Krishna, Pravin and D. Mitra, "Trade Liberalization, Market Discipline and Productivity Growth: New Evidence from India," *Journal of Development Economics*, 56(2), 1998, 447–62.

Kugler, Maurice and E. Verhoogen, "The Quality-Complementarity Hypothesis: Theory and Evidence from Colombia," NBER Working Paper 14418, 2008.

Mitter, Bhaskar, "The Metal Box Company of India Limited: Review by the Chairman, Mr Bhaskar Mitter," *Economic and Political Weekly*, 5(28), 1970.

Mukerji, Purba, "Trade Liberalization and the Extensive Margin," *Scottish Journal of Political Economy*, 56(2), 2009.

Nouroz, H., *Protection in Indian Manufacturing: An Empirical Study* (Delhi: MacMillan India Ltd., 2001).

Panagariya, Arvind, "India's Trade Reform," *India Policy Forum*, 2004, 1, 1–57.

Panagariya, Arvind, *India: The Emerging Giant* (New York: Oxford University Press, 2008).

Rivera-Batiz, Luis and Paul M. Romer, "Economic Integration and Endogenous Growth," *Quarterly Journal of Economics*, 106(2), 1991, 531–55.

Romer, Paul M., "Growth Based on Increasing Returns Due to Specialization," *American Economic Review*, 77(2), 1987, 56–62.

Romer, Paul M., "Endogenous Technological Change," *Journal of Political Economy*, 98(5), 1990, 71–102.

Schott, Peter K, "Across-Product versus Within-Product Specialization in International Trade," *Quarterly Journal of Economics*, 119(2), 2004, 647–78.

The Economist, "Plain Tales of the License Raj," May 4, 1991.

Topalova, Petia and A. K. Khandelwal, "Trade Liberalization and Firm Productivity: The Case of India," *The Review of Economics and Statistics*, 93(3), 2011, 995–1009.

CHAPTER 8

Reforms and the Competitive Environment

LAURA ALFARO AND ANUSHA CHARI

INTRODUCTION

In the mid-1980s, India's growth rate began accelerating, culminating at a rate of over 9 percent per annum by 2005. Thus far the extensive empirical literature has focused on characterizing India's aggregate economic performance. However, aggregate data do not shed light on the channels through which policy reform can transform the economy at the microlevel. In this chapter we examine the impact of the massive reforms that began in 1991 on the competitiveness of the Indian industrial environment using firm-level data.

The end of the License Raj and the implementation of pro-market reforms have had far-reaching implications for India's industrial structure. Significant sectors of the economy were opened up for private participation. India began to integrate into the world economy: import licensing was abolished in many sectors, import duties were sharply reduced, and many restrictions on foreign direct investment (FDI) were lifted. New firms emerged and many Indian firms established an international presence. Data from the Centre for Monitoring the Indian Economy (CMIE) record the birth of thousands of new private firms as the economy opened up. Within industries reforms have therefore had the capacity to transform the competitive environment in which firms operate.

Schumpeter (1942) argued that creative destruction, the replacement of old firms by new firms and of old capital by new capital, happens in waves. We argue that system-wide reform such as that implemented in India may be the shock that prompts a creative destruction wave and therefore provides an ideal backdrop against which to investigate the firm-level response to a changing competitive environment. In this chapter we survey recent evidence about the impact of these reforms on the competitive environment in India.

In previous research (Alfaro and Chari 2010), using a firm-level dataset, we document detailed stylized facts about the evolution of India's microeconomic industrial structure against the backdrop of the reforms (albeit piecemeal in nature) that began in the mid-1980s. We present information about the average number of firms and firm size (assets, sales) for the firms in our sample by sector as well as by owner-category of firm: state-owned enterprises, private firms incorporated before 1985 (old private firms), private firms incorporated after 1985 (new private firms), and foreign firms.

The data portray a dynamic economy driven by the growth of private and foreign firms. Consistent with the rapid growth observed after the mid-1980s, overall firm activity measured by the number of firms grew substantially relative to the beginning of the sample period. While one cannot infer causality from our findings, the increasing number of private and foreign firms suggests that the liberalization measures enacted to allow domestic entry through delicensing and de-reservation, combined with the liberalization of FDI, promoted ease of entry for firms other than the pre-reform incumbents (state-owned and traditional private firms incorporated before 1985). Indeed, the doubling (albeit from very low pre-reform levels) of the average number of foreign firms in this period suggests substantial foreign entry. This pattern is broadly mimicked for average assets and sales, by ownership type and sector.

Recent research predicts that the reforms related to liberalizing firm entry will lead to more firms and less incumbent power (Blanchard and Giavazzi 2003, Alesina et al. 2005). Other studies show that liberalization can lead to (i) increases in average firm size; (ii) increasing dispersion in sales, assets, profits; and (iii) increasing turnover and firm age distributions tilting towards younger firms (Melitz and Ottaviano 2008, Campbell and Hopenhayn 2005, Syverssen 2004, Asplund and Nocke 2006).[1]

Several studies have focused on the effects of trade liberalization on indigenous firms and have also uncovered substantial heterogeneity in firm performance within narrowly defined industries in both developed and developing countries (see Goldberg and Pavcnik 2004). Trade liberalization is found to have a positive effect in terms of efficient allocation of resources, in other words, higher output and productivity in manufacturing industries. In the case of India, Krishna and Mitra (1998) find that low-productivity plants contract and industry-level productivity increases following liberalization. Sivadasan (2006) and Topalova (2007) show similar results, while Arnold et al. (2008) find positive productivity effects from India's policy reform in services.

Firm-level data in several micro-studies come from the Prowess database collected by the CMIE from company balance sheets and income statements. Prowess covers both publicly listed and unlisted firms from a wide cross section of manufacturing, services, utilities, and financial industries from 1989–2005. About one-third of the firms in Prowess are publicly listed firms. The companies covered account for more than 70 percent of industrial output,

75 percent of corporate taxes, and more than 95 percent of excise taxes collected by the Government of India (CMIE). Prowess covers firms in the organized sector, which refers to registered companies that submit financial statements. (The fourth section of this chapter describes in detail the advantages and shortcomings of the dataset.)

The advantage of firm-level data is that detailed balance sheet and ownership information permit an investigation of a range of variables such as sales, profitability, and assets for more than 10,800 firms across our sample period (1989–2005). In Alfaro and Chari (2011), for instance, we focus on firms that are classified across sixty-two three-digit industries in the manufacturing sector. As Goldberg et al. (2009) note, unlike the Annual Survey of Industries (ASI), the Prowess data is a panel of firms, rather than a repeated cross section, and is therefore particularly well suited for understanding how firms adjust over time and how their responses may be related to policy changes. The data are also classified by incorporation year, so that distinctions can be made across firms by age. As a result, the data contain rich detail to characterize changes in firm size distributions, as well as differentiate across types of firms such as incumbents and new entrants.

The main findings in Alfaro and Chari (2011) are as follows. First, average firm size declines significantly in manufacturing industries that liberalize entry (domestic, foreign) consistent with small firm entry combined with import competition. Second, firm entry occurs from the left-hand tail of the size distribution with more small firms entering the market, while the largest incumbent firms get significantly bigger following deregulation. Third, the shift in the distribution of firm size is non-linear, with average firm size increasing till around the fifteenth percentile, and then getting significantly smaller till the ninetieth percentile, while the largest percentile (95 percent) gets significantly bigger over the same time period. Consistent with a decline in monopoly power, the Herfindahl index of firm sales also shows a significant decline.

A feature of firm entry and exit in India documented by some studies is the observation in Topalova (2007) that there seems to be very little exit at the firm level in India's industry. Goldberg et al. (2008) also find that net product creation following trade liberalization is almost exclusively driven by product addition as opposed to discontinuation of product lines, consistent with arguments in Panagariya (2008) about the slow transformation of the country following reforms. In concurrence with these findings, Alfaro and Chari (2010) document that creative destruction does not appear to characterize firm activity in the Indian context following liberalization. Consistent with the addition of product lines in Goldberg et al. (2009), there was substantial firm entry across all sectors and in particular in the services sectors. However, it does not appear that firm entry was also accompanied by firm exit.

The micro-evidence from firm-level data in Alfaro and Chari (2010, 2011) is related to research that has focused on different aspects of the recent evolution of the Indian economy (see for example Bosworth, Collins, and Virmani 2007; Rodrik and Subramanian 2005; Kochhar et al. 2006; Panagariya, 2004, 2008). Aghion et al. (2008) study the effects of the progressive elimination of the system of industrial regulation on entry and production (License Raj), registered manufacturing output, employment, entry and investment across Indian states with different labor market regulations. The effects vary depending on the institutional environment. Other recent work examines the effects of India's 1990s liberalization with an emphasis on bank lending (Cole 2009) and product mix and imported intermediate inputs (Goldberg et al. 2008, 2009). The authors find little evidence of "creative destruction" and no link between declines in tariffs on final goods induced by India's 1991 trade reform and product dropping.

The chapter is organized as follows. The second section provides a brief survey of recent empirical and theoretical literature on reforms and the competitive environment. The third section offers an overview of the main reforms in India. The fourth section describes the data, and the fifth presents summary statistics about the birth of new firms after reforms. The sixth section presents the main findings from Alfaro and Chari (2011), while the seventh section concludes.

THE RELEVANT LITERATURE

This study relates to the literature on the recent performance of the Indian economy as well as research studying the impact of liberalization on firm entry and the number of firms. It also refers more generally to work analyzing the effects on allocation of resources and economic growth. We discuss a few examples most closely related to our work.

There is an extensive empirical literature analyzing different aspects of India's economic growth. Work in this literature has focused on characterizing India's economic performance at the aggregate level to examine the relative contributions of factor accumulation and total factor productivity. Bosworth, Collins, and Virmani (2007), for example, use growth accounting techniques to analyze India's economic growth experience during 1960–2004, focusing on the post-1973 acceleration.

Aggregate data, however, cannot be used to examine the micro-channels that can impact economic growth. Firm-level data, on the other hand, offer a lens through which to examine transmission mechanisms that impact growth at the microlevel. Until recently, the literature focusing on firm-activity using micro-data, has however, predominantly focused on developed economies. The lack of data availability is an obvious constraint (see Tybout 2000).

More importantly, firms in developed economies operate in relatively unconstrained environments; in contrast, firms in developing countries often face constraints such as excessive regulation and underdeveloped financial markets. These constraints become particularly problematic when it comes to the ease with which resources can be reallocated across sectors and within firms. Liberalization policies in many emerging and developing nations have relaxed some of these constraints and changed the environment in which firms operate. These reforms provide an ideal setting to investigate the firm-level response to a changing economic environment.

Theories emphasizing the role of creative destruction highlight rapid output and input reallocation, product obsolescence, and changes in productivity levels as necessary ingredients for the pace of reallocation to play an important role in aggregate productivity growth. Schumpeter (1942) describes creative destruction in the following way: "The fundamental impulse that keeps the capital engine in motion comes from the new consumers' goods, the new methods of production and transportation, the new markets... [The process] incessantly revolutionizes from within, incessantly destroying the old one, incessantly creating a new one. This process of Creative Destruction is the essential fact of capitalism. It is what capitalism consists in and what every capitalist concern has got to live in." In addition to technological change, a system-wide reform or deregulation may prompt the creative destruction wave. Industries then go through a shakeout phase during which the number of producers in the industry declines, as incumbents and new entrants replace the firms that exit (see Caballero and Hammour 1996). Restructuring is one manifestation of creative destruction, by which the production structure weeds out unproductive segments; upgrades its technology, processes, and output mix; and adjusts to the evolving regulatory and global environment.

In macro-models of entry liberalization and deregulation, theoretical predictions about firm activity are ambiguous (see Blanchard and Giavazzi 2003, Alesina et al. 2009). Blanchard and Giavazzi (2003) develop a model of both labor market and product market regulation and their interconnection. Alesina et al. (2009) analyze a monopolistic competition model and show that deregulation of product markets has a positive effect on capital accumulation if it generates a reduction in the mark-up of prices over marginal costs (for instance through a reduction in entry barriers) or if it lowers costs of adjusting the capital stock. Reducing entry barriers and implementing reforms that lead to a reduction in price markups in excess of marginal cost are likely to lead to an increase in the number of firms. Reduction in red tape, for example, can also affect the desired number of firms, while for certain firms, removing constraints on rates of returns (especially ceilings restrictions) could have a negative impact.[2]

In the trade literature, recent work using monopolistic competition models with heterogeneous firms highlights the point that opening up trade leads to reallocation of resources across firms within an industry. Trade liberalization is widely believed to have pro-competitive effects that are ruled out by assumption in most models (constant elasticity of substitution preferences implying constant markups). In contrast, in a world of variable markups, import competition could have differential effects on firms of different productivities through endogenous changes in markups. In Melitz (2003), for example, opening up trade leads to changes in firm composition within industries, along with improvements in aggregate industry productivity under exogenously determined levels of firm productivity: low productivity firms exit; surviving intermediate productivity firms contract; and high productivity firms enter export markets and expand. In the standard version of the model, there is firm selection into export markets but no feedback from exporting to firm productivity (see Bustos 2011 and Lileeva and Trefler 2010). In a world of variable markups, import competition could have differential effects on firms of different productivities and pro-competitive effects through endogenous changes in mark-ups (see Melitz and Ottaviano 2008).

For the Indian case, theory suggests that the number of firms operating within industries can change through entry and exit in the face of deregulation. Most models, however, assume that firms are able to efficiently allocate resources within the firm and that factor markets are frictionless. Goldberg et al. (2009) argue that remnants of industrial regulation still affect the operation of Indian firms and may constrain their flexibility to adjust to new economic conditions. Some of their results also suggest that declines in tariffs are associated with somewhat bigger changes in firms' product scope in industries that were no longer subject to licenses at the onset of the 1991 reform compared to those that were still regulated.

In India, evidence suggests that despite the extensive industrial deregulation in the early 1990s, remnants of industrial licensing and rigid labor market regulations may continue to affect the daily operations of Indian firms, potentially precluding them from eliminating unprofitable product lines. For example, a federal amendment to the Industrial Disputes Act (1947) in 1982 required firms with more than one hundred employees to seek government approval to dismiss workers (Kochhar et al. 2006).

In addition, liquidation procedures are cumbersome and long. As noted by Panagariya, "India operates in a world with virtually no exit doors" (2008). According to the World Bank (2005), India's bankruptcy rate was 4 per 10,000 firms, compared with 15 in Thailand and 350 in the United States. Our findings corroborate this observation. While there was dynamism in firm entry following liberalization, particularly by private and foreign firms, we observe little incumbent firm exit. Taken together, traditional incumbents like state and group-owned firms account for almost 80 percent of firms assets, sales, and profits throughout our sample period.

As mentioned, many studies have emphasized the gains in aggregate output that arise when policy reforms or changes in market fundamentals induce reallocation of resources. In the case of India, Krishna and Mitra (1998) find a contraction of low-productivity plants and an increase in industry-level productivity following liberalization. Similar results are shown in Sivadasan

(2006) and Topalova (2007), while Arnold et al. (2008) find positive productivity effects from India's policy reform in the services sector as well.

Aghion et al. (2008) find differential effects of liberalization on manufacturing output, employment, entry, and investment across Indian states with different labor market regulation. Besley and Burgess (2004) show that Indian states which amended their labor regulations in a pro-worker direction experienced lowered output, employment, and productivity. Hsieh and Klenow (2009) use plant-level information from Indian census data to measure dispersion in the marginal products of capital and labor within four-digit manufacturing sectors. When capital and labor are hypothetically reallocated to equalize marginal products to the extent observed in the United States, the authors find efficiency gains of 50–60 percent in India.[3] As noted by Klenow (2008), the importance of allocative efficiency has been validated by the fact that growth took off in India in the wake of policy reforms.

Our work contributes to this literature by analyzing both the evolution of firm entry and measures of competitiveness as proxies for the efficiency-enhancing role of reforms and thus provides an understanding of the effectiveness of reforms. In fact, a growing literature argues that not only the level of factor accumulation, but also how these factors are allocated across heterogeneous production units, matters in trying to understand income differences (see Hsieh and Kelnow 2009, Restruccia and Rogerson 2008, Alfaro et al. 2008). In other words, the great divide between rich and poor countries may not be explained merely by the lack of capital and skilled labor but also as a consequence of the misallocation or misuse of available resources.

In addition to the literature studying the evolution of India's economy and the effects of current reforms, our work more generally relates to literature studying effects of liberalization (in particular those that use firm-level data). Alfaro and Charlton (2007) study the effects on firm activity for capital account liberalization in a sample of developed and developing economies after 1999. Chari and Henry (2008) and Galindo et al. (2007) study whether capital account liberalization has increased the efficiency of the allocation of investment in publicly traded firms in the liberalizing economies. The literature also suggests that reforms may be captured by powerful interests (Kroszner and Strahan 1999, Chari and Gupta 2008), so new firms may not benefit from liberalization.

The next section provides a brief overview of the reforms that impacted new firm entry in India.

REFORMS IN INDIA

Liberalization in India encompassed a series of reforms including foreign entry and trade liberalization, industrial delicensing, and de-reservation measures.

In this section, we provide a broad overview of the reforms and refer the reader to studies that provide in-depth detail about specific reform measures.

Topalova (2007) provides a detailed overview of trade policy reform following the conditionalities imposed by the 1991 IMF program. Benchmarks set forth under those conditions included reduction in the level and dispersion of tariffs, removal of quantitative restrictions on imported inputs and capital goods for export production, and elimination of public-sector monopoly on imports of almost all items.

It is important to note that the most significant initial trade reform was the removal of import licensing for capital and intermediate goods. However, tariff rates remained extremely high in the initial reform period. For example, the top tariff was brought down from 350 percent to 150 percent. Moreover, the 22 percent devaluation of the rupee further shielded the domestic industry from import competition, at least temporarily (Panagariya 2008).

The government's export-import policy plan (1992–97), however, dramatically reduced the use of quantitative restrictions. The share of products subject to quantitative restrictions decreased from 87 percent in 1987–88 to 45 percent in 1994–95; all twenty-six import-licensing lists were eliminated and a "negative" list was established. Restrictions on exports were also relaxed, with the number of restricted items falling from 439 in 1990 to 210 in 1994 (Topalova 2007).

Tariff reductions took place in seventy-seven industrial categories, and tariffs across a wide range of industries fell from a simple average of about 85 percent in 1990 to a value of approximately 12 percent in 2007 (Panagariya 2008). The top tariff dropped from 50 percent in 1995–96 to 40 percent in 1997–98, 35 percent in 2000–01, 30 percent in 2002–03, 25 percent in 2003–04, 20 percent in 2004–05, 15 percent in 2005–06, 12.5 percent in 2006–07, and 10 percent in 2007–08. Since some tariff peaks were outside the top rate, the simple average of tariffs on industrial goods in 2007 was approximately 12 percent. Custom duty collection in 2005–06 as a proportion of merchandise imports was just 4.9 percent (Panagariya 2008). Topalova (2007) also notes that the standard deviation of tariffs dropped by approximately 63 percent during the period between 1987–2001 (figure 8.1, panel A).[4] At the industry level, although there was variation across industries, the sharpest drop in tariffs took place between 1991 and 1992.

Historically, the Industrial Development and Regulation Act (IDR) was enacted in 1951 with the objective of empowering the government to take necessary steps to regulate the pattern of industrial development through licensing. This paved the way for the Industrial Policy Resolution of 1956, which was the first comprehensive statement on the strategy for industrial development in India and outlined steps for extensive state ownership.

The trend toward delicensing and de-reservation began with the industrial policy statements in 1985 that outlined many liberalization measures,

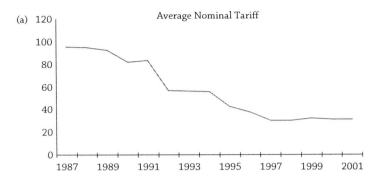

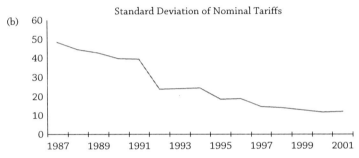

Figure 8.1
Trade Reform in India, 1987–2001

including not restricting business houses to Appendix 1 industries provided they moved to industrially backward regions, and allowing business houses to expand their asset base. The pace of these policy trends accelerated with the New Industrial Policy outlined in the Industrial Policy Resolution of 1991.

Compulsory industrial licensing was abolished for all except eighteen industries. Large companies no longer needed Monopolies and Restrictive Trade Practices Act (MRTP) approval for capacity expansions. The number of industries reserved for the public sector in Schedule A from the Industrial Policy Resolution of 1956 was cut from seventeen to eight.[5] Schedule B, which listed industries open to the private sector but with increasing involvement from the state—particularly for new establishments—was abolished altogether. These industries included minerals, aluminum, and other non-ferrous metals not listed in schedule A; machine tools; basic intermediate products required by the chemicals industries; antibiotics and other essential drugs; synthetic rubber; fertilizers; and road and sea transport. Importantly, limits on foreign equity holdings were raised from 40 to 51 percent (for industries listed in Annexure III of the Statement of Industrial Policy in 1991) under the "automatic approval route." The Industrial Policy Resolution of 1991 (Office of the Economic Advisor 2001) provides information about the list of manufacturing industries in which the state liberalized foreign entry and also a list of industries for which domestic entry restrictions continued to be in effect.

FIRM-LEVEL DATA FROM THE PROWESS DATASET

Firm-level data come from the Prowess database; its sample period is from the year of inception of dataset, from 1989 to 2005. The Prowess database has now been used in several studies, including Bertrand et al. (2002), Khanna and Palepu (1999), Fisman and Khanna (2004), Khanna and Palepu (2005), Topalova (2007), Chari and Gupta (2008), and Goldberg et al. (2008, 2009). The data are collected by the CMIE from company balance sheets and income statements and cover both publicly listed and unlisted firms from a wide cross section of manufacturing, services, utilities, and financial industries. About one-third of the firms in Prowess are publicly listed firms. The companies covered account for more than 70 percent of industrial output, 75 percent of corporate taxes, and more than 95 percent of excise taxes collected by the Government of India.

Prowess covers firms in the organized sector, which refers to registered companies that submit financial statements. According to the government, "The organized sector comprises enterprises for which the statistics are available from the budget documents or reports etc. On the other hand the unorganized sector refers to those enterprises whose activities or collection of data is not regulated under any legal provision or do not maintain any regular accounts" (Government of India 2000). Indian firms are required by the 1956 Companies Act to disclose in their annual reports information on capacities, production, and sales. All listed companies are included in the database whether financials are available or not. Unlisted companies are not required to disclose their financials. (CMIE asks permission to include these companies in Prowess, but cannot do so if they refuse.)

The Indian National Industrial Classification (NIC) (1998) system is used to classify firms in the Prowess dataset into industries. The data include firms from a wide range of industries, including mining, basic manufacturing, financial and real estate services, and energy distribution. The evidence in the sixth section of this chapter focuses on the manufacturing sector.

The main advantage of firm-level data is that detailed balance sheet and incorporation information allow an analysis of new firm entry as well as how incumbent firms are impacted by policy changes that allow new firm entry, such as liberalization. In contrast, industry-level databases usually do not provide information about sales, assets, and profits by incorporation year, and hence firm age. Since firms are not required to report employment in their annual reports, we observe employment data for only a more restricted sample of firms. Financial Services is the only industry that is mandated by law to disclose employment information. Since the sample of firms that report employment is small, we do not focus on these numbers.

The data allow us to examine a variety of firm characteristics by incumbent and new entrant status and by industry. For example, we can examine changes in the number and size of firms, the fractions of sales, and assets by ownership category or by industry. We can also examine changes in firm activity and market dynamics in industries where entry restrictions, both foreign and domestic, were lifted. Appendix table 8.A1 provides a description of variables used in the data analysis.

Goldberg et al. (2009) argue that the Prowess dataset is not a manufacturing census and, given that it includes only larger firms for which entry and exit are not important margins of adjustment, it may not be ideal for studying firm entry and exit. However, it is pertinent to note that unlike the ASI, which is a survey of manufacturing, the Prowess data is a panel of firms, rather than a repeated cross section. Prowess is therefore particularly well suited to examining how firm characteristics—including entry and exit—evolve over time and may respond to policy changes. For instance, Goldberg et al. (2009) use the Prowess dataset to examine how firms adjust their product mix over time. New products that are introduced into the market by firms not covered by Prowess are also excluded from their study. In our analysis, firms that no longer report sales or assets are assumed to have exited. We also classify firms that do not report data because of mergers and acquisitions as firms that exit due to consolidation.

REFORMS AND THE BIRTH OF NEW FIRMS

We study five subperiods: 1988–90, 1991–94, 1994–98, 1999–2002, and 2003–05. These periods broadly match the different waves of liberalization. Our objective is to provide the reader with an overview of new firm entry in the manufacturing sector in the last twenty years. We present deflated data using the GDP deflator from the World Bank's World Development Indicators. Appendix table 8.A2 presents detailed information on the industries included in each sector and the number of firms by sector.

The columns in table 8.1 present data on the average number of firms by sector. The table shows information for the full sample of data consolidated by sector. Consistent with the rapid growth observed in India after the mid-1980s, overall firm activity as proxied by the number of firms grew substantially relative to the beginning of the sample period.

Alfaro and Chari (2010) show that growth rates in the average number of new private firms across sectors (agriculture, manufacturing, and services) increased from 3,031 in 1988–1990 to close to 8,864 by 2005. The number of foreign firms increased from an average of 533 in 1988–1990 to 748 by 2005.

Table 8.1 INDUSTRIAL COMPOSITION—AVERAGE NUMBER OF
MANUFACTURING FIRMS, 1988–2005

Industry/Period	1988–1990	1991–1994	1995–1998	1999–2002	2003–2005
Food, Text., Pap. Mfg	1,983	2,494	2,637	2,473	2,144
Chem., Plastics Mfg.	1,853	2,242	2,309	2,128	1,901
Metals, Ind. Mfg	2,204	2,578	2,747	2,545	2,272
Misc. diversified	246	338	506	559	547

Source: Prowess Data Set. See Appendix tables A1 and A2 for detailed explanation of variables.

While one cannot infer causality from this pattern, following the different wave of reforms in the mid-1980s and early 1990s, the increasing number of not just private but also foreign firms suggests that the liberalization measures promoted more dynamic firm entry than before the reforms (state-owned and traditional private firms incorporated before 1985).

In this previous work, we also show that these patterns are broadly mimicked within sectors. For example, in food production, textiles and paper manufacturing, chemicals and plastic manufacturing, and metals and industrial manufacturing, the number of private and foreign firms increased substantially between 1988 and 2005. Overall, table 8.1 presents a picture of a dynamic economy witnessing the birth of many new firms following reforms. In fact, the data suggest that 1988–1990 was already a period of great activity in terms of the number of firms. We examined growth in the number of firms for this particular period and found it to be substantial, ranging from 35 percent for foreign firms to 115 percent for new private firms. As mentioned, while the firm-level data precludes comparisons with the pre-1985 period, the evidence is consistent with arguments in Panagariya (2008) that the reforms of the 1980s opened wider the door to entry of new firms. Consistent with previous evidence, the data also suggest that the regime shift in India's growth path began in the mid-1980s.

We note that there was acceleration in entry in the period following 1991 that continued through the rest of the decade. Further, our findings corroborate observations of lingering exit restrictions. While the data in Alfaro and Chari (2010) present clear evidence of dynamism in firm entry—particularly by private and foreign firms—we observe little incumbent firm exit (notwithstanding methodological issues in the collection of the data).

Alfaro and Chari (2010) also present information on average assets of ownership type and sector (in constant rupees crore). Average assets have also grown in the last two decades, particularly for new private firms and firms in the foreign sector, although the initial values of assets under foreign ownership and private firms incorporated after 1985 were very low (the latter by construction). The evidence shows high accumulation of assets by private and foreign firms in all manufacturing sectors of the economy but particularly in food, textiles, and paper manufacturing. For sales (in constant rupees crore), much the same pattern emerges; new private firms also stand out in terms of the growth rate of their average profits.

REFORMS AND COMPETITION

Table 8.2 includes information on industry concentration (the Herfindahl index), firm size, and dispersion measures (coefficient of variation calculated by assets and sales). We present data for the full sample first and then by incumbents and new entrants. Note that the Herfindahl index is an indicator of the degree of competition among firms in an industry. It is defined as the square

Table 8.2 THE EVOLUTION OF FIRM SIZE AND FIRM PROFITS (CONSTANT RS. CRORE)

	1989 –1990	1991 –1995	1996 –1998	1999 –2002	2003 –2005
			Full Sample		
NIC3 Herfindahl index (sales)	0.33	0.28	0.25	0.25	0.24
Average firm size (assets Rs. crore)	69.15	58.11	64.77	62.70	57.56
Average firm size (sales Rs. crore)	73.63	62.11	61.46	58.11	60.96
Coefficient of variation of firm size (assets)	5.39	5.39	7.11	8.89	10.11
Coefficient of variation of firm size (sales)	5.49	5.49	6.32	6.77	7.88
			Incumbents		
Total market share (sales)	0.99	0.97	0.92	0.87	0.79
Average firm size (assets Rs. crore)	67.64	59.35	71.86	73.46	73.73
Average firm size (sales Rs. crore)	70.75	54.61	65.15	69.07	80.14
Coefficient of variation of firm size (assets)	5.32	6.11	5.63	6.18	7.27
Coefficient of variation of firm size (sales)	5.40	5.98	7.04	9.38	9.95
			New Entrants		
Total market share (sales)	0.01	0.04	0.10	0.16	0.24
Average firm size (assets Rs. crore)	22.71	14.76	21.26	42.72	25.77
Average Firm Size (sales Rs. crore)	27.90	12.24	10.85	19.08	22.64
Coefficient of variation of firm size (assets)	5.92	6.52	6.04	6.55	6.66
Coefficient of variation of firm size (sales)	1.88	2.55	2.64	5.91	4.59

Appendix 2 provides variable definitions.

of the market shares of each firm in an industry. (The value of the Herfindahl index can range from zero in perfectly competitive industries to 1 in single-producer monopolies.) All data are first expressed in constant rupees crore.

For the overall economy, table 8.2 shows a reduction in market concentration for the average firm throughout the sample period. The Herfindahl indices suggest an increased degree of competition among firms in India. This finding is consistent with the earlier evidence on increased firm activity and a more dynamic economy overall (Alfaro and Chari 2010).

The coefficient of variation (for both sales and assets) also indicates increased dispersion. In sum, what emerges is a picture of the average manufacturing firm in India growing smaller in terms of assets and sales, along with a substantial increase in heterogeneity among firms over the period.

We construct the average firm sales and assets measures by taking firm averages by year and industry and then averaging these measures across industries and years within a given time period. For example, the average firm asset size of Rs. (crore) 69.15 was constructed by taking the average of average firm assets by industry across industries and over the two year period 1989–90.

In terms of the differences in incumbent status, for the average incumbent firm, dispersion has also increased while the average incumbent firm has grown bigger. Although new entrants have also grown significantly in terms of sales and assets, it is striking to note that the incumbent firms are considerably bigger than the new entrants. This suggests, consistent with international evidence, that young firms tend to be small in size and that entry takes place from the left-hand tail of the size distribution. For new entrants, dispersion also increases during the sample period.

The total market share variable here refers to the fraction of sales accounted for by incumbent and new firms relative to the total sales in a particular industry. It is interesting to note that the average market share of incumbent firms in total sales declines from 99 percent to 79 percent between 1989 and 2005. Over the same period, the average market share of new entrants incorporated after 1991 increased from 1 percent to 24 percent.[6]

Table 8.3 presents information by year of incorporation (pre-1947, 1947–85, 1985–2005) for number of firms, firm size, assets, sales, and employment, as well as their evolution in the different periods of study. The oldest firm in the sample (Howrah Mills Company Ltd.) was incorporated in 1825; there are over 390 other manufacturing firms in the sample that were incorporated before independence. Some firms exit the sample through mergers. Many of these older firms (pre-independence), however, remain in operation following the reforms.

Tables 8.4a–c describe how firms evolved before and after in industries that enacted specific reforms: liberalization of foreign direct investment, trade liberalization, and domestic market deregulation.[7]

One interesting pattern that emerges from all three panels is that market concentration seems to have diminished dramatically for the affected industries

Table 8.3 YEAR OF INCORPORATION

	I	II	III	IV	V
Incorporation/	1988–	1991–	1996–	1999–	2003–
Period	1990	1995	1998	2002	2005
Pre-independence					
Assets (Rs. crore)	87	97	130	129	134
Sales (Rs. crore)	103	98	116	109	113
No. of firms = 390					
c1947–1985					
Assets (Rs. crore)	87	85	98	103	109
Sales (Rs. crore)	83	67	79	93	107
No. of firms = 1,486					
c1985–2005					
Assets (Rs. crore)	32	25	31	43	44
Sales (Rs. crore)	19	11	15	25	30
No. of firms = 3,303					

Source: Prowess Dataset. See Appendix tables 8.A1 and 8.A2 for detailed explanation of variables.

following domestic market deregulation, FDI deregulation, and trade liberalization. These results are consistent with declining incumbent monopoly power following liberalization and are perhaps not very surprising given the extent of previous regulation. The value of the Herfindahl index declines from 0.43 to 0.27 for industries that liberalized FDI, and from 0.48 to 0.27 and 0.26 for industries that liberalized trade and deregulated domestic entry, respectively.

The FDI reforms in 1991 reduced barriers to foreign entry in a subset of industries. According to the IPR of 1991, automatic approval was granted for foreign direct investment of up to 51 percent in forty-six of ninety-six three-digit industrial categories (Office of the Economic Advisor 2001). In the remaining fifty industries, the state continued to require that foreign investors obtain approval for entry.

Table 8.4a shows measures of market share, firm size, and dispersion averaged across sectors that were deregulated before FDI liberalization in the first column and after FDI liberalization in the second one. The top panel of the table shows the results for the whole sample, and the lower ones by incumbent. The sample is between 1989 and 1995 and restricted to industries that deregulated foreign investment; the policy of FDI liberalization was implemented in 1991.

For the average firm, market shares declined significantly in liberalized industries as did average firm sales and assets. Dispersion (both in terms of assets and sales) increased following the reforms. The average incumbent firm in the liberalized industries also experienced a decline in market shares and firm size. The coefficient of variation for incumbent firms increased somewhat.

Table 8.4 THE EVOLUTION OF FIRM SIZE & MARKET CONCENTRATION IN MANUFACTURING (LIBERALIZED INDUSTRIES)

Panel 3a: FDI Deregulation

	1989–1990	1991–1995
	Full Sample	
Herfindahl index	0.43	0.27
Market share (sales)	3.31	1.69
Firm size (assets Rs. crore)	65.47	49.87
Firm size (sales Rs. crore)	64.50	42.30
CV firm size (assets)	2.58	3.02
CV firm size (sales)	2.24	3.03
	Incumbents	
Market share (sales)	3.32	2.003
Firm size (assets Rs. crore)	67.1	61.58
Firm size (sales Rs. crore)	65.9	53.68
CV firm size (assets)	2.56	2.79
CV firm size (sales)	2.22	2.72

Panel 3b: Trade Liberalization

	1989–1990	1991–1995
	Full Sample	
Herfindahl index	0.48	0.27
Market share (sales)	2.69	1.36
Firm size (assets Rs. crore)	86.19	65.79
firm size (sales Rs. crore)	101.33	62.46
CV firm size (assets)	5.59	6.63
CV firm size (sales)	5.99	7.59
	Incumbents	
Market share (sales)	2.74	1.68
Firm size (assets Rs. crore)	89.75	84.9
Firm size (sales Rs. crore)	105.74	83.55
CV firm size (assets)	5.51	6.06
CV firm size (sales)	5.89	6.7

Panel 3c: Domestic Delicensing

	1989–1990	1991–1995
	Full Sample	
Herfindahl index	0.48	0.26
Market share (sales)	3.32	1.64
Firm size (Assets Rs. crore)	68.96	52.59
firm size (sales Rs. crore)	65.47	43.22
CV firm size (assets)	4.91	5.81
CV firm size (sales)	3.50	4.09
	Incumbents	
Market share (sales)	3.31	2.01
Firm size (assets Rs. crore)	71.8	66.3
Firm size (sales Rs. crore)	68.18	55.42
CV firm size (assets)	4.84	5.38
CV firm size (sales)	3.45	3.71

Source: Prowess Dataset. See Appendix tables 8.A1 and 8.A2 for detailed explanation of variables.

Table 8.4b presents similar results for trade liberalization. First, it is important to note that trade liberalization in 1991 was inversely related to industry concentration before 1991. Second, the market share and size of the average firm in industries that liberalized trade declined significantly in the five years following the policy change. Third, dispersion also increased following trade liberalization. A similar pattern emerges for incumbent firms. Finally, table 8.4c shows similar summary statistics for pre- and post-domestic market deregulation, showing a similar pattern of declining market shares and average firm size, as well as increased dispersion.

In conclusion, summary statistics suggest that industry concentration, average market shares, and firm size all declined in industries that experienced either delicensing or FDI trade liberalization. The coefficient of variation in average firm sales and assets increased, suggesting that there is greater dispersion in firm size within liberalized industries.

REFORMS, NEW ENTRANTS, AND INCUMBENTS: THE DISTRIBUTION OF FIRM SIZE

Table 8.5 presents detailed distributional statistics for firm size in terms of log sales and log assets before and after liberalization. For both assets and sales, the mean and median numbers suggest that firm size declined over the sample period; the pattern holds for incumbent firms as well. New entrants, on the other hand, experience an increase in firm size, perhaps not surprisingly.

Examining the tails of the size distribution reveals two interesting patterns. First, we see that the smallest firms in the left-hand tail of the size distribution have become smaller over time. The firms in the tenth percentile have grown considerably smaller over the post-liberalization period. The data also indicate that new entrants are much smaller than the incumbent firms in the lowest percentiles for both assets and sales.

Second, the largest firms have grown bigger. For all three samples—the full sample, incumbents, and new entrants—the largest firms in the ninety-ninth percentile have grown larger over time. It is particularly interesting to note the increase in the size of the largest new entrants.

These two patterns from the distributional data (small firms getting smaller and big firms bigger) are consistent with an increase in the standard deviation in the size distribution. Also, given the increase in the standard deviation of firm size and the fall in average firm size, it is perhaps not surprising that dispersion measured by the coefficient of variation in firm size rises.

While the largest firms increase in size, there also appears to be considerable entry from the left-hand tail of the distribution. The smallest incumbent firms also appear to get smaller. In addition, the average firm size falls, rather than rising as the trade models predict. The marginal entry of small firms is consistent with an increase in competition following entry deregulation.

Table 8.5 DISTRIBUTIONAL STATISTICS OF FIRM SIZE

	N	p10	Mean	p50	p99	Max	SD	CV	Skewness
				Log Sales					
				Full Sample					
1989–1990	3,084	1.63	3.14	3.03	6.83	9.59	1.42	0.45	0.02
1991–1995	14,675	0.23	2.41	2.51	6.37	9.91	1.83	0.76	−0.62
1991–2005	62,776	−0.49	2.12	2.33	6.42	10.81	2.10	0.99	−0.70

	N	p10	Mean	p50	p99	Max	SD	CV	Skewness
				Log Sales					
				Incumbents					
1989–1990	3,045	1.63	3.14	3.03	6.83	9.59	1.43	0.45	0.03
1991–1995	13,463	0.52	2.54	2.61	6.47	9.91	1.74	0.69	−0.55
1991–2005	48,454	−0.14	2.34	2.51	6.58	10.81	2.05	0.88	−0.73

	N	p10	Mean	p50	p99	Max	SD	CV	Skewness
				Log Sales					
				New Entrants					
1991–1995	1212	−1.86	0.93	1.17	4.72	5.86	2.04	2.19	−0.62
1991–2005	14,322	−1.39	1.40	1.68	5.53	9.33	2.10	1.50	−0.70

(*Continued*)

Table 8.5 CONTINUED

	N	p10	Mean	p50	p99	Max	SD	CV	Skewness
				Log Assets					
				Full Sample					
1989–1990	3,120	1.41	2.97	2.82	6.97	9.20	1.41	0.48	0.42
1991–1995	15,597	0.67	2.48	2.39	6.65	9.45	1.58	0.64	0.13
1991–2005	70,902	0.27	2.29	2.25	6.73	10.15	1.83	0.80	-0.30

	N	p10	Mean	p50	p99	Max	SD	CV	Skewness
				Log Assets					
				Incumbents					
1989–1990	3081	1.42	2.98	2.82	6.99	9.20	1.42	0.48	0.43
1991–1995	11,779	0.82	2.59	2.46	6.72	9.45	1.54	0.59	0.27
1991–2005	53,948	0.53	2.51	2.44	6.91	10.15	1.76	0.70	-0.09

	N	p10	Mean	p50	p99	Max	SD	CV	Skewness
				Log Assets					
				New Entrants					
1991–1995	1718	-0.40	1.44	1.47	4.90	7.00	1.52	1.06	-0.37
1991–2005	16,954	-0.45	1.58	1.67	5.65	8.93	1.87	1.18	-0.76

Source: Prowess Dataset. See Appendix tables 8.A1 and 8.A2 for detailed explanation of variables.

The final column of table 8.5 shows that the size distribution flattens and becomes negatively skewed following liberalization with the magnitude of skewness increasing over time. The size distribution in the early years following liberalization (1991–95) is more skewed in comparison to the pre-liberalization period (1989–1990), and the size distribution in the later years following liberalization (2003–05) is more skewed in comparison to the early years (1991–95). The shift in the pattern of skewness holds for both log assets and log sales, as well as for the incumbent firms. We do not conduct this analysis for the new entrants because they did not exist before liberalization.

CONCLUSION

India has engaged in a massive reform effort since 1991. The end of the License Raj and implementation of pro-market reforms have had far-reaching implications for competitiveness in the Indian economy. Significant sectors of the economy have been opened up for private participation through delicensing and allowing entry to industries previously reserved exclusively for the state-owned sector. Trade liberalization has also been considerable. Furthermore, many sectors of the economy have been opened to foreign entry via direct investment.

Nearly twenty years after the reforms began we ask whether liberalization in the manufacturing sector has led to more competition. We argue that an increase in competition may be measured in several ways. Deregulating entry may imply an increase in dispersion in firm size distributions, a reduction in concentration ratios, or a decline in average firm size. To examine the competitive effects of deregulating entry, we use firm-level data from the CMIE's Prowess database to examine the changes in firm size distributions.

The evidence suggests several interesting patterns. Average firm size declines significantly in industries that deregulated entry. Small firms enter the market from the left-hand tail of the size distribution, while the incumbent firms get significantly bigger following deregulation. Consistent with a decline in monopoly power, the Herfindahl index of firm sales also shows a significant decline. The dispersion of firm size (sales and assets) also rises following deregulation, consistent with Melitz and Ottaviano (2008), Campbell and Hopenhayen (2005), and Asplund and Nocke (2003).

On balance, the evidence suggests that the distributional changes in firm size reveal the more nuanced effects of deregulation. The marginal entry of small firms and the decline in the average size of firms in the middle percentiles appear consistent with the hypothesis that deregulation leads to entry, a larger number of firms in the long run, and the reduction in the monopoly power of incumbent firms. However, the increase in the size of the largest firms suggests that it is important to take into account the possible non-linear effects of entry reforms on competition.

ACKNOWLEDGMENT

Work on this chapter has been supported by Columbia University's Program on Indian Economic Policies, funded by a generous grant from the John Templeton Foundation. The opinions expressed in the chapter are those of the authors and do not necessarily reflect the views of the John Templeton Foundation.

APPENDIX

Table 8.A1 DESCRIPTION OF VARIABLES

Variables	Definition
State-owned (SOE)	Firms majority owned by the federal and state governments.
Traditional private firms	Includes firms majority owned by a business group and private firms not affiliated to a group incorporated before 1985. Indian business groups or family-owned firms are groups of companies that are controlled by the same shareholders, usually all members of a family.
New private firms	Includes firms majority owned by a business group and private firms not affiliated to a group incorporated after 1985.
Foreign firms	Firms incorporated overseas.
Sales	Sales generated by a firm from its main business activity measured by charges to customers for goods supplied and services rendered. Excludes income from activities not related to main business, such as dividends, interest, and rents in the case of industrial firms, as well as non-recurring income. Data in constant Rs. crore (deflated by GDP deflator from World Bank, WDI).
Assets	Gross fixed assets of a firm, which include movable and immovable assets as well as assets which are in the process of being installed. Data in constant Rs. crore (deflated by GDP deflator from World Bank, WDI).
Firm size (assets & sales)	Average firm assets, sales, and profits in an industry. For the full sample, the industry-level averages are averaged across industries. Data in constant Rs. crore (deflated by GDP deflator from World Bank, WDI).
SOE share	The ratio of total sales and assets accounted by state-owned firms in an industry to industry sales and industry assets in that industry.
Traditional firms share	The ratio of total sales and assets accounted by private firms incorporated before 1985 in an industry to industry sales and industry assets in that industry.

Table 8.A1 DESCRIPTION OF VARIABLES

Variables	Definition
New private firms share	The ratio of total sales and assets accounted for by private firms incorporated after 1985 in an industry to industry sales and industry assets in that industry.
Foreign share	The ratio of total sales and assets accounted by foreign firms in an industry to industry sales and industry assets in that industry.
Herfindahl index	Sum of the squares of the market share of all firms in an industry in each 3-digit industrial category.
Coefficient of variation	Ratio of standard deviation to mean of assets and sales at the industry level.
Tade liberalization measure	Percentage decrease in tariffs at the 3-digit industry level between 1986–90 and 1991–95.
NIC code	Three-digit industry code includes manufacturing, financial, and service sectors.

Table 8.A2 MANUFACTURING INDUSTRY CLASSIFICATIONS

Industry	3-digit NIC Code	# Firms	Industry	3-digit NIC Code	# Firms
Abrasives	269	13	Dyes & pigments	241, 242	99
Air-cond. & refrigerators	291, 293	23	Dyes & pigments	242	13
Alkalies	241	17	Fertilizers	241	77
Alum. & alum. products	272	76	Footwear	192	73
Automobile ancillaries	343	424	Gems & jewelry	369	121
Bakery products	154	29	General purpose machinery	291	109
Beer & alcohol	155	137	Generators & switchgears	289, 291, 311, 312, 319	143
Books & cards	210, 221, 222	80	Glass & glassware	261	68
Castings & forgings	273, 289	173	Industrial machinery	291, 292, 300	185
Cement	269	159	Inorganic chemicals	241, 242	115
Ceramic tiles	269	72	Inorganic chemicals	242	1
Cloth	171	218	Lubricants, etc.	232	66
Coal & lignite	231	16	Machine tools	292	75
Cocoa products	154	12	Marine foods	151	101
Coffee	154	21	Media-print	221	46
Commercial vehicles	341	8	Metal products	271, 281, 289, 361	283

(Continued)

Table 8.A2 CONTINUED

Industry	3-digit NIC Code	# Firms	Industry	3-digit NIC Code	# Firms
Communication equipment	319, 322, 331	71	Milling products	153, 155	76
Comp., perip. & storage dev.	221, 252, 300	79	Misc. electrical machinery	269, 291, 292, 312, 319	64
Construction equipment	291, 292	53	Misc. manufactured articles	232, 331, 332, 333, 361, 369	99
Consumer electronics	300, 321, 323	43	Organic chemicals	241	176
Copper & copper products	272	45	Other agricultural products	155	4
Cosmetics, toiletries, soaps & detergents	242	118	Other chemicals	241, 242, 293, 300, 311, 312, 314, 319, 321, 323, 331	441
Cotton & blended yarn	171	453	Other industrial machinery	172, 291, 292	30
Dairy products	152, 154	69	Other leather products	191	62
Domestic elec. appliances	289, 292, 293, 315	76	Other non-ferrous metals	272	43
Drugs & pharmaceuticals	242	626	Other non-metallic mineral prod.	269	37
Dry cells	314	7	Other recreational services	223, 253	3
Processed/packaged foods	151–155	55	Other storage & distribution	232	7
Prod., distrib. & exh. films	242	1	Other textiles	171–173, 181, 252	261
Readymade garments	181	199	Other transports equipment	351–353, 359	48
Polymers	241	83	Paints & varnishes	242	44
Poultry & meat products	151, 154	18	Paper	210	205
Prime movers	281, 291	37	Paper products	210	66
Prime movers	291	26	Pass. cars & multi-utility vehicles	341	12
Processed/packaged foods	151–155	55	Pesticides	241, 242	115
Prod., distrib. & exh. films	242	1	Pig iron	271	13

Table 8.A2 CONTINUED

Industry	3-digit NIC Code	# Firms	Industry	3-digit NIC Code	# Firms
Readymade garments	181	199	Plastic films	252	56
Refinery	232	15	Plastic packaging goods	252	137
Refractories	269	43	Plastic tubes & sheets, others	252	219
Rubber & rubber products	241, 251	105	Polymers	241	83
Sponge iron	271	32	Poultry & meat products	151, 154	18
Starches	153	13	Prime movers	281, 291	37
Steel	271	488	Prime movers	291	26
Steel tubes & pipes	271	111	Storage batteries	314	12
Sugar	154	147	Trading	293	1
Synthetic textiles	171–172, 243	158	Two & three wheelers	359	22
Tea	154	214	Tyres & tubes	251	42
Textile processing	171, 243	176	Vegetable oils & products	151–153	307
Tobacco products	155, 160, 369	30	Wires & cables	313	110
Tractors	292	14	Wood	201, 202	53
Housing construction	452	177		261	1
Industrial construction	452	156		343	1
Infrastructural construction	452	91	Diversified	970	63
Other constr. & allied act.	452, 453	159	Misc. manufactured articles	970	695

NOTES

1. A monopolistic competition assumption in the goods market determines the size of rents.
2. In some network industries, such as utilities and telecommunications, reforms entailing service liberalization and price rules for accessing networks can have conflicting influences on investment.
3. Hsieh and Klenow (2009) use data from India's Annual Survey of Industries (ASI) from 1987–88 through 1994–95.

4. Data for Figure 8.1 were generously provided by Petia Topalova.
5. According to the Industrial Policy Resolution (1948), Schedule A comprised among others (i) industries exclusively reserved for the state (atomic energy, arms and ammunition, and railways) and (ii) basic industries where the state would have the exclusive right to undertake new investments (iron and steel, mineral oils, coal, shipbuilding, aircraft production, and telecommunications equipment). Other categories included eighteen industries of national importance regulated and licensed in cooperation with state governments and industries open to private-sector participation. The Industrial Policy Resolution (1956) included the nine industries in categories (i) and (ii) of IPR 1948 and added eight additional industries including mining sectors, air transportation, and some heavy industries.
6. Note that the market shares of incumbents and new entrants do not sum to exactly 100 percent for the following reason. The total market share measure for incumbents was constructed by taking the ratio of total incumbent sales to total industry sales by NIC3 industry and taking an average of this ratio across industries. Similarly, the total market share of new entrants was constructed by taking the ratio of total new entrant sales to total industry sales by NIC3 industry and then averaging this ratio across industries.
7. Variations in the number of industries in table 8.4a before and after liberalization reflect entry or exit by different owner categories into industries that were liberalized. The number of industries in the results for the full sample gives the maximum number of liberalized industries.

REFERENCES

Aghion, P., R. Burgess, S. Redding, and F. Zilibotti, 2008. "The Unequal Effects of Liberalization: Evidence from Dismantling the License Raj in India," *American Economic Review* 94, 1397–1412.

Alesina, A., S. Ardagna, G. Nicoletti, and F. Schiantarelli, 2005. "Regulation and Investment," *Journal of the European Economic Association* 3, 791–825.

Alfaro, L., and A. Chari, 2010. "India Transformed? Insights from the Firm Level 1988–2007," *Brookings India Policy Forum Journal* 6, 155–228.

Alfaro, L., and A. Chari, 2011. "Deregulation, Competition and Firm Size: Evidence from India," working paper.

Alfaro, L., and A. Charlton, 2007. "International Financial Integration and Entrepreneurial Firm Dynamics." NBER Working Paper No. 13118.

Alfaro, L., A. Charlton, and F. Kanczuk, 2008. "Plant-Size Distribution and Cross-Country Income Differences." In *NBER International Seminar on Macroeconomics*, edited by Jeffrey A. Frankel. Cambridge, Mass: NBER.

Arnold J., B. Javorcik, M. Lipscomb, and A. Mattoo, 2008. "Services Reform and Manufacturing Performance: Evidence from India," University of Oxford working paper.

Asplund, M., and V. Nocke, 2006. "Firm Turnover in Imperfectly Competitive Markets," *Review of Economic Studies* 73, 295–327.

Bertrand, M., P. Mehta, and S. Mullainathan, 2002. "Ferreting out Tunneling: An Application to Indian Business groups," *Quarterly Journal of Economics* 117, 121–48.

Besley, T., and R. Burgess, 2004. "Can Labor Regulation Hinder Economic Performance? Evidence from India," *Quarterly Journal of Economics* 119, 91–134.

Blanchard, O., and F. Giavazzi, 2003. "Macroeconomic Effects of Regulation and Deregulation in Goods and Labor Market," *Quarterly Journal of Economics* 118, 879–908.

Bosworth, B., S. Collins, and A. Virmani, 2007. "Sources of Growth in the Indian Economy," *Brookings India Policy Forum Journal* 3, 1–69.

Bustos, P., 2011. "Trade Liberalization, Exports and Technology Upgrading: Evidence on the Impact of MERCOSUR on Argentinean Firms," *American Economic Review* 101, 304–40.

Caballero, R., and M. Hammour, 1996. "On the Timing and Efficiency of Creative Destruction," *Quarterly Journal of Economics* 446, 805–52.

Campbell, J. R., and H. A. Hopenhayn, 2005. "Market Size Matters," *Journal of Industrial Economics* 53, 1–25.

Chari, A., and N. Gupta, 2008. "Incumbents and Protectionism: The Political Economy of Foreign Entry Liberalization," *Journal of Financial Economics* 88, 33–656.

Chari, A. and P. B. Henry, 2004. "Risk Sharing and Asset Prices: Evidence from a Natural Experiment," *Journal of Finance* 59, 1295–1324.

Centre for Monitoring the Indian Economy, Prowess Dataset. http://www.cmie.com/database/?service=database-products/firm-level-data-services/prowess-corporate-database.htm.

Cole, S. A., 2009. "Financial Development, Bank Ownership, and Growth. Or, Does Quantity Imply Quality?" *The Review of Economics and Statistics* 91, 33–51.

Fisman, R., and T. Khanna, 2004. "Facilitating Development: The Role of Business Groups," *World Development* 32, 609–28.

Galindo, A., F. Schiantarelli, and A. Weiss, 2007. "Does Financial Reform Improve the Allocation of Investment? Micro Evidence from Developing Countries," *Journal of Development Economics* 83, 562–87.

Goldberg, P., A. Khandelwal, N. Pavcnik, and P. Topalova, 2008. "Imported Intermediate Inputs and Domestic Product Growth: Evidence from India," NBER Working Paper 14416.

Goldberg, P., A. Khandelwal, N. Pavcnik, and P. Topalova, 2009. "Trade Liberalization and New Imported Inputs," *American Economic Review* 99, 494–500.

Goldberg, P., and N. Pavcnik, 2004. "Trade, Inequality, and Poverty: What Do We Know? Evidence from Recent Trade Liberalization Episodes in Developing Countries." In *Brookings Trade Forum*, edited by Susan Margaret Collins and Carol Graham. Washington, DC: Brookings Institution Press, 223–69.

Government of India, 2000. http://labour.nic.in/ss/INFORMALSECTORININDIA-approachesforSocialSecurity.pdf.

Hsieh, C.-T., and P. J. Klenow, 2009. "Misallocation and Manufacturing TFP in China and India," *Quarterly Journal of Economics* 124, 1403–48.

Industrial (Development and Regulation) Act, 1951. http://dipp.gov.in/English/Policies/Industries_act1951.pdf.

Industrial Policy Resolution, 1956. http://www.fipbindia.com/changes_files/changes/chap001.pdf.

Khanna, T., and K. Palepu, 1999. "Policy Shocks, Market Intermediaries and Corporate Strategy: The Evolution of Business Groups in Chile and India," *Journal of Economics & Management Strategy* 8, 271–310.

Khanna, T., and K. Palepu, 2005. "The Evolution of Concentrated Ownership in India: Broad Patterns and a History of the Indian Software Industry," in Randall Morck (ed.), *A History of Corporate Governance around the World: Family Business Groups to Professional Managers* (Chicago: University of Chicago Press).

Klenow, P., 2008. "Discussion On Big Answers for Big Questions: The Presumption of Macro," paper presented at The Brookings Institution Conference on "What Works in Development? Thinking Big and Thinking Small."

Kochhar, K., U. Kumar, R. Rajan, A. Subramanian, and I. Tokatlidis, 2006. "India's Pattern of Development: What Happened, What Follows," *Journal of Monetary Economics* 53, 981–1019.

Krishna, P., and D. Mitra, 1998. "Trade Liberalization, Market Discipline and Productivity Growth: New Evidence from India," *Journal of Development Economics* 56, 447–62.

Kroszner, R., and P. E. Strahan, 1999. "What Drives Deregulation? Economics and Politics of the Relaxation of Bank Branching Restrictions," *Quarterly Journal of Economics* 114, 1437–67.

Lileeva, A., and D. Trefler, 2010 "Improved Access to Foreign Markets Raises Plant-Level Productivity ... for Some Plants," *The Quarterly Journal of Economics* 125, 1051–99.

Melitz, M., 2003. "The Impact of Trade on Intra-Industry Reallocations and Aggregate Industry Productivity," *Econometrica* 71, 1695–725.

Melitz, M., and G. Ottaviano, 2008. "Market Size, Trade, and Productivity," *Review of Economic Studies* 75, 295–316.

Office of the Economic Advisor, 2001. *Handbook of Industrial Policy and Statistics*. Government of India, New Delhi.

Panagariya, A., 2004. "India in the 1980s and 1990s: A Triumph of Reforms," *IMF Staff Country Reports*, 1–37.

Panagariya, A., 2008. *India, the Emerging Giant* (New York: Oxford University Press).

Restuccia, D., and Rogerson, R. 2008. "Policy Distortions and Aggregate Productivity with Heterogeneous Plants," *Review of Economic Dynamics* 11, 707–20.

Rodrik, D., and A. Subramanian, 2005. "From Hindu Growth to Productivity Surge: The Mystery of the Indian Growth Transition," *IMF Staff Papers*, Vol. 52, No. 2, 193–228.

Schumpeter, J. A., 1942. *Capitalism, Socialism and Democracy* (London: Unwin University Books).

Sivadasan, J., 2006. "Productivity Consequences of Product Market Liberalization: Microevidence from Indian Manufacturing Sector Reforms," working paper.

Syverson, C., 2004. "Market Structure and Productivity: A Concrete Example," *Journal of Political Economy* 112, 1181–222.

Topalova, P., 2007. "Trade Liberalization and Firm Productivity: The Case of India," IMF Working Paper, WP/04/28.

Tybout, J., 2000. "Manufacturing Firms in Developing Countries: How Well Do They Do and Why?" *Journal of Economic Literature* 38, 11–44.

World Bank, 2005. "Improving the Investment Climate in India," South Asia Region and Investment Climate Unit. Washington, DC: World Bank.

PART THREE

Reforms and Social Transformation

CHAPTER 9

The Post-reform Narrowing of Inequality across Castes

Evidence from the States

VIKTORIA HNATKOVSKA AND AMARTYA LAHIRI

INTRODUCTION

One of the most enduring legacies of Indian society is the caste system. This social arrangement wherein groups are segmented into various "castes" has been around in various degrees of rigidity for over fifteen hundred years. The system originally was devised as a way of organizing the workforce by occupations. Over time, however, it gradually morphed into a social division by birth; that is, one was born into a caste rather than opting into it based on one's occupational choice. Given the implicit social ordering of different occupations, the system opened the door to systemic discrimination and social ostracization of groups that belonged to the castes that were typically associated with the most menial tasks. These groups, who are referred to as Dalits in modern India, were thus subjected to horrific social abuses as well as systemic economic discrimination as the upper castes denied them access to even basic amenities like local water and land, educational opportunities, and so on. The typical pretext for these acts was that these groups were "unclean"; upper castes would get "polluted" if they interacted with these lower castes.

Upon independence from Britain, India adopted a new constitution in 1950 in which special provision was made for these lowest castes by setting aside a certain proportion of seats in institutions of higher education, in public sector jobs, and in parliament. These reservations were intended to correct the thousands of years of social and economic discrimination endured by the "lowest" castes. The castes that received this affirmative action protection were listed under a specific schedule of the constitution and hence came to be known over time as Scheduled Castes and Tribes or SC/STs.

At the aggregate level, India has had two distinctly different phases. After over three decades of relatively tepid growth following independence in 1947, the period since the mid-1980s has been characterized by a sharp change in the economic fortunes of the country as a whole. Induced in part by a sequence of economic reforms, the average growth rate of GDP rose from around 3 percent to upwards of 6 percent annually. Such rapid aggregate changes often accompany large underlying distributional changes, with some sections gaining and others losing out in the process. Indeed, the effect of the reforms and aggregate changes on poverty has been the subject of some spirited debate among academics, observers, and policymakers alike.

In this chapter we focus on the fortunes of SC/STs since 1983. This period is particularly interesting to us due to its overlap with the economic takeoff of India. Given that SC/STs are historically the poorest and among the least educated groups, this focus allows us to potentially shed light on the effects of aggregate changes on the poor and disadvantaged. It has the additional benefit of possibly yielding insights regarding the efficacy of affirmative action programs, specifically the ones targeted toward SC/STs in India. This is of independent importance since it has now been over sixty years since the introduction of such constitutional protection for SC/STs, which means that about three generations of SC/STs have potentially been covered by them. Clearly, some empirical feedback regarding the performance of these programs is desirable.

In recent work on this topic, we have shown that the overall gaps between SC/STs and non-SC/STs in education and wages declined sharply between 1983 and 2004–05 (see Hnatkovska, Lahiri, and Paul 2012). Panel A of figure 9.1 shows the evolution of the ratio of mean years of education of non-SC/STs to SC/STs between 1983 and 2008. Panel B shows the evolution of the non-SC/ST mean and median wages relative to SC/ST wages. The two graphs reveal a similar pattern: the caste gaps in both education and wages have been declining secularly since 1983. A key finding in Hnatkovska, Lahiri, and Paul (2012) was that most of the measured wage convergence was due to convergence in the educational attainment levels of the two groups. Moreover, the occupation distributions and consumption levels of the two groups have also been converging, though the process has been more muted.

In related work, we also examined the intergenerational mobility rates of SC/STs and non-SC/STs during this period in terms of education, occupation, and wages (see Hnatkovska, Lahiri, and Paul 2011). There too we found that the overall intergenerational mobility rates of the two groups converged sharply between 1983 and 2004–05. In other words, SC/ST children were changing their status relative to their parents at faster rates than the non-SC/ST children. Moreover, we also found that education has played a key role in this process.

Our main conclusion from this work is that the past three decades have been special in the sense that they have been a period in which large historical caste disparities have begun to shrink sharply. Moreover, the educational

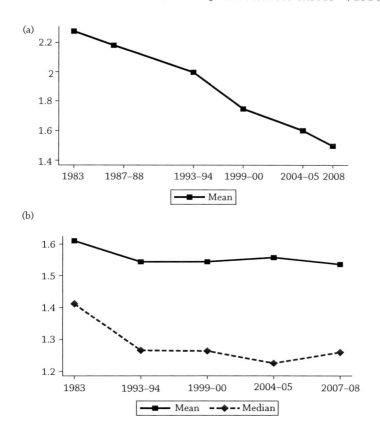

Figure 9.1
Education and Wage Convergence

convergence across the castes is particularly heartening, as it signals that disparities along caste lines are unlikely to widen in the near future. The big question though is what accounts for these dramatic changes? There are a number of candidate explanations. The aggregate growth takeoff may clearly have been important. The reservations policies in place since 1950 may have been another contributing factor as they may have aided the SC/STs in taking advantage of new opportunities that were opening up in a growing dynamic economy. The increasing political empowerment of Dalits over the past three decades may also have been influential.

In this chapter we attempt to evaluate these alternative explanations by exploiting the cross-state variation in the outcomes. Specifically, we use National Sample Survey (NSS) data from rounds 38 (1983), 43 (1987–88), 50 (1993–94), 55 (1999–2000), and 61 (2004–05). Our focus is on the comovements of the caste convergence indicators with state level indicators of growth and reservation quotas. Additionally, we also examine outcomes in some outlier states where Dalit political empowerment was particularly marked during this period.

We find that higher growth was almost always associated with faster convergence of educational attainment rates, wages, and consumption. However, the initial income levels of the states in 1983 tended to comove negatively with subsequent education and wage convergence. Our examination of the relationship between quotas and convergence suggests that quotas may have been an important contributing factor. However, what seems to have mattered more at the margin was the level of the quota in the state during the period rather than changes in the level of the quota.

The data also revealed a couple of outlier states. Andhra Pradesh and Himachal Pradesh stood out during this period as states where there was the most rapid and broad-based reduction in the caste gaps in education and wages. Orissa, on the other hand, was the worst performing state on the convergence metric across almost all the indicators that we examined. The large presence of STs in Orissa suggests that there may be an important distinction between SCs and STs with most of the convergence being concentrated on SCs. The relatively poor performance in education convergence of Madhya Pradesh, another state with a relatively large share of STs, indicates some support for this view. We should add, though, that Madhya Pradesh's performance in other indicators such as median wage convergence is better. Hence, this aspect of the evidence requires more detailed analysis.

One state which has seen rising Dalit political power since the mid-1980s is Uttar Pradesh. A Dalit-based party called the Bahujan Samaj Party (BSP) has in fact been in power in the state for significant periods since the 1990s. One might expect that this would have made the caste convergence process faster/stronger in Uttar Pradesh due to the increasing political empowerment of SC/STs. Exploiting the time series variations in the caste gaps and the vote share of the BSP, we do indeed find some evidence suggesting an important role for political empowerment. In spite of these findings, it is difficult to draw any conclusions regarding the effect of political empowerment from the Uttar Pradesh experience for a couple of reasons. First, we don't really have a comprehensive way of evaluating the counterfactual of what might have happened to caste gaps in Uttar Pradesh had the Dalit political empowerment not occurred. Second, the popular appeal of the BSP in Uttar Pradesh may itself have been due to the perceived absence of upward mobility of the backward castes. Lastly, since the convergence patterns are nationwide, the importance of political empowerment can be gauged fully only with an India-wide study as opposed to one that considers only Uttar Pradesh.

Our work is related to some existing work on caste gaps in wages, consumption, and employment. Thus, Banerjee and Knight (1985) and Madheswaran and Attewell (2007) studied the wage discrimination faced by SC/STs in the urban India. Similarly, Borooah (2005) studied employment discrimination in the urban areas, while Ito (2009) focused simultaneously on wage and employment discrimination by examining data from Bihar and Uttar Pradesh. Consumption inequality of SC/ST households was the focus of work by Kijima (2006). Lastly, Munshi and Rozensweig (2009) documented the low degree of labor mobility in India. Our study differs from these in that we examine the data for all states and for both rural and urban areas. Moreover, by using data from five rounds of the NSS, we are also able to provide a time series perspective on the evolution of the caste gaps, a feature that other studies have typically not included.

In terms of political empowerment, our work relates to Pande (2003), who showed that greater political representation for SC/STs in India through reservations tended to change the composition of public expenditures. However, her results do not provide much guidance about whether these changes were beneficial for the targeted minorities. Our study measures some concrete outcomes and hence potentially sheds light on the welfare aspects of such representation.

The rest of the chapter is organized as follows: The next section presents the basic cross-state data facts. This is followed by a section that examines the potential explanatory factors underlying these trends. The last section concludes.

CROSS-STATE FACTS

We start with an examination of the patterns across the states in terms of convergence between SC/STs and non-SC/STs. There are five primary variables of interest: education, wages, consumption, occupation distributions, and employment distribution across industries. We compare the gaps between the groups in 1983 with the corresponding gaps in 2004–05 for each of these indicators. Our goals are twofold: (1) determine whether the gaps in 2004–05 were systematically smaller for all states relative to 1983, and (2) identify which states showed the sharpest narrowing of the gaps for the most indicators.

Our data comes from the NSS, which includes all of India except for a few inaccessible areas. We use rounds 38 (1983), 43 (1987–88), 50 (1993–94), 55 (1999–2000), and 61 (2004–05). The NSS provides household-level data on approximately 600,000 individuals on education, employment, consumption, and wages, as well as other social characteristics. We restrict the sample to individuals in the age group 16–65 who, at the time of the survey, belonged to male-headed households, were not enrolled full time in any educational degree or diploma, and were working full time. The sample is restricted to those individuals who provided their occupation and industry of employment code information as well as their education information.[1] Full-time working individuals are defined as those who work at least 2.5 days per week and who are not currently enrolledin any educational institution. This selection leaves us with a working sample of around 165,000–182,000 individuals, depending on the survey round. The wage data is more limited due to the presence of self-employed individuals. As a result, the subsample with wage data is limited to about 48,000 individuals, on average, across rounds.[2] For the state domestic product information we use real per capita state domestic product data available from the *Handbook of Statistics on Indian Economy*, published by the Reserve Bank of India. Reservation quotas for SC/STs in Indian states for various years are obtained from the Report of the Commissioner for Scheduled Castes and Scheduled Tribes, published by the Government of India. Finally, BSP voting shares are obtained from the statistical reports of the Election Commission of India.

Our measure of caste gaps for any variable is non-SC/STs divided by SC/STs. Thus, the education gap is average years of education of non-SC/STs divided by the average years of education of SC/STs in the sample. The gaps for wages and consumption are computed analogously. Note that the consumption numbers reported in the NSS refer to consumption of a household. We use them to compute the per capita consumption of that household. The consumption gaps reported here thus refer to the mean per capita monthly consumption expenditure of non-SC/ST households divided by the corresponding measure for SC/ST households.

Before proceeding it is worth presenting some basic cross-state sample statistics regarding our key measures of caste gaps. Table 9.1 shows the caste gaps for education, wages, and consumption for 1983 (round 38 of the NSS employment survey) and 2004–05 (round 61) across all the constituent states. Two features are worth noting. First, the gaps, averaged across all the states, fell for both education years and wages while staying relatively unchanged for consumption, indicating a broad trend toward convergence in the country as a whole. Second, the dispersion in the gaps across the states (as measured by the standard deviation) fell for both the education and median wage gaps.

Table 9.1 SUMMARY CROSS-STATE STATISTICS FOR CASTE GAPS

Variable		Mean	St. Dev	Max	Min
Education years gap	1983	2.22	0.42	3.01	1.37
	2004–05	1.58	0.25	2.11	1.04
Median wage gap	1983	1.43	0.33	2.47	1
	2004–05	1.19	0.19	1.85	1
Consumption gap	1983	1.34	0.1	1.54	1.13
	2004–05	1.35	0.15	1.71	1.07

Note: The table presents the mean of the caste gaps across the constituent states and the dispersion of the caste gaps across the states, as well as the max and the min for each variable for rounds 38 and 61 of the NSS employment survey.

This suggests a pattern of cross-state convergence for these two indicators. The dispersion in the consumption gap, on the other hand, increased between 1983 and 2004–05. This is a recurrent feature of the data: consumption patterns are often at odds with those in education and wages.

We start our detailed analysis of the time series patterns with education. Panel A of figure 9.2 shows the gaps in educational attainment between the groups. The diagonal line is the 45 degree line. Observations along the 45 degree line indicate no change in the education gaps during the period, while observations below the line indicate convergence since the gaps in 2004–05 were smaller than in 1983. The key feature to leap out from panel a of figure 9.2 is the sharp convergence in the educational attainment levels of the two groups during this period. Moreover, this pattern is almost uniform across the different states. In terms of strong and weak performers, Andhra Pradesh appears to have outperformed almost everyone in narrowing the caste education gap, while Orissa showed little change during this period.

Panel B of figure 9.2 shows the gaps in the mean per capita monthly consumption expenditure (MPCE) between the groups. This reveals a slightly different picture relative to the education plot. Specifically, while there is convergence in the consumption levels in some states, there is also divergence in other states. Obviously, the convergence in education hasn't always carried over into convergence in consumption. However, as we have shown in Hnatkovska, Lahiri, and Paul (2012), consumption has converged at the aggregate level for the country as a whole. These results show that the aggregate picture masks significant underlying state-level variation. Individually, the consumption gap between the castes fell the fastest in Jammu and Kashmir, while the gap actually rose in the northern belt states of Punjab, Haryana, and Delhi.

The next variable of interest is wages. Panel A of figure 9.3 depicts the mean wage convergence in each of the states between 1983 and 2004–05, while panel B shows the corresponding patterns for median wages. An overwhelming majority of states show a sharp convergence in median wages between the groups during this period. The convergent trends in mean wages are bit more muted. Relative to median wages, more states show divergence, while the size of the improvement is often smaller in the states with convergent trends. However both measures suggest an overall convergence of wage gaps between the groups. In terms of individual states, Himachal Pradesh was an outstanding performer in terms of narrowing the caste wage gaps; Orissa again performed the worst.

Lastly, we turn to the evidence on employment patterns for the two groups. We examine two indicators: the occupation distribution and the employment distribution by industry. We measure the gaps in distributions of the two groups by using the dissimilarity index, $d = \frac{1}{2}\sum_{i=1}^{N}\left|\frac{N_1}{N} - \frac{S_1}{S}\right|$, where $\frac{N_i}{N}$ indicates the share of non-SC/STs in occupation (or industry) i, and $\frac{S_i}{S}$

(a)

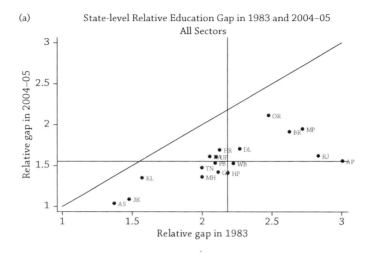

(b)

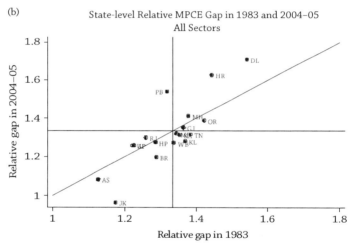

Figure 9.2
Cross-state Education and Consumption Convergence

measures the corresponding share for SC/STs. The distributions are completely similar when $d = 0$, while $d = 1$ indicates complete segmentation or dissimilarity.[3] Figure 9.4 plots the dissimilarity indices for the occupation and industry distributions of the labor force of the two groups. The main pattern that emerges from the two panels of the figure is that cross-state evidence on convergence in the employment distribution of the groups is very mixed. While our previous study at the aggregate level suggests overall convergence, albeit muted, in the employment distribution, there is clearly huge underlying variation across states. On both indicators, Punjab and Orissa performed the worst; that is, they showed the largest increase in the

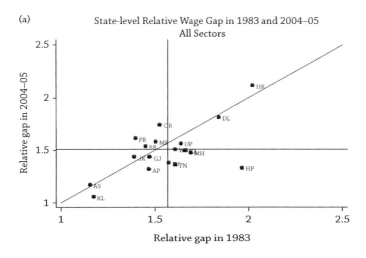

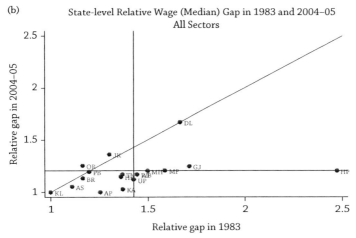

Figure 9.3
Wage Convergence Across States

dissimilarity index over time for both the occupation and industry distributions of the two groups.

The preceding results have three main takeaways. First, educational attainment and median wages converged not just at the aggregate level but in
almost all the constituent states of India—this was a broad-based, countrywide phenomenon. Second, the evidence on employment and consumption
convergence is more mixed. While both these indicators showed overall convergence at the aggregate level, there has been significant cross-state variation in the patterns. Third, Himachal Pradesh (and to a lesser extent, Andhra
Pradesh) was one of the better performing states on this margin as it showed
widespread decreases in caste gaps across a variety of indicators. On the flip

(a)   State-level Occupational Dissimilarity Index in 1983 and 2004–05

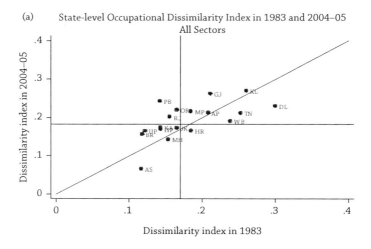

(b)   State-level Industrial Dissimilarity Index in 1983 and 2004–05

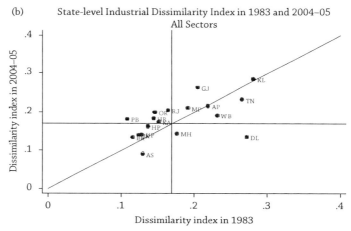

Figure 9.4
Occupation and Industry Convergence

side, Orissa (and to a lesser extent, Punjab and Haryana) performed relatively poorly across all states in narrowing the caste gaps.

The heterogeneity in outcomes across states suggests that one might learn much more about the key drivers of the observed aggregate changes by exploiting these state-level variations in outcomes. This is precisely what we do next.

EXPLANATIONS FOR THE TRENDS

While the overall trends toward shrinking gaps between SC/STs and non-SC/STs are encouraging, it is equally important to determine the proximate factors that may have been responsible for the changes. There are a few obvious explanations. The first is the role of the economic reforms, which translated to high growth rates in India during this period. A second factor may have been the reservations policy enshrined in the constitution that provided affirmative action protection for SC/STs with regard to education, jobs, and political representation. A third factor could be the increasing political empowerment of SC/STs during this period. We examine each of these below more systematically.

Growth and Convergence

We start by examining the relationship between the cross-state convergence patterns and the growth performance of the states. Of key interest is whether the states that grew the fastest were also the ones where the caste gaps narrowed the most. Figure 9.5 shows the relationship between the educational gaps and the GDP of the states.

Panel A of the figure shows the relationship between the change in the educational gaps (in years) and the average annual growth rate of GDP for each state during the period 1983–2005. Shaded areas on all figures below indicate 95 percent confidence interval. There is a mild but clear negative relationship, illustrating the fact that the states which grew faster during this period were also the ones where the education gaps declined relatively more. Among the states with the highest GDP growth as well as the largest reduction in the education gap was Andhra Pradesh. Contrarily, Orissa stands out in terms of poor performance. Its growth rate during this period was about average, but the caste gap in education barely changed.[4]

A related issue of interest is the importance of the initial income of the states in accounting for the observed convergence patterns. Panel B of the figure shows that the relationship between the education gaps and initial income was positive; that is, the initially richer states saw a slower decline in the education gaps between SC/STs and non-SC/STs. This graph also highlights the dramatic contrast between Andhra Pradesh and Orissa. The two states are neighbors and had fairly similar income levels in 1983. The subsequent performance of the two in terms of narrowing the education gap between the SC/STs and non-SC/STs, however, was diametrically different.

Next, we examine the joint evolution of wage convergence and GDP of the states. Figure 9.6 shows the patterns for median wage convergence. Panel A of the figure plots the change in the wage gap against the average GDP growth of the concerned state between 1983 and 2005. Clearly, wage gaps declined at a faster rate in states which grew faster during this period, corroborating the pattern for education convergence. Himachal Pradesh was among the top

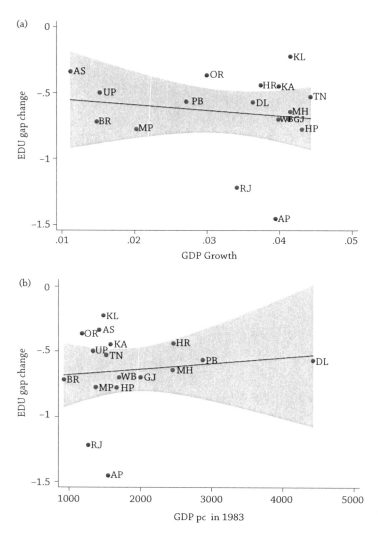

Figure 9.5
Educational Convergence and GDP

performers, while Orissa again stood out in terms of underperforming (the wage gap actually rose) despite a middling performance in terms of growth.

Panel B of figure 9.6 shows the scatter plot of changes in the wage gaps against GDP in 1983 of the states. The graph shows an upward sloping relationship indicating that the states that were relatively richer in 1983 showed smaller declines in the wage gaps over this period. This pattern is similar to that for education, for which the richer states also showed the smallest reduction in the gaps.

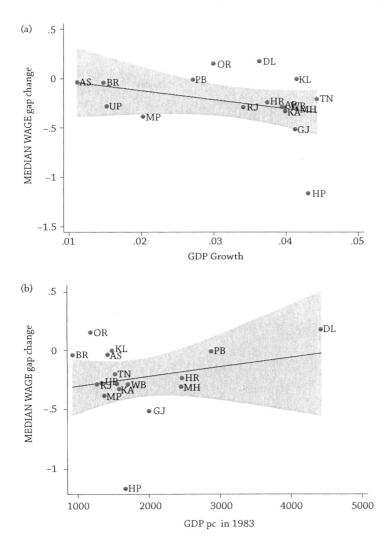

Figure 9.6
Median Wage Convergence and GDP

A third metric of interest is consumption convergence. Figure 9.7 shows the relationship between changes in GDP and in the gap in average per capita consumption expenditures of non-SC/STs and SC/STs. Panel A of the figure shows that the relationship between changes in consumption gaps and GDP growth is almost flat; there is barely any discernible trend. However, panel B of the figure shows that the relationship between changes in the consumption gaps and GDP in 1983 is positive: the consumption gap tended to decline more in the relatively poorer states. This was similar to the pattern for wage convergence.

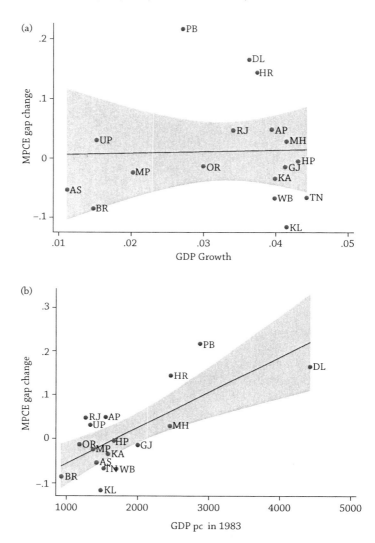

Figure 9.7
Consumption Convergence and GDP

The positive relationship of all three indicators of caste convergence with initial income could indicate some sort of decreasing returns in the process if the gaps were small to start with in the richer states. However, this seems unlikely since both the consumption and wage gaps actually widened in some of the more well-off states in 1983 like Delhi, Haryana, and Punjab. Moreover, as indicated in figures 9.2 and 9.3, Delhi and Haryana were the two states with the largest initial gaps between the groups in both consumption and wages.

Our principal conclusion from the above is that aggregate growth was clearly a key factor associated with the declining caste gaps in education and wages during the period under study.

Reservations and Convergence

We now turn to the potential effects of the reservations in educational institutions and public sector employment on the caste gaps. India enshrined these reservations in the constitution that it adopted in 1950; they are among the largest affirmative action programs implemented anywhere in the world. The quotas were determined for SC/STs in proportion to their population representation both at the federal and state levels. These quotas are periodically revised in every state based on the latest census results. This procedure for adjusting the quotas leads to lags between changes in the population representation of SC/STs and changes in the quotas set aside for them. One reason for this is that the censuses are conducted every ten years while the population representation of these groups changes continuously. Moreover, there are administrative lags in translating the population share numbers of the latest census into changes in the implemented quotas.

Our study is related to a recent work by Prakash (2009) who exploits the exogenous variation in changes in the quotas to study the impact of reservations on employment patterns, wages, and consumption of SC/STs. His principal findings are that reservations did not significantly affect wages or consumption but they did affect the composition of the employment of SC/STs; quotas tended to increase the probability of salaried employment of SC/STs. However, Prakash's focus was not on examining the convergence patterns between the groups; neither did it study the cross-state variation in the patterns. Lastly, we are also interested in overall educational outcomes such as total years of schooling. Prakash focused on school enrollment rates in order to measure education outcomes.

We start by examining the cross-state comovements of quotas and education gaps. Panel A of figure 9.8 shows the scatter plot of the changes in the education gaps (in years) and the change in the quotas allocated to SC/STs between 1983 and 2005. The relationship is basically flat, indicating the absence of any clear relationship between the two. Panel B of figure 9.8 shows the relationship between the initial level of the quota in each state and the change in the education gaps that followed during 1983–2005. This relationship is clearly negative; states with larger quotas in 1983 saw larger declines in the education gaps between the castes. The key suggestion from figure 9.8 is that the initial level in the quota was more important for changing education gaps than the fluctuations in the quotas.

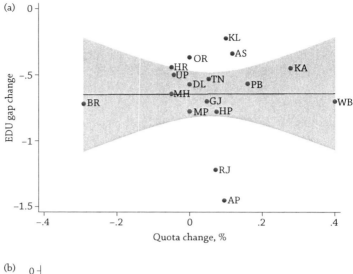

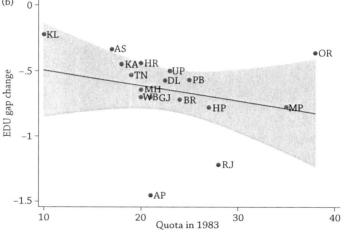

Figure 9.8
Educational Convergence and Reservation Quotas

How important were quotas for the convergence in wages? Figure 9.9 shows the relationship between the change in the median wage gaps and quotas. The pattern is the same for both mean and median wages. Larger increases in the quotas were accompanied by bigger declines in the wage gaps between the groups (panel A). On the other hand, akin to the result for education gaps, higher initial levels of the quota were typically also associated with larger reductions in the caste wage gaps.

The relationship between the initial level of the quotas and the subsequent changes in the education and wage gaps we have identified are in the spirit of

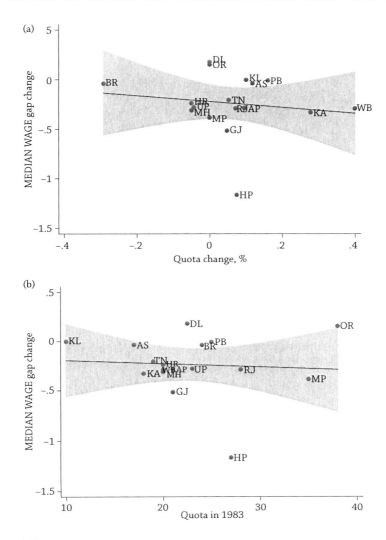

Figure 9.9
Wage Convergence and Reservation Quotas

Hnatkovska and Lahiri (2011) who developed a skill and occupation choice model to show that caste gaps can decline in response to a rise in aggregate growth without any change in reservations for SC/STs as long as the preexisting affirmative action inducements are sufficiently strong.

Lastly, figure 9.10 shows the relationship between quotas and the changes in the consumption gaps between SC/STs and non-SC/STs. The relationship between changes in the quota and the consumption gap is similar to that between the change in quotas and the wage gap. The difference lies in the relationship between the initial level of the quotas and changes in the gaps. Panel

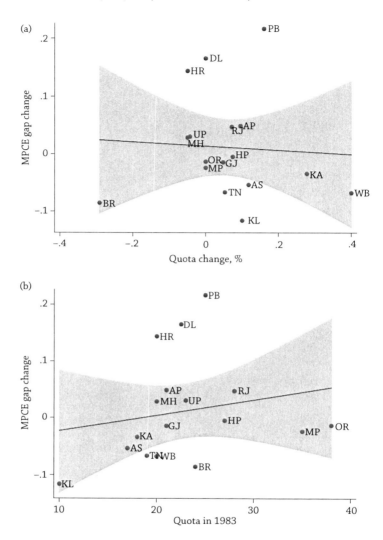

Figure 9.10
Consumption Convergence and Reservation Quotas

B of figure 9.10 shows a positive relationship, but the corresponding relationships for education and wage gaps are negative. This is an intriguing feature of the data and reinforces our previous impression that consumption dynamics at the household level are often at odds with some of the individual-level movements in education and wages.

Overall, we conclude from this analysis that reservation quotas may well have been important in explaining the declining caste gaps. However, the effect is nuanced in that the initial levels of the quotas were possibly more influential than the effects of changes in the quotas on the cross-state variation in the caste gaps in education, wages, and consumption. It is worth noting that these results are consistent with the findings of Prakash (2009), who found fairly muted effects of quotas.

Political Empowerment: The Case of Uttar Pradesh

A third possible explanation for the declining overall caste gaps is that SC/STs have become more politically empowered over the course of the past thirty years. This political empowerment has translated into less discrimination, more opportunities, and—consequently—better relative outcomes. Indeed, Pande (2003) and Duflo (2005) document how political representation of minorities influences public policy in terms of expenditure patterns on public goods. However, those papers do not examine the effect of these changes on the welfare of the targeted groups.

Is there any evidence to suggest that political empowerment and representation may have played a role in narrowing the caste gaps? We approach this question by looking at the case of Uttar Pradesh. Uttar Pradesh is special among the states because of the BSP, which is essentially an SC/ST- and other-backward-castes-supported party. If political empowerment is indeed an important factor underlying the overall trends, one would expect to see Uttar Pradesh among the states that performed the best in narrowing the caste gaps.

As can be seen from figures 9.2 and 9.3 above, Uttar Pradesh did not show any dramatic decline in the gaps between SC/STs and non-SC/STs in education, consumption, or wages between 1983 and 2004–05. On most of the indicators, the state has an average caste gap in both 1983 and 2004–05. However, this picture is potentially a bit misleading since the BSP was only formed in 1984 and began to be a serious political contender in 1989. The political rise of the party was quite swift; it actually became part of a coalition government in 1992 and continued to be in power through different coalition governments off and on until 2007 when it was voted in to power on its own. The key questions, then, is how the caste gaps have evolved since 1992 and whether there are any differences in the patterns before and after 1992.

Figure 9.11 shows the paths of the median and mean wage gaps (panels a and b) and the vote share of the BSP in the Uttar Pradhesh assembly elections since 1989 (the first year that the BSP ran for elections in the state in any major organized way). The figure reveals two interesting features. First, the wage gaps between the two groups actually widened between 1983 and 1993–94 (left axis of the graphs). Second, wage gaps have been declining since 1993, which was the first year the BSP was actually part of the government's ruling coalition.

Is this pattern restricted to the caste wage gaps? Figure 9.12 shows the education gaps (in years) and the per capita mean consumption gaps (panels A

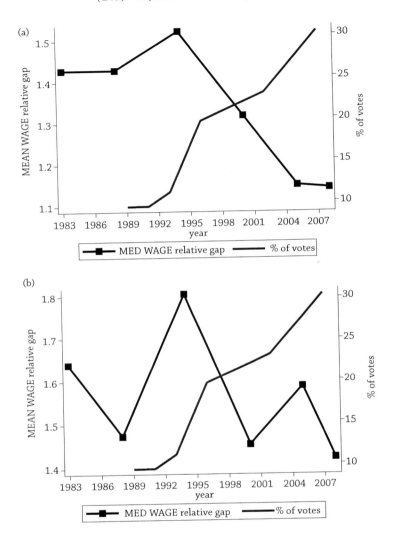

Figure 9.11
Uttar Pradesh: Wage Convergence and Political Empowerment

and B) between the castes against the BSP vote share. This figure corroborates the impression given by figure 9.11. The education convergence was weaker before 1993 than after 1993, while consumption gaps widened until 1993 before beginning to fall. Clearly, even though Uttar Pradesh began and finished the period 1983–2007 as an average performer in terms of the caste gap trends, there was significant underlying time variation in the trends, suggesting a key role of political empowerment of SC/STs in accounting for the overall trends.

Clearly, there could be other factors accounting for the time trends in the caste gaps documented above. First, it could be that widening gaps between the groups during 1983–93 was a nationwide trend. But figure 9.1 shows that that was most certainly not the case. Both education and wage gaps fell between 1983–93. Hence, Uttar Pradesh behaved differently from the norm during that period. Second, it could be that Uttar Pradesh's growth performance during 1983–93 and post-1993 could account for the different behavior of the caste gaps in education and wages in these two phases. However, per capita income in Uttar Pradesh grew at an average annual rate of 1.6 percent from 1983–93 and at 1.5 percent from 1993–2005. Thus, there was hardly any difference in the growth rates during the two phases. Between 2005–2008,

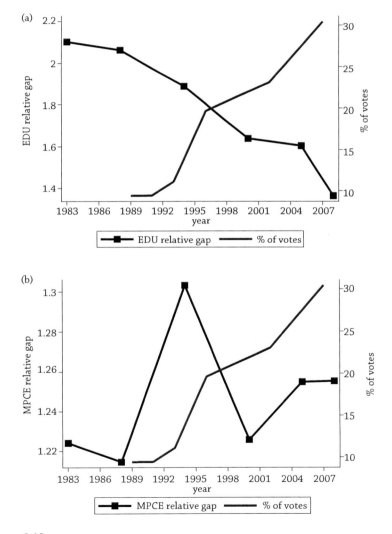

Figure 9.12
Uttar Pradesh: Caste Convergence and Political Empowerment

Uttar Pradesh has grown at a much faster per capita annual rate of 5.6 percent. But this is precisely the period when the rate of decline of the wage gap between SC/STs and non-SC/STs has slowed down. Based on this, we do not believe that growth has been the key underlying driver of the caste gaps in Uttar Pradesh since 1983. Lastly, it is important to point out that the reservation quotas in Uttar Pradesh stayed unchanged over the sample. Hence, additional affirmative action protection cannot account for the reduction in the caste gaps in the state since 1992.

While our results from Uttar Pradesh are most certainly not definitive regarding the effect of political empowerment of SC/STs on the caste gaps, they do suggest that this may have been an important factor nationwide. This deserves more in-depth and careful analysis, which—while beyond the scope of this study—is an issue that we intend to pursue in future research.

CONCLUSION

The past three decades have been a period of rapid and historic changes in India at the aggregate level. In recent work, Hnatkovska, Lahiri, and Paul (2011 and 2012) have shown that this period has also proven historic in terms of the changes that have occurred in the fortunes of SC/STs. Between 1983 and 2004–05, SC/STs have dramatically narrowed the gaps with non-SC/STs in educational attainment rates, wages, and consumption. Moreover, gaps in the occupation distributions have also narrowed. In this chapter we have examined the potential contributions of three factors to these trends, namely, aggregate growth effects, reservations, and political empowerment. The key innovation of the study is to exploit the cross-state variation in outcomes (the key measures of convergence across castes) to ascertain the explanatory potential of the different channels.

Our primary finding is that aggregate growth effects are usually important for education and wage convergence across the castes. Interestingly, we find that the initially richer states saw a slower reduction in the education, wage, and consumption gaps. We also find relatively mixed associations of reservations with our measures of convergence. The initial levels of quotas seem to correlate positively with the subsequent convergence of the education and wage gaps. In other words, larger initial quotas appear to coincide with faster subsequent convergence. The change in the quotas during the period, however, have a more muted relationship with caste convergence rates. Education convergence, for example, appears to be uncorrelated with changes in the quotas.

We also examine the potential effect of political empowerment of the SC/STs by examining in greater detail the caste gaps in Uttar Pradesh. Examining the joint patterns of the vote share of the Dalit party (the BSP) and the caste gaps in education, wages, and consumption in Uttar Pradesh since the mid-1980s, we do find some evidence of greater political empowerment of SC/STs inducing a narrowing of the caste gaps in these indicators. This is a topic that deserves closer examination due to issues associated with identification of political empowerment as well as reverse causality. We intend to pursue it in future work.

One last point is worth stressing. A common feature of a number of our results is that the consumption patterns are often at odds with the patterns in education and wages. This probably partially reflects the fact that the consumption data reflect the household, while the education and wage data are at the individual level. However, whether or not there are interesting intrahousehold redistribution and insurance mechanisms at play is an issue of independent interest, which may be worth pursuing in future research.

ACKNOWLEDGMENT

Second author's research on this chapter has been supported by Columbia University's Program on Indian Economic Policies, funded by a generous grant from the John Templeton Foundation. The opinions expressed in the chapter are those of the authors and do not necessarily reflect the views of the John Templeton Foundation.

NOTES

1. We also consider a narrower sample in which we restrict the sample to only males and find that our results remain robust.
2. Wages are computed as the daily wage/salaried income received by respondents for the work done during the previous week (relative to the survey week). Wages can be paid in cash or kind. If paid in kind, wages are evaluated at the current retail prices. We convert wages into real terms using state-level poverty lines that differ for rural and urban sectors. We express all wages in 1983 rural Maharashtra prices.
3. While there is no uniformly accepted metric for comparing distributions, this index is often used in analyzing intergroup heterogeneity.
4. Kerala too showed a very small decline in the caste gap in education years. However, the initial gap in 1983 in Kerala was itself very small—it was among the three states with the smallest caste gaps in education.

REFERENCES

Banerjee, B., and J. Knight (1985): "Caste Discrimination in the Indian Urban Labour Market," *Journal of Development Economics*, 17(3), 277–307.

Borooah, V. K. (2005): "Caste, Inequality, and Poverty in India," *Review of Development Economics*, 9(3), 399–414.

Duflo, E., (2005): "Why Political Representation," *Journal of the European Economic Association*, 3(2–3), 668–78.

Government of India, "Report of the Commissioner for Scheduled Castes and Scheduled Tribes."

Hnatkovska, V., and A. Lahiri (2011): "Convergence Across Castes," working paper, University of British Columbia and International Growth Center.

Hnatkovska, V., A. Lahiri, and S. Paul (2011): "Breaking the Caste Barrier: Intergenerational Mobility in India," working paper, University of British Columbia.

Hnatkovska, V., A. Lahiri, and S. Paul (2012): "Castes and Labor Mobility," *American Economic Journal: Applied Economics*, 4(2), 274–307.

Ito, T. (2009): "Caste Discrimination and Transaction Costs in the Labor Market: Evidence From Rural North India," *Journal of Development Economics*, 88(2), 292–300.

Kijima, Y. (2006): "Caste and Tribe Inequality: Evidence from India, 1983–1999," *Economic Development and Cultural Change*, 54(2), 369–404.

Madheswaran, S., and P. Attewell (2007): "Caste Discrimination in the Indian Urban Labour Market: Evidence from the National Sample Survey," *Economic and Political Weekly*, 42(41), 41–6.

Munshi, K., and M. Rosenzweig (2009): "Why is Mobility in India So Low? Social Insurance, Inequality, and Growth," working paper, Brown University, Department of Economics.

Pande, R. (2003): "Can Mandated Political Representation Increase Policy Influence for Disadvantaged Minorities? Theory and Evidence from India," *American Economic Review*, 93(4), 1132–51.

Prakash, N. (2009): "The Impact of Employment Quotas on the Economic Lives of Disadvantaged Minorities in India," working paper, Dartmouth College, Department of Economics.

Reserve Bank of India. *Handbook of Statistics on the Indian Economy.*

CHAPTER 10

Entrepreneurship in Services and the Socially Disadvantaged in India

RAJEEV DEHEJIA AND ARVIND PANAGARIYA

INTRODUCTION

Writing in the *Indian Express*, a leading national daily, editor Shekhar Gupta narrates an interesting episode that highlights the absence of entrepreneurs among the socially disadvantaged groups—the Scheduled Castes (SCs) and Scheduled Tribes (STs)—in India (2011). He observes that when speaking to a crowd of nearly five hundred of "the best paid, globalized Indian finance whiz-kids" at an institutional investors' conference a few weeks prior to writing, he was repeatedly quizzed about the "curse" of caste-based reservations in India. Disconcerted, he decided to turn the tables on the audience and asked: "We have here fellow Indians with the finest jobs in the world, mostly with an IIT/IIM education. Both institutions have also had caste-based reservations forever. So how many of you here are tribal or Dalit?"[1] Gupta continues, "Not a single hand came up."

While Gupta uses this episode as prologue to a critical examination of the search for short-cut and extra-democratic solutions to every problem, it makes an important statement about entrepreneurship among the socially disadvantaged in India: despite all the affirmative action programs during the last sixty years, the SCs and STs remain absent from entrepreneurial activity, at least in the high-end financial sector.

At the highest end of business activity, the absence is of course across a much wider spectrum than just the financial sector: out of fifty-five Indian billionaires in US dollars on the latest Forbes list, not one is from the SCs or STs. Yet, it would be incorrect to conclude from either the episode narrated by Gupta or this fact that the system has produced no entrepreneurs from the socially disadvantaged groups. While it is true that during the years of slow growth, the economy produced few significant entrepreneurial successes among the socially disadvantaged, the recent acceleration in growth is beginning to pull them into its fold. The "pull-up" has not yet brought them all the way to the top and therefore into the Forbes billionaire list, but it has produced rupee billionaires from among at least the SCs if not STs.

In fact, newspapers have recently widely reported on thirty "dalit crorepatis" who were invited for a meeting that the Planning Commission specially organized for them. Among the invitees was Milind Kamble, who serves as chairman of the Dalit Indian Chamber of Commerce and Industry (DICCI) formed in 2005. Kamble is reported to have said, "Including mine, most of the big Dalit-owned businesses are fifteen years old. With the emergence of globalization and the disappearance of the License-Permit Raj, many opportunities appeared and many of us jumped on them." Describing the meeting at the Planning Commission, he went on to note, "The Planning Commission was stunned when they asked how many of us used government schemes to build their businesses. Only one entrepreneur from Mumbai raised his hand and described how he'd applied for $20,000, spent three years visiting government offices to chase his money and finally got $15,000."[2] Beginning on July 21, 2011, *The Economic Times*, India's leading financial daily, has been profiling some of the most prominent Dalit entrepreneurs.

While anecdotes of entrepreneurship among the Dalit are thus beginning to filter through, almost nothing is known of entrepreneurship among the STs. More generally, systematic data on entrepreneurship among either of these disadvantaged groups is entirely lacking. There is no information about their shares in the number of enterprises, value added, and employment; the sectors in which they operate; and the states in which they are concentrated. Nor do we know how they fare relative to each other, the other backward castes (OBCs), or the remaining castes—sometimes called the forward castes (FCs). And finally, we lack systematic information on how the accelerated growth under the reforms has impacted entrepreneurship among these groups in both absolute and relative terms.

Therefore, the purpose of the present chapter is to provide systematic evidence of the role played by entrepreneurs belonging to various social groups. We identify the shares of various social groups in the number of enterprises, gross value added (GVA), and workers employed. We also analyze these shares according to enterprise size in terms of workers. In addition, we identify the shares of entrepreneurs by social group in different sectors and states. Finally, we throw light on growth in GVA; the number of enterprises; and employment by social groups, sectors, and states between two specific years for which data are available, 2001–02 and 2006–07.

Our analysis is based on two extensive India-wide surveys of service sector enterprises conducted by the National Sample Survey Organization (NSSO) in 2001–02 and 2006–07 (rounds 57 and 63 respectively). Both these surveys identify the social group of the owner of proprietary and partnership enterprises, though not of cooperative and corporate enterprises, unfortunately. Insofar as the latter set of enterprises account for a very substantial proportion of services output and also represent the more successful enterprises, their exclusion naturally distorts the picture we draw of the relative importance of various social groups as entrepreneurs. But given that we currently have almost no systematic data on this subject, our analysis constitutes an important step forward.[3]

Our findings are systematically summarized in the concluding section of the chapter; here we state their main thrust. A small scholarly literature by economists on the impact of reforms and accelerated growth on poverty and inequality among the traditionally disadvantaged groups now exists. Mukim and Panagariya (2012) provide a comprehensive analysis of poverty among the SC and ST populations relative to the general population since the early 1980s. They find that, while the levels of poverty for the SC and ST populations remain significantly higher than that for the general population, higher growth has been associated with steadily declining poverty not just for the general population but for these socially disadvantaged groups as well.[4] They find no evidence that rising incomes have left the disadvantaged groups behind.

In an earlier paper, Kijima (2006) studied whether the gap between the average consumption levels of the SC/ST and non-scheduled households declined between 1983 and 1999–2000 and, if so, whether this decline could be attributed to reduced discrimination. She answered the former question in the affirmative but the latter in the negative. More recently, Hnatkovska, Lahiri, and Paul (2012) offer an analysis of intergroup inequality, asking whether the wages, education levels, and occupational structure of the SCs and STs as a group converged with those of the non-scheduled groups. They answer forcefully in the affirmative on each count, and cite competitive pressures unleashed on markets via the economic liberalization as a possible cause of the convergence (Hnatkovska, Lahiri, and Paul 2012, p. 300).[5]

Coming from the entrepreneurship angle, our results reinforce these findings. We find that the SC and ST groups do lag behind other social groups in terms of their shares in GVA, workers employed, and number of enterprises owned in a large number of services sectors covered by our data. But the presence of these groups in entrepreneurial activity is far from negligible. More importantly, there is no truth whatsoever to the assertions by many left-of-center observers that growth is leaving these groups behind. The ST entrepreneurs, who have been at the greatest disadvantage, have also made the largest gains between 2001–02 and 2006–07. Overall, in terms of workers employed and enterprises owned, SC entrepreneurs have a presence in the services sectors that is not far out of line with the SC share in the population, but they are in enterprises with below-average productivity. As a result, their share in GVA is well below their population share. But they, too, have grown alongside other entrepreneurs.

Interestingly, during the five years we analyze, the FC groups, which consist of the "privileged" castes, are in retreat in virtually all dimensions in the services sector. The major gains have been reaped by the OBCs. Indeed, much of our analysis shows that the most important source of competition for SC entrepreneurs are OBC entrepreneurs.

THE SURVEYS

Although Dehejia and Panagariya (Chapter 4 of this volume) provide a detailed description of the surveys, we review their key features here briefly. It is convenient to begin with the surveys' sectoral coverage. Round 63 covers all services except construction, wholesale and retail trade, and public administration and defense. It includes hotels and restaurants; transport, storage, and communications; financial intermediation; real estate, renting, and business activities; education; health and social work; and other community, social, and personal services. It excludes all government and public sector enterprises, educational institutions in which the entire salary of teaching and non-teaching staff is borne by the government, and service enterprises registered under the Factories Act of 1948. Round 57 has the same coverage with one major difference: it does not cover financial intermediation. For consistency over time, we entirely exclude the financial sector from our analysis.

The surveys are highly stratified. They cover the entirety of India and sharply distinguish between rural and urban areas. The first stage units (FSUs) are villages in rural areas and urban frame survey blocks in urban areas. After the first-stage units are selected, the ultimate stage units (enterprises) are selected. In turn, the latter are divided into two types: own-account enterprises (OAEs), which do not employ any workers on a regular basis, and establishment enterprises, which employ one or more workers on a regular basis.

There are 15,869 FSUs in round 57, of which 41 percent are from rural and the remainder from urban areas. Altogether, the survey covered 244,376 enterprises with 37.85 percent in rural and 62.15 percent in urban areas. Round 63 selected 13,271 FSUs, of which 42 percent were in rural and 58 percent in urban areas. It surveyed 190,282 enterprises with 43.8 percent in rural and 56.2 percent in urban areas. The union territories typically had fewer observations, with Lakshadweep having the fewest: 171 in round 57 and 187 in round 63.

SETTING THE STAGE

We noted in the introduction that the social group of the owner is identified only for proprietary and partnership enterprises and not for cooperative and corporate enterprises. Therefore, as the first step, it is important to identify the proportion of economic activity for which the social group information on the owner is available. Services covered by the surveys represent approximately one-quarter of GDP and one-tenth of the labor force (Chapter 4 of this volume, table 4.2). Because of the exclusions, especially of government and public enterprises even within the included sectors, the actual shares are lower. For instance, the total number of workers employed in the included enterprises common to the two surveys was 26.6 million in round 57 and 27.7 million in round 63. Their numbers are considerably less than 10 percent of the total countrywide workforces of 417 and 408 million in 2001–02 and 2007–08 reported in employment-unemployment surveys.

Excluding the financial sector, the total number of enterprises was approximately 14.5 million in round 57 and 15 million in round 63. The vast majority of the enterprises are tiny OAEs. Indeed, even within the establishment enterprises, the vast majority are smaller enterprises. Thus, enterprises typically have an informal character.

Given that the social group of the owner is identified only for proprietary and partnership enterprises, our first step is to identify their share of the total number of enterprises, GVA, and workers employed. Remembering that the surveys generate all values at current prices, we convert them into constant 1999–2000 prices using the deflators implicit in the sectoral GDP data as described in Chapter 4 of this volume. Table 10.1 reports the proportions of GVA, workers employed, and the number of enterprises in proprietary or partnership enterprises and those in cooperative and corporate enterprises. In the last two columns, it also reports the growth in the three variables over the two surveys.

In 2001–02, proprietary or partnership enterprise types accounted for 82.2 percent of GVA, 92.5 percent of workers, and 98.7 percent of enterprises. In five years, there was a large shift in the GVA share toward cooperative and corporate enterprises, though not as much in workers and the number of

Table 10.1 PROPRIETARY AND PARTNERSHIP VERSUS COOPERATIVE AND CORPORATE ENTERPRISES

Item	2001–02		2006–07		Percent growth	
	Prop/Part	Coop/Corp	Prop/Part	Coop/Corp	Prop/Part	Coop/Corp
Gross value added (real)	82.2	17.8	50	50	30	498.5
Total workers employed	92.5	7.5	89.6	10.4	1.3	44.4
Number of enterprises	98.7	1.3	98.8	1.2	3.7	-5.1

Source: Author calculations from the surveys mentioned in the text.

enterprises. The shift in the shares leaves unclear whether the change represents a decline of proprietary and partnership enterprises or simply slower growth. To clarify this, the last two columns show the growth in the three variables over the two surveys. These columns show that the shift in shares resulted from a very large growth in the GVA of cooperative and corporate enterprises between the two surveys. As we discuss in Chapter 4 of this volume, some of this growth may well reflect the activities of the largest enterprises in round 63, but this is by no means decisive.

From the perspective of the present chapter, the key point to note is that in terms of the number of enterprises and workers employed, we have information on the social group of owners of a very large segment. Indeed, even by GVA, we have ownership information on 82.2 percent of the activity in round 57 and 50 percent in round 63. What our data do not allow us to analyze, of course, is the role played by disadvantaged social groups in cooperative and corporate enterprises. But going by the number of members of the DICCI, which stood at approximately one thousand in July 2011, the share of the socially disadvantaged in these enterprises is likely to be tiny (Narasimhan 2011).

SOCIALLY DISADVANTAGED IN PROPRIETARY AND PARTNERSHIP SERVICES ENTERPRISES

We next consider the ownership of proprietary and partnership enterprises by social groups. The natural background against which we must evaluate this distribution is the distribution of population according to social groups. Table 10.2, excerpted from Mukim and Panagariya (2012, table 5.1), provides this information from three sources: the 2001 census and the NSSO expenditure surveys conducted in 1999–2000 and 2004–05. While census data are generally regarded as more reliable, we also report the data from the two NSSO surveys because they provide the breakdown of the non-scheduled-caste population into OBCs and FCs.

It is readily gleaned from the table that the share of the STs in the population according to all three sources is a little above 8 percent. But the shares of other social groups vary according to the source. The SC population is approximately 16 percent of the total according to the 2001 census but between 19 and 20 percent

Table 10.2 SHARES OF SOCIAL GROUPS IN THE NATIONAL POPULATION

Survey/Census Year	ST	SC	OBC	FC	Total Population (Million)
1999–2000	8.3	19	36.1	36.6	904.5
2004–05	8.1	19.7	41.2	30.9	968
Census 2001	8.2	16.2			1029

Source: Mukim and Panagariya (2012, table 5.1).

according to the NSSO surveys. Likewise, the proportion of the OBCs is 36.1 percent according to the 1999–2000 survey but 41.2 percent according to the 2004–05 survey. Perhaps one safe way to read these numbers is to say that, *minimally*, the ST population is 8 percent of the total; the SC, 16 percent; and the OBC, 36 percent.

Table 10.3 shows the distribution of GVA, workers employed, and the number of proprietary and partnership enterprises by social groups in rounds 57 and 63, as well as growth in these variables over the two rounds. Consistent with the data in other spheres of life such as poverty alleviation (Mukim and Panagariya 2012) and wage and education outcomes (Hnatkovska, Lahiri, and Paul 2012), the SC and ST groups are behind other social groups in entrepreneurship, but their presence is not negligible in relation to their population shares. At least at the aggregate level, the SCs account for approximately the same proportion of enterprises and worker employment as their share in the total population according to the 2001 census. Their share in GVA, however, is only half of their share in the population implying that the enterprises they own are less productive than an average enterprise. This is a theme to which we will continue to return in this chapter.

As regards the STs, their presence is considerably below their share in the total population. As we will see shortly, this in part reflects the disproportionate concentration of the STs in rural areas. The OBCs do much better than the SCs and STs, though not as well as the FCs. By 2006–07, the OBCs' share in GVA had risen to almost 37 percent, slightly above their share in the population according to the 1999–2000 round of the expenditure survey, but significantly below that according to the 2004–05 round. The average productivity of OBC enterprises is below that of FC enterprises but above those of SC and ST enterprises. On the whole, the sharpest differences are those between the SCs and STs on the one hand and the OBCs and FCs on the other, rather than those between the OBCs and the FCs.

Table 10.3 PROPRIETARY AND PARTNERSHIP ENTERPRISES IN AGGREGATE BY SOCIAL GROUPS

Item	ST	SC	OBC	FC	Total
Share (round 57)					
Gross value added (real)	1.7	8.8	32.7	56.8	100
Total workers employed	2.1	13	41.1	43.8	100
Number of enterprises	2.6	16.1	42.1	39.2	100
Share (round 63)					
Gross value added (real)	2.3	8.5	36.9	52.3	100
Total workers employed	3	13.8	40.7	42.4	100
Number of enterprises	3.5	16.4	41.6	38.4	100
Percent growth between rounds					
Gross value added (real)	82.1	26.2	46.2	19.3	29.8
Total workers employed	44.1	7.3	0.1	−2	1.1
Number of enterprises	41.4	5.5	2.5	1.4	3.6

Source: Author calculations from the surveys mentioned in the text.

Finally—and perhaps most importantly—the SCs and STs have shared in the growth that has taken place between the time periods of the two surveys. Although starting from a low base, ST enterprises have gained the most in terms of GVA and employment. But even the SCs, with their larger base, have gained more than the FCs both in terms of GVA and workers employed. Excluding the STs, the OBCs have made the largest gains in terms of GVA growth and, given their small gain in employment and number of enterprises, their gains in output per capita and output per enterprise have been perhaps the largest as well. In some ways, the OBCs are probably the most intense competitors of SC and ST entrepreneurs. The FCs have gained the least in terms of GVA; their share actually declined.

DISTINGUISHING BETWEEN THE OAES AND ESTABLISHMENT ENTERPRISES

Our next step is to begin disaggregating enterprises. The first such disaggregation is between OAEs and establishment enterprises. As one would expect, among OAEs, virtually all enterprises belong to the proprietary and partnership category. But within establishment enterprises, a significant proportion belong to the cooperative/corporate category. Table 10.4 provides the breakdown of GVA, workers employed, and the number of enterprises between the two categories.

Two main observations follow from table 10.4. Within establishment enterprises, approximately 70 percent of GVA and 82 percent of employment were in proprietary and partnership enterprises in round 57. Although these shares fell significantly to 35 and 76 percent, respectively, in round 63, they were still

Table 10.4 SHARES AND GROWTH OF PROPRIETARY/PARTNERSHIP AND COOPERATIVE/CORPORATE ENTERPRISES IN THE ESTABLISHMENTS

Item	Proprietary/Partnership	Cooperative/Corporate	Total
Round 57			
Gross value added (real)	69.5	30.5	100
Total workers employed	82.2	17.8	100
Number of enterprises	92.8	7.2	100
Round 63			
Gross value added (real)	35.1	64.9	100
Total workers employed	75.9	24.1	100
Number of enterprises	93.2	6.8	100
Growth			
Gross value added (real)	41.8	499.4	181.2
Total workers employed	−1.4	44.3	6.8
Number of enterprises	−5.6	−11.3	−6

Source: Author calculations from the surveys mentioned in the text.

substantial. Second, while both proprietary/partnership and cooperative/corporate enterprises experienced healthy growth in terms of GVA between the two surveys, the latter grew much faster. It was this much faster growth in cooperative/corporate enterprises that drove down the share of proprietary/partnership enterprises in GVA by such a large margin. Notably, the shift in the proportion of workers employed between the two categories was much smaller. This fact reflects the larger increase in output per worker in cooperative/corporate enterprises. Interestingly, the total number of enterprises fell in both categories, perhaps reflecting some consolidation.

Our next step is to examine how GVA, workers, and enterprises are divided between OAEs and establishments within proprietary and partnership enterprises. We do this in table 10.5. In very approximate terms, the output is divided equally between OAEs and establishment enterprises, while workers and enterprises are heavily concentrated in OAEs. These features imply relatively low productivity in OAEs both in terms of output per worker and output per enterprise. Growth figures further show that output per worker and output per enterprise have gone up in both OAEs and establishments. The increase in the latter has been larger, however. Finally, the absolute number of workers as well as enterprises has declined in establishments.

We are now in a position to consider the distribution of each type of enterprise by social group. Table 10.6 shows the division of GVA, workers employed, and the number of enterprises within OAEs among the STs, SCs, OBCs, and FCs. In these enterprises, the SC population finds representation in terms of GVA, workers, and the number of enterprises owned that is close to its share of the general population, especially as revealed by the 2001 census. The ST

Table 10.5 COMPOSITION OF GVA, WORKERS, AND NUMBER OF PROPRIETARY/PARTNERSHIP ENTERPRISES ACROSS THE OAES AND ESTABLISHMENTS

Item	OAE	Establishment	Total
Round 57			
Gross value added (real)	50.6	49.4	100
Total workers employed	64.1	35.9	100
Number of enterprises	84.5	15.5	100
Round 63			
Gross value added (Real)	46.1	53.9	100
Total workers employed	65.1	34.9	100
Number of enterprises	85.9	14.1	100
Percent growth between rounds			
Gross value added (real)	18.2	41.6	29.8
Total workers employed	2.5	−1.6	1
Number of enterprises	5.3	−5.8	3.6

Source: Author calculations from the surveys mentioned in the text.

Table 10.6 SHARES OF SOCIAL GROUPS IN OAES

Item	ST	SC	OBC	FC	Total
Round 57					
GVA (real)	2	14.3	40.4	43.2	100
Total workers employed	2.5	17.4	46.8	33.3	100
Number of enterprises	2.7	18.2	43.5	35.6	100
Round 63					
GVA (real)	3.1	15	42.3	39.7	100
Total workers employed	3.5	18.2	44.3	34.1	100
Number of enterprises	3.7	18.1	42.3	35.9	100
Percent growth between rounds					
GVA (real)	80.4	23.7	23.6	8.4	18.2
Total workers employed	41.8	6.7	-3	5	2.5
Number of enterprises	41.6	4.9	2.4	6.2	5.3

Source: Author calculations from the surveys mentioned in the text.

population lags behind, however. Both SCs and STs have grown faster than the total across all social groups between 2001–02 and 2006–07 in terms of GVA and workers employed. Thus, significant improvement in the status of the SCs and STs is observed. Interestingly, the competition to SCs and STs is coming more from the OBCs than from the FCs. While the latter have lost ground in GVA, the former have gained despite their high initial share.

As one would expect from their historically disadvantaged position, the shares of the SCs and STs are significantly lower in establishments (see table 10.7), which employ one or more hired workers on a regular basis and therefore have a more formal structure. The good news, however, is that their progress over time in these enterprises is even more impressive than in OAEs. They have grown faster than their OAE counterparts along virtually all dimensions and also as fast as or faster than the total activity across all groups within establishment enterprises. Tables 10.6 and 10.7 together imply that, while the SCs and STs remain behind the OBCs and FCs in terms of entrepreneurial activity, they are most surely sharing in the growth that has taken place during the period of analysis. Once again, the OBCs seem to provide the most intense competition to the SCs and STs. The disadvantaged but improving positions of the SCs and STs are consistent with evaluations of their gains along other dimensions such as poverty (Mukim and Panagariya 2012) and wages and education (Hnatkovska, Lahiri, and Paul 2012).

LOCATION: RURAL VERSUS URBAN

Our next step is to disaggregate the data between rural and urban locations. Before doing so, however, it is useful to provide the location of various social

Table 10.7 SHARES OF SOCIAL GROUPS IN PROPRIETARY/PARTNERSHIP ESTABLISHMENTS

Item	ST	SC	OBC	FC	Total
Round 57					
GVA (real)	1.3	3.1	24.8	70.8	100
Total workers employed	1.4	5.2	31	62.5	100
Number of enterprises	1.6	5	34.5	58.9	100
Round 63					
GVA (real)	1.7	3	32.2	63	100
Total workers employed	2.1	5.8	34.1	58	100
Number of enterprises	2.4	6.2	37.8	53.6	100
Percent growth between rounds					
GVA (real)	84.8	38	83.9	26.2	41.6
Total workers employed	51.6	10.4	8.3	−8.7	−1.6
Number of enterprises	40	16.3	3.3	−14.3	−5.8

Source: Author calculations from the surveys mentioned in the text.

groups in rural and urban areas. Ceteris paribus, enterprise location by social group depends on the location of the social groups themselves. Table 10.8, derived from table 5.2 in Mukim and Panagariya (2012), provides the relevant information on the basis of the 2004–05 NSS expenditure survey. It may be recalled that the shares in this survey do not match those in the 2001 census. Specifically, the share of SC population is an order of magnitude higher than in the latter.

The upper half of table 10.8 shows the shares of social groups by region. For example, the SC population in rural locations is 21.1 percent of the total rural population. The lower half of the table shows the within-group split between urban and rural locations. From the lower half of the table, we can gather that SC, ST, and OBC populations are concentrated significantly more heavily in rural areas than is the FC population. In the case of the ST population, only 8.1 percent of it is in urban areas. This translates to the ST population being only 2.8 percent of the total urban population. The composition of population across rural and urban regions suggests that SC, ST, and OBC enterprises are more likely to be concentrated in rural areas.

Table 10.9 shows the shares and growth by social groups in rural and urban regions in GVA, workers employed, and number of enterprises in OAEs. Three features of the table stand out. First, shares of the SC population in GVA, the number of workers, and the number of enterprises in both rural and urban areas, especially in 2006–07, are approximately in line with their shares in the general population. This conclusion is considerably strengthened if we go by the SC population shares as measured by the 2001 census rather than the 2004–05 NSSO survey.

Table 10.8 SOCIAL GROUPS IN RURAL AND URBAN AREAS, 2004–05

Region	ST	SC	OBC	FC	All groups
Group share within the region					
Rural	10	21.1	43.1	25.8	100
Urban	2.6	15.7	35.7	46	100
Rural + urban	8.1	19.7	41.2	30.9	100
Rural-urban split within the group					
Rural	91.9	79.8	78.1	62.4	74.7
Urban	8.1	20.2	21.9	37.6	25.3
Rural + urban	100	100	100	100	100

Source: Mukim and Panagariya (2012).

Table 10.9 SHARES AND GROWTH BY SOCIAL GROUPS IN THE OAE IN RURAL AND URBAN REGIONS

Item	ST	SC	OBC	FC	Total	ST	SC	OBC	FC	Total
			Rural					Urban		
Round 57										
GVA (real)	2.7	15.8	46.8	34.7	100	1.3	12.6	33.3	52.8	100
Total workers employed	3.2	19	51.6	26.2	100	1.4	14.7	38.6	45.2	100
Number of enterprises	3.5	19.9	47.8	28.8	100	1.4	15.3	36.3	47	100
Round 63										
GVA (real)	4.3	17.7	44.4	33.6	100	1.7	11.9	40	46.4	100
Total workers employed	4.7	21.1	45.1	29.1	100	1.5	13.5	43	41.9	100
Number of enterprises	5	20.8	42.8	31.4	100	1.6	13.8	41.4	43.2	100
Percent growth between rounds										
GVA (real)	90.1	32.1	11.7	14.1	17.9	57.7	11.9	42.5	4.2	18.6
Total workers employed	49.1	10.9	–12.4	11.6	0.3	14.3	–2.3	18.2	–1.5	6.2
Number of enterprises	45.8	8.6	–6.9	13.3	3.9	23.4	–3	22.6	–1.1	7.6

Source: Author calculations from the surveys mentioned in the text.

Second, and by comparison, the shares of the ST population in OAEs in GVA, workers employed, and the number of enterprises substantially lag behind their shares in both the rural and urban population. But the good news is that the ST population has seen its shares in GVA and workers rise uniformly and sharply in both rural and urban areas. The shares of the SC population, on the other hand, have risen in rural areas but declined in urban areas. The latter does not imply a lack of growth but rather slower-than-average growth.

Finally, in urban OAEs, the OBCs have emerged as a serious competitor to the FC population. Beginning with shares approximately commensurate to population share, the OBC group has significantly expanded its share in GVA from 33.3 to 40 percent over the five years we examine. Though much of its gain has come at the expense of the FCs, it has also wrested some share from the SCs.

Next, table 10.10 reports the shares of different social groups in rural and urban areas in establishment enterprises. Two features of the table stand out. First, while the shares of the SC and ST populations are uniformly lower than the corresponding shares in OAEs, they have uniformly risen. GVA, workers

Table 10.10 SHARES AND GROWTH BY SOCIAL GROUPS IN THE ESTABLISHMENTS IN RURAL AND URBAN REGIONS

Item	ST	SC	OBC	FC	Total	ST	SC	OBC	FC	Total
			Rural					Urban		
Round 57										
GVA (real)	2.7	5.1	40.6	51.5	100	0.7	2.3	18.5	78.5	100
Total workers employed	2.3	7.9	40.7	49.2	100	0.8	3.5	25.1	70.5	100
Number of enterprises	2.4	6.4	43.5	47.6	100	1	3.9	27.5	67.6	100
Round 63										
GVA (real)	4.5	5.2	42.7	47.6	100	0.9	2.4	29.2	67.5	100
Total workers employed	4.4	9.6	40.9	45.2	100	1	4	31	64	100
Number of enterprises	4.5	8.7	43.2	43.6	100	1.2	4.7	34.9	59.2	100
Percent growth between rounds										
GVA (eal)	85.7	11.9	17.1	3	11.4	83.5	61.4	143	32.3	53.8
Total workers employed	62.7	0.8	−15.9	−23.1	−16.3	33.3	23.6	32.1	−2.6	7.4
Number of enterprises	45.6	5.2	−23.2	−29.1	−22.5	29.8	30.8	35.7	−6.3	7

Source: Author calculations from the surveys mentioned in the text.

employed, and the number of enterprises owned by the SCs and STs in the establishment category in both rural and urban regions have risen faster than the corresponding averages. Growth is not leaving the SCs and STs behind, but they do have a significant amount of catching up to do.

Second, in urban areas, the shares of both SCs and STs in establishment enterprises have been low in all categories. But both groups have also experienced very impressive growth rates. This said, one aspect of the pattern observed in OAEs repeats here. The OBC population has experienced phenomenal growth. In enterprises owned by the OBCs, GVA rose an extraordinary 143 percent over the five years we examine. That growth led to an increase in the OBC share in total GVA from 18.5 to 29.2 percent within five years. In comparison, the FC share fell from 78.5 to 67.5 percent over the same period.

MORE ON SMALL VERSUS LARGE ENTERPRISES

The division of enterprises between OAEs and establishments already gives us some idea of how the disadvantaged social groups fare in small versus large enterprises. The distinction can be made sharper, however, by the division of enterprises according to the number of workers employed.

Therefore, in the next step, we divide enterprises into those with fewer than five workers and those with five or more workers. In table 10.11, we first show the division of economic activity between these two types of enterprises according to both NSS survey rounds. In 2001–02, three-quarters of

Table 10.11 DIVISION OF ACTIVITY BETWEEN ENTERPRISES WITH FEWER THAN FIVE WORKERS AND FIVE OR MORE WORKERS

Item	Fewer than Five Workers	Five or More Workers	Total
Round 57			
GVA (real)	72.2	27.8	100
Total workers employed	80.3	19.7	100
Number of enterprises	96	4	100
Round 63			
GVA (real)	69.1	30.9	100
Total workers employed	80.5	19.5	100
Number of enterprises	96.1	3.9	100
Growth			
GVA (real)	24.1	44.5	29.8
Total workers employed	1.3	0	1
Number of enterprises	2.8	-1.7	2.6

Source: Author calculations from the surveys mentioned in the text.

GVA and four-fifths of workers in proprietary or partnership enterprises were in units with fewer than five workers. The share of GVA in these smaller enterprises declined slightly in 2006–07 but, at 69 percent, was still very large. The decline in share reflected slower growth in smaller rather than larger enterprises.

In table 10.12, we depict the social groups' shares in smaller and larger enterprises. This table strongly reinforces the pattern we noted across OAEs and establishments. Both the SC and ST populations do significantly better in smaller enterprises. Between the two rounds, the ST population improves its position across all indicators in both small and large enterprises. But the achievements of the SC population differ between enterprise types: it improves its position in the smaller enterprises for all indicators, but not in the larger ones. Its share in GVA and workers employed fell in the larger enterprises.

Table 10.12 also brings out the dominance of the FC population in larger enterprises more sharply. Over time, this dominance has declined, but even in 2006–07, this group's share in GVA in larger enterprises was 72.6 percent

Table 10.12 RELATIVE SHARES OF DIFFERENT SOCIAL GROUPS IN ENTERPRISES WITH FEWER THAN FIVE AND FIVE OR MORE WORKERS

	Fewer than Five Workers					Five or More Workers				
Item	ST	SC	OBC	FC	Total	ST	SC	OBC	FC	Total
Round 57										
GVA (real)	2	10.9	37.6	49.5	100	0.8	3.4	20	75.8	100
Total workers employed	2.4	14.6	44.1	38.9	100	0.9	6.6	29.1	63.3	100
Number of enterprises	2.7	17	43.7	39.3	100	1	6.8	29.6	62.5	100
Round 63										
GVA (real)	2.8	11.3	42.7	43.1	100	1.2	2.4	23.8	72.6	100
Total workers employed	3.3	15.7	43.4	37.7	100	1.9	6.3	29.7	62.1	100
Number of enterprises	3.7	17.4	43.6	39	100	2	7.3	32.2	58.5	100
Percent growth between rounds										
GVA (real)	76.7	29.1	40.9	8.1	24.1	116.3	1.9	72.2	38.4	44.5
Total workers employed	38.6	8.6	−0.2	−2.1	1.3	101.8	−4.8	2	−1.9	0
Number of enterprises	40.6	5.4	2.4	2	2.8	93.6	5.5	6.9	−8.1	−1.7

Source: Author calculations from the surveys mentioned in the text.

compared with only 43.1 percent in smaller enterprises. The OBC population has improved its position in both small and large enterprises, but it still lags relative to its population share in the large enterprises.

WHICH SECTORS?

The surveys allow us to follow the social group of the owner by broad NIC (National Industrial Classification) sectors called "sections" and denoted by uppercase letters. The exhaustive list of the sections ranges from A, B, C,...,to N, O, and Q. The initial letters represent agriculture and industrial sectors and the later ones services. Services sections that both surveys covered include H (hotels and restaurants), I (transport, storage, and communications), K (real estate, renting, and business activities), M (education), N (health and social work), and O (other community, social, and personal service activities).

Table 10.13 gives the composition of and growth in the services included in the surveys at the national level when we restrict ourselves to proprietary and partnership enterprises. Section I—which represents transport, storage, and communications—accounts for the most GVA, workers employed, and number of enterprises by far, followed by section H, which includes hotels and restaurants. Together, these sections account for more than half of GVA,

Table 10.13 COMPOSITION OF AND GROWTH IN SERVICES SECTORS

Item	H	I	K	M	N	O	Total
Round 57							
GVA (real)	18.8	35.7	13.8	8.7	11.2	11.7	100
Total workers employed	20.2	29.3	9.5	11.8	7.9	21.3	100
Number of enterprises	15	37.5	8.8	8.1	9.3	21.3	100
Round 63							
GVA (real)	18.8	37.8	12.5	8.7	9.8	12.5	100
Total workers employed	19.9	33	9.7	10.7	7	19.7	100
Number of enterprises	13.8	42.3	9.3	6.5	7.2	20.9	100
Growth							
GVA (real)	29.5	37.3	17.1	29.2	13.7	37.8	29.8
Total workers employed	−0.5	13.6	4.1	−8.7	−10.3	−6.6	1
Number of enterprises	−4.8	16.8	9.5	−17.4	−19.3	1.5	3.5

Source: Author calculations from the surveys mentioned in the text.

workers, and enterprises in the services covered by both surveys. At the other extreme, we have Section M, comprising education and accounting for less than 10 percent of GVA.

We next document the shares of different social groups in GVA, workers employed, and number of enterprises in each of the sections. This is presented in table 10.14. Perhaps the single clearest pattern emerging from this table is the across-the-board gain made by the STs. In five out of six sectors, GVA growth associated with the ST-owned enterprises exceeds that associated with any other social group. In the remaining sixth case, Section H, GVA growth of 34.1 percent in ST-owned enterprises is barely edged out by the 34.2 percent growth in the SC-owned enterprises. In terms of workers employed, ST-owned enterprises show higher growth (or lower decline) than any other group in any section. Going by value-added share in 2006–07 (round 63), ST enterprises have the greatest presence in Section I (transport, storage, and communications) followed by Section M (education).

The presence and performance of SC-owned enterprises show greater variance across sectors. Going by value-added share in 2006–07, they have the greatest presence in Section O (other community, social, and personal service activities) followed by Section I (transport, storage, and communications). An interesting contrast between these two sectors, however, is that whereas the SCs marginally increased their presence in Section I, they lost substantial ground in Section O between the two surveys. Surprisingly, the latter development is a welcome one. A key service included in Section O is Division 90, which comprises sewage and refuse disposal, sanitation, and similar activities. Our strong suspicion is that the heavy SC presence in Section O is due to its traditional dominance of Division 90. Their exit from this set of activities is desirable, since it is likely to help undermine stereotyping of the SCs.

The third section in which the SC population has a major presence is N (health and social work). Here also, its share in GVA declined from 6.3 percent in 2001–02 to 5.0 percent in 2006–07, with a 10.2 percent absolute decline in real terms. Once again, it is possible that the SC involvement in this sector was largely in low-end cleaning and sweeping activities from which they are now exiting. But this is only a conjecture.

The SC population has made its greatest gains in Section K (real estate, renting, and business activities). No doubt, with 4.4 percent share in GVA in 2006–07, its presence in the sector is far below its potential as reflected by its share in the population. But 97.6 percent growth in real terms over five years in a sector that includes computer services and outsourcing activities suggests that the SC population is fast entering the modern sectors where it has traditionally not had a presence.

Next, we may make some brief remarks about the OBCs. The data in table 10.14 offer little support to any notion that they are at a disadvantage. They have large shares in almost all sectors and have either held or improved these

Table 10.14 SHARES AND GROWTH BY SOCIAL GROUPS AND BY SECTORS

Item	ST	SC	OBC	FC	ST	SC	OBC	FC
		Section H				Section I		
Round 57								
GVA (real)	1.9	4.2	39	54.9	2.3	12.2	33.3	52.1
Total workers employed	2.5	6	46.2	45.3	2.6	16.8	35.8	44.8
Number of enterprises	2.9	8	49.8	39.3	2.8	20.5	35.9	40.9
Round 63								
GVA (real)	2	4.4	38.9	54.8	3.3	12.4	37.3	47.1
Total workers employed	3.3	7.1	46.7	42.9	3.5	16.4	38.4	41.7
Number of enterprises	3.9	9.5	50.1	36.5	3.6	19.3	38.1	39
Growth								
GVA (real)	34.1	34.2	29.2	29.1	92	39.1	53.8	24
Total workers employed	34.8	17.4	0.6	−5.9	50.4	10.3	22	5.9
Number of enterprises	27.4	13.4	−4.2	−11.7	51.1	9.9	24.2	11.5
		Section K				Section M		
Round 57								
GVA (real)	0.6	2.9	19.4	77.1	1.6	4.3	24.3	69.8
Total workers employed	1.4	5.6	33.1	59.9	1.4	6.2	26.4	66
Number of enterprises	1.9	6.8	35.3	56	2.2	8.6	25.8	63.4
Round 63								
GVA (real)	1	4.8	29.4	64.8	3.1	3.5	23.4	70.1
Total workers employed	2.3	7.5	37.6	52.6	2.4	5.8	29	62.7
Number of enterprises	2.3	8.1	39.6	50	4.3	10.3	27.3	58.1
Growth								
GVA (real)	97.8	97.6	76.9	−1.6	151.3	4.4	24.4	29.6
Total workers employed	69.6	40.3	18.1	−8.6	57.2	−13.2	0.4	−13.3
Number of enterprises	31.4	30.8	22.8	−2.1	63.2	−1.4	−12.8	−24.2
		Section N				Section O		
Round 57								
GVA (real)	1	6.3	22.1	70.6	1.2	18.4	52.8	27.6
Total workers employed	3.5	8.8	28.4	59.4	1.3	23.2	60.1	15.4

Table 10.14 CONTINUED

Item	ST	SC	OBC	FC	ST	SC	OBC	FC
		Section N				Section O		
Round 57								
Number of enterprises	4.8	10.9	31.6	52.8	1.4	23.1	61	14.4
Round 63								
GVA (real)	1.7	5	24.9	68.4	1.4	13.3	58.7	26.6
Total workers employed	3.8	9.1	28.7	58.3	2.3	25.5	50.7	21.4
Number of enterprises	5.7	12.9	31	50.4	2.6	22	52.2	23.2
Growth								
GVA (real)	93.6	−10.2	27.9	10.2	58.2	−0.1	53.3	32.4
Total workers employed	−0.3	−6.8	−9.3	−11.9	67.2	3	−21.1	29.5
Number of enterprises	−4.1	−4.1	−20.8	−23	88.4	−3.5	−13.1	63

Source: Author calculations from the surveys mentioned in the text.

shares over the two surveys. Quite remarkably, in Sections H and I, which together account for more than half of the GVA covered by the two surveys, they had shares approaching 40 percent in 2006–07. Equally important, in fast-growing Section K, they expanded their GVA share from 19.4 to 29.4 percent.

Finally, it can be seen that the FC population has been uniformly losing ground to the other three groups. Its value-added share has fallen in five out of six sections covered by the two surveys over the five-year period. In the sixth case, Section M (education), its gain is marginal, from 69.8 percent in 2001–02 to 70.1 percent in 2006–07. Overall, it simply cannot be denied that shifts in favor of the disadvantaged groups are taking place in the rapidly growing private economy. One may complain about the pace of the shift but not the direction.

WHICH STATES?

Our last step in the analysis is to consider the presence and progress of the disadvantaged social groups by states. In all, India has thirty-five politically separate entities: twenty-eight states and seven union territories. The inclusion of all these entities would clutter the analysis. Therefore, we choose to focus on the twenty-one largest states. For the convenience of terminology, we count Delhi as a state, although it is formally a union territory. We exclude six other union territories, six smaller northeastern states, Sikkim, and the tiny state of Goa. Table 10.15 shows the shares of various social groups in the twenty-one states using the 2004–05 NSS expenditure survey data.

Several observations follow from this table. First, Chhattisgarh, Orissa, Jharkhand and Madhya Pradesh—in that order—have the largest presence of SCs and STs taken together. The two groups combined account for 46.6 percent of the population in Chhattisgarh and approximately 40 percent in the remaining three states. The SCs and STs also account for a significant proportion (34 percent) of the population in Rajasthan. Second, the SCs account for 20 percent or more of the population in as many as ten states. These include some of the largest states such as Uttar Pradesh, West Bengal, Bihar, Tamil Nadu, and Rajasthan. Third, the five most populous states—Uttar Pradesh, Maharashtra, West Bengal, Bihar, and Andhra Pradesh—account for more than half of the SC population. In evaluating the presence of the SC population among entrepreneurs, it is crucial to assess their presence in these five

Table 10.15 SHARES OF GROUPS WITHIN EACH STATE

State	ST	SC	OBC	FC	Population (Millions)
Andhra Pradesh	7	18.3	46.9	27.8	72.9
Assam	17.8	9.9	17.6	54.6	25.2
Bihar	0.6	21.9	59.7	17.8	73.6
Chhattisgarh	32.4	14.2	44.1	9.3	21.5
Delhi	1.6	24.6	11.4	62.5	12.4
Gujarat	14.8	10.5	39.2	35.5	47.2
Haryana	0.3	25.5	30.3	44	21.6
Himachal Pradesh	4.9	26.2	14.9	54.1	6.1
Jammu and Kashmir	0.6	12.7	12.5	74.2	6.8
Jharkhand	26.6	12.9	45	15.5	24.3
Karnataka	6.6	17.9	39	36.4	49.3
Kerala	1.6	10.5	60.2	27.7	30.8
Madhya Pradesh	21.2	17.4	39.4	22	60.1
Maharashtra	9.4	15.8	30.9	43.9	92.3
Orissa	23.4	17	38.2	21.4	37.2
Punjab	0.4	35.9	20.4	43.3	23.2
Rajasthan	13.1	20.9	44.6	21.4	55.3
Tamil Nadu	0.6	22.2	72.2	5	56.1
Uttar Pradesh	0.5	23.1	52.8	23.6	165
Uttarakhand	4.8	21.4	18	55.8	8.3
West Bengal	6.5	26.8	6.5	60.3	78.9
All 21 states	8.1	19.7	41.2	30.9	968

Source: Mukim and Panagariya (2012, table 5.4).

Table 10.16 GVA AND WORKER SHARES OF SOCIAL GROUPS IN THE STATE

State	GVA Shares				Worker Shares			
	ST	SC	OBC	FC	ST	SC	OBC	FC
Andhra Pradesh	1.7	6.4	36.1	55.8	2.2	8	50.6	39.3
Assam	13.7	8.2	24.9	53.1	19	9	27.1	44.9
Bihar	0.7	16.2	51.3	31.8	0.8	24.3	51.4	23.4
Chhattisgarh	4.4	7	47.5	41.1	5	8	52.6	34.4
Delhi	0.7	7	10.6	81.7	0.7	9.2	12.9	77.2
Gujarat	2.4	6.3	26.1	65.2	3.7	8.5	35.6	52.2
Haryana	0.1	10.9	30.3	58.7	0.2	14.4	31.9	53.5
Himachal Pradesh	11.2	9.3	11.9	67.6	7.3	12.2	12.6	67.9
Jammu & Kashmir	1.4	6.3	13.1	79.1	0.9	6.7	18.7	73.7
Jharkhand	5.7	5.9	42.8	45.6	7.9	7.8	49.6	34.6
Karnataka	1.7	3.5	39.6	55.2	3.2	4.4	48.9	43.5
Kerala	0.1	1.9	67.5	30.5	0.2	3.5	61.7	34.6
Madhya Pradesh	1	3.3	33.1	62.7	2	5.6	44.6	47.8
Maharashtra	1.5	5.7	23	69.8	3.2	8	32.5	56.4
Orissa	6.1	8.5	40	45.4	8.9	21.3	38.5	31.3
Punjab	0.1	18.4	17.6	63.8	0.2	23	17.6	59.2
Rajasthan	1.8	6	37.8	54.4	2.3	9.7	41	47
Tamil Nadu	0.2	6.9	76.6	16.2	0.2	8.7	80.1	11
Uttar Pradesh	0.5	14.1	42.8	42.6	0.5	21.5	44.3	33.7
Uttaranchal	1.2	6	18.5	74.3	1	8.9	16.2	73.8
West Bengal	1.6	23.7	5.6	69.2	1.8	29.6	6.4	62.2

Source: Author calculations from the surveys mentioned in the text.

states. Finally, the OBCs form the largest single social group in eleven out of the fourteen most populous states. The FC populations also form the largest single group in nine states, but these are mostly small states. Among these nine states, only Maharashtra and West Bengal make the list of the twelve largest states.

We are now in a position to consider the presence of various social groups in the services enterprises in different states. To economize on space, we only report the share of various social groups in GVA and workers employed in 2006–07. These are shown in table 10.16 for the same states shown in table 10.15. Broadly speaking, the representation of SCs and STs as entrepreneurs bears a close relationship to their presence in the states.

Consistent with what we already know, the STs consistently lag more than the SCs in relation to their population shares. But in some states, the gaps are truly large. The ST population has very large shares of the population in Chhattisgarh (32.4 percent), Jharkhand (26.6 percent), Orissa (23.4 percent), Madhya Pradesh (21.2 percent), and Assam (17. 8 percent). But only in Assam do its shares in GVA and workers employed reach double digits. Somewhat anomalously, the ST share in GVA in Himachal Pradesh is 11.2 percent, well above the population share of the group, which is only 4.9 percent. The shares in GVA in Chhattisgarh (4.4 percent), Jharkhand (5.6 percent), and Orissa (6.1 percent) suggest some presence of ST entrepreneurs, but they remain substantially below their population shares. The GVA share in Madhya Pradesh is especially low at only 1 percent.

In comparison, the SC population has a more significant presence in many states, especially when we consider workers employed. West Bengal has the most impressive presence of this social group: 23.7 percent in GVA and 29.6 percent in workers employed in comparison with a 26.5 percent share of the population. But there are other states with a significant presence of SC entrepreneurs. In each of Bihar, Punjab, Haryana, and Uttar Pradesh, the SC populations have double-digit shares in both GVA and workers employed. Indeed, 6 percent or higher shares in GVA and 8 percent or higher shares in workers employed are common across the states. Three states that stand out for their low shares of SC entrepreneurs are Kerala, Karnataka, and Madhya Pradesh.

The shares of the OBCs in both GVA and workers approximately match their shares in the population in nearly all states. Where they are lower, the gaps are small. Indeed, it is difficult to conclude from these data that they are in any way disadvantaged. Any advantage the FC population enjoys in GVA and workers employed relative to their population shares largely reflects the disadvantage to the STs and SCs.

CONCLUDING REMARKS

While substantial literature now exists on poverty and inequality among social groups, until now, almost nothing has been known about how the socially disadvantaged groups fare in entrepreneurship in terms of shares in the GVA, workers employed, and number of enterprises owned. Our chapter provides a first comprehensive look at these measures of entrepreneurship. We analyze the presence of the socially disadvantaged groups in proprietary and partnership enterprises in the economy as a whole, according to enterprises size, in rural and urban areas, according to sectors, and in different states.

Our analysis exploits two services sector surveys of enterprises, which identify ownership according to three caste groups: STs, SCs, OBCs, and "other," which we label as the FCs. Our main findings may be summarized as follows:

- Consistent with the data in other spheres of life, such as poverty alleviation and wage and education outcomes, the SC and ST groups are behind other social groups in entrepreneurship but their presence is not negligible. At the aggregate level, the SCs account for approximately the same proportion of enterprises and worker employment as their share in the total population according to the 2001 census. Their share in GVA is, however, only half of their share in the population implying that the enterprises they own are less productive than an average enterprise.

- The entrepreneurial presence of the STs is considerably below their share of the total population. In part, this reflects the disproportionate concentration of the STs in the rural areas, often outside the mainstream of even the rural economy.

- The OBCs do much better than the SCs and STs, though not as well as the FCs. By 2006–07, their share in the GVA had risen to almost 37 percent, approximately equal to their share in the population. On the whole, the sharpest differences are those between the SCs and STs on the one hand and the OBCs and FCs on the other hand rather than those between the OBCs and the FCs.

- All groups have shared in growth though not to an equal extent. In terms of GVA, ST enterprises grew the fastest followed by OBC, SC, and FC enterprises in that order. The STs started with low shares in GVA, workers employed, and the number of enterprises owned in 2001–02 but experienced the sharpest increases in all shares. The SCs, by contrast, increased shares in workers employed and enterprises owned but lost in terms of GVA. The main competition to the SCs came from the OBCs rather than the FCs.

- The shares of the SCs and STs steadily decline as we move from smaller to larger enterprises. Their shares are much smaller in establishment enterprises, which employ one or more hired workers on a regular basis, than in own-account enterprises, which do not employ any hired workers on a regular basis. The shares decline even further when we limit ourselves to enterprises with five or more workers. Thus, the SCs and STs are heavily concentrated in smaller enterprises, which are characterized by lower productivity on average.

- The OBCs do particularly well in urban areas. Whereas the SCs and STs gained shares at the expense of both OBCs and FCs in the rural areas, the SCs lost shares to the latter groups in urban areas. Remarkably, the ST group gained shares in both rural and urban areas though starting from a very low level.

- The ST group made very substantial gains in all six sectors covered by our data between 2001–02 and 2006–07. In five out of six sectors, growth in GVA in ST-owned enterprises exceeded that associated with any other social group. In the remaining sixth case, SC-owned enterprises barely edged it out.

- An extremely interesting feature of the data is that the SC group seems to now be exiting sewage and refuse disposal, sanitation, and similar activities while entering transport, storage, and communications in a major way.

This development can be expected to contribute to the breaking down of stereotypical attitudes that associate SC members with sewage and refusal disposal.

- The OBC group has a strong presence in all six broad sectors. Moreover, they either maintained their shares or improved them in all of the sectors between 2001–02 and 2006–07. At least these data do not support the hypothesis that they are seriously disadvantaged.

The short conclusion from this study is that the SCs and STs are well behind the OBCs and FCs in the area of entrepreneurship, as in other areas such as poverty, wages, and educational achievement. But there is no support whatsoever for the assertions often made by many left-of-center commentators that growth has left these disadvantaged groups behind. Both groups have shared in economic growth, with the ST group—which is farther behind than the SC group—gaining the most in the service enterprises we have studied. We also find at best limited evidence that the OBC population is at a significant disadvantage. Indeed, it has a presence commensurate with its population share and has been rapidly displacing the FC entrepreneurs in the enterprises we have studied.

ACKNOWLEDGMENT

The authors thank Nandini Gupta for extremely helpful comments and Shaheen Lavie-Rouse for excellent research assistance. Work on this chapter has been supported by Columbia University's Program on Indian Economic Policies, funded by a generous grant from the John Templeton Foundation. The opinions expressed in the chapter are those of the authors and do not necessarily reflect the views of the John Templeton Foundation.

NOTES

1. The word *dalit* means the "downtrodden" in Hindi and refers to the class of people in South Asia formerly known as "untouchable."
2. See   http://mobile.globalpost.com/dispatch/news/regions/asia-pacific/india/110421/india-untouchable-dalit-business-entrepreneur (accessed January 18, 2012).
3. It is probable that the SCs and STs were entirely absent from corporate enterprises in 2001–02. Even in 2006–07, their presence was so sparse that identification of the social group would have identified the enterprise, thus violating confidentiality laws.
4. Sundaram and Tendulkar (2003) had earlier compared the poverty levels among the socially disadvantaged groups between 1993–94 and 1999–2000.

5. A recent study by Shukla, Jain, and Kakkar (2010) also focuses on the prevailing inequality among various social groups and offers a rich set of indicators drawn from the National Survey of Household Income and Expenditure conducted by the National Council on Applied Economic Research. But they do not track the fortunes of the groups over time. Additional references to earlier studies on inequalities between scheduled and non-scheduled groups can be found in the reference lists in Kijima (2006) and Hnatkovska, Lahiri, and Paul (2010).

REFERENCES

Dehejia, Rajeev, and Arvind Panagariya. (2010). "Services Growth in India: A Look Inside the Black Box." Working Paper 2010-2, Columbia Program on Indian Economic Policies, Columbia University. Forthcoming in Bhagwati, Jagdish, and Arvind Panagariya, eds. *Reforms and Economic Transformation in India*. New York: Oxford University Press.

Gupta, Shekhar. (2011). "Our Singapore Fantasy," *Indian Express*, June 25.

Hnatkovska, Viktoria, Amartya Lahiri, and Sourabh B. Paul. (2012). "Castes and Labor Mobility." *American Economic Journal: Applied Economics* 4(2), 274–307.

Kijima, Yoko. (2006). "Caste and Tribe Inequality: Evidence from India, 1983–1999." *Economic Development and Cultural Change* 54(2), 369–404.

Mukim, Megha, and Arvind Panagariya. (2012). "Growth, Openness and Socially Disadvantaged," in Bhagwati, Jagdish, and Arvind Panagariya, eds. *India: Trade, Poverty, Inequality and Democracy*. New York: Oxford University Press, pp. 186–246.

Narasimhan, T. E. (2001). "CII Members to Step Up Sourcing from Dalit-owned SMEs." *Business Standard*. July 12. Available at http://www.business-standard.com/sme/storypage.php?autono=442322.

Shukla, Rajesh, Sunil Jain, and Preeti Kakkar. (2010). *Caste in a Different Mould*. New Delhi: Business Standard.

Sundaram, K., and S. Tendulkar. (2003). "Poverty among Social and Economic groups in India in 1990s." *Economic and Political Weekly* 38(50), 5263–76.

INDEX

Tables and figures are indicated by an italic *t* or *f*, respectively.